MW00604423

UN**FAIR LABOR?**

UNFAIR LABOR?

American Indians and the 1893
World's Columbian Exposition in Chicago

DAVID R. M. BECK

UNIVERSITY OF NEBRASKA PRESS | LINCOLN

Library of Congress Cataloging-in-Publication Data
Names: Beck, David, 1956– author.
Title: Unfair labor?: American Indians and the
1893 World's Columbian Exposition in Chicago /
David R. M. Beck.
Description: Lincoln: University of Nebraska
Press, [2019] | Includes bibliographical
references and index.
Identifiers: LCCN 2018051871
ISBN 9781496206831 (cloth: alk. paper)
ISBN 9781496214843 (epub)
ISBN 9781496214850 (mobi)
ISBN 9781496214867 (pdf)
Subjects: LCSH: Indians of North America—
Economic conditions—19th century. | Indians
of North America—Employment—History—
19th century. | Indians of North America—Social
conditions—19th century. | World's Columbian
Exposition (1893: Chicago, Ill.)—Influence.
Classification: LCC E98.E2 B43 2019 |
DDC 970.004/97—dc23
LC record available at
https://lccn.loc.gov/2018051871

Set in Whitman by E. Cuddy.

I dedicate this work to the memory
of Michael Chapman, a generous
leader, mentor, colleague, and friend.

Contents

Illustrations

Figures

ix

Maps

Tables

Acknowledgments

Throughout my career I have been fortunate to have the support and aid of so many generous people that I would be remiss not to recognize that without them, my research and writing would not be possible. Friends and relatives have opened their homes to me time and again, which has permitted me to spend significant amounts of time in archival collections across the country. Friends and colleagues have offered me access to office space and library privileges when I worked away from home. Colleagues and friends have guided me to record collections and published articles and books that have enriched my work in ways I would not have imagined. Some have even shared their own research with me, giving me access to records that I would not otherwise have seen. Others have read portions or all of my works with a critical eye, in the process saving me from errors of omission and commission, and strengthening my own understanding of the materials I have been immersed in with their insights. I am truly fortunate to be working in a field, and in communities, that are so filled with this generosity.

For this book, I would like to especially thank the following people, who generously supported this work in their own various ways, with hospitality, aid in chasing funding, guidance to resources, help in preparation, or critique: JoAllyn Archambault, Grant Arndt, John Aubrey, Ann Baker, Joel Beck, Katy Beck, Matt Bokovoy, Willie Brown, Michael Chapman, Rich Clow, Daniel Cobb, Philip Deloria, Ken Egan, Armand Esai, Dan Flores, Neil Froemming, Peter Hoffenberg, Brian Hosmer, Fred Hoxie, Lucien Liz-Lepiorz, Amy Lonetree, Michael

Mayer, Castle McLaughlin, Haley Mendlik, Elaine Nakahashi, Patricia Norby, Elaine Durham Otto, Jody Pavilak, Tammy Ravas, Mary Frances Ronan, LaVonne Ruoff, Robert Smale, Heather Stauffer, Scott Stevens, Jodi Todd, Mike Turcotte, Aura Wharton-Beck, and Geoff White. I would especially like to thank Wade Davies, Nancy Parezo, and the anonymous reviewer for the press for their close readings and critique of the full manuscript.

Portions of this work were presented in various venues, and I would like to thank all who commented on it in the following places: the Peabody Museum of Harvard University (2015), Salish-Kootenai College (2015), the 2015 American Society for Ethnohistory Annual Conference, a University of Hawaii history department 2015 colloquium, the 2016 Canadian History Association Annual Conference, the 2016 Montana Historical Society Conference, and the 2016 "Indians in the Midwest" symposium sponsored by the D'Arcy McNickle Center for American Indian and Indigenous Studies at the Newberry Library. Portions of this work were published in *World History Connected.*

A work such as this would not be possible without the guidance of dedicated, knowledgeable, and helpful archivists, librarians, and staff at the various repositories that I visited. Special thanks therefore to those who helped me at the American Philosophical Society, Bishop Museum Archives, the Buffalo Bill Center of the West McCracken Research Center, the Chicago Public Library Harold Washington Library Center Special Collections, the Chicago History Museum Research Center, the Field Museum of Natural History Archives, the Harvard University Archives, the Hawaii State Archives, Library and Archives Canada, the Minnesota Historical Society, the National Anthropological Archives, the National Archives and Records Administration in Chicago, College Park, and Washington D.C., the Newberry Library, the Peabody Museum Archives, the Smithsonian Institution Archives, the University of Chicago Library Special Collections Research Center, and the University of Montana Interlibrary loan desk.

I would also like to acknowledge generous support from the American Museum of Natural History's American Indian Program, Humanities Montana, the University of Hawaii-Manoa Department of Anthropology, the University of Montana Faculty Professional

Enhancement Program, the University of Montana Native American Studies Department, the University of Montana Office of International Programs, the University of Montana Office of the Provost, the University of Montana Office of Research and Sponsored Programs, and a University of Montana Small Grant.

I want to thank my children, Abaki and Iko'tsimiskimaki, who once asked whether we would ever take a family vacation where Mom and Dad were *not* working. They have been interested in and supportive of, as well as occasionally inconvenienced by, my scholarship for their entire lives. Above all, I would like to thank my wife and life partner, Rosalyn LaPier, who has supported my work with strength and enthusiasm for all of our time together.

Introduction

In conjunction with the 1893 World's Columbian Exposition in Chicago, Frederick Jackson Turner famously declared that the frontier had closed. Arguments regarding the accuracy of his declaration aside, the seminal change it represented was an outcome of the American project of expansion from a small nation hugging the Atlantic seaboard to a transcontinental entity on the cusp of becoming the greatest world power. In a settler/colonial or settler/indigenous context, this outcome was achieved by the dispossession of the land's original inhabitants of the bulk of their real estate and resources.[1] This ushered in an abrupt new era for American Indians who suddenly found themselves impoverished, with their populations and communities decimated.

By the late nineteenth century, American Indian economies across the continent, and indeed across the Americas, had been largely destroyed by a combination of imperial expansion and colonial and federal governmental policies. Indian communities were under severe assault on a number of fronts—economic, political, religious, and social.

As a result of these rapid transformations, Americans viewed Indians as the last remnants of a dying race. Indians still viewed America as their home and sought new ways to survive in it. The 1893 world's fair provides a lens through which we can view the ways in which American Indians were continuing to adapt to the changes and challenges they faced as the nineteenth century drew to a close. A variety of interests, from politicians to reformers to entrepreneurs to scientists to Indians themselves worked to define the place of American Indians in U.S. society, even as the American nation was coming to grips with its own evolving self-definition. The forces working to control Native lives were particularly strong at this time. That Native peoples were able to gain even a modicum of control over their destiny and the definition of their place in American society is in itself remarkable. This is true in relation to not only their social, religious, and political activities but their economic fortunes as well.

This book explores the place of American Indian labor and economy in the context of the changing economic landscape of late nineteenth-century America. By then most American Indian tribal economies had been devastated, so Indians became increasingly focused on adapting to their new circumstances. To a large degree their purposes were twofold—on an individual level to support their families, and on a community-based level to maintain their separate place in American society. To do this, individual tribal members needed to find new ways to make a living. The development of the nascent field of anthropology in conjunction with the World's Columbian Exposition provided a variety of opportunities for American Indians from across the United States and Canada—and even from Latin America—to participate in the American economy. This book explores the ways in which the fair reflects a pivotal moment in history as American Indians increasingly entered a cash economy that was extending even beyond the nation's borders.

No book-length study of the labor that American Indians did leading up to and during the fair has been written. Most of the scholarship on Indians at the World's Columbian Exposition focuses on their experiences at the fair itself, or the ways they were portrayed. Lee Baker has aptly observed that "no other site of cultural production during the late nineteenth century can better demonstrate the conflict and confluence that occurred between educators, entertainers, and ethnologists over the image of the Indians." They "vied, competed, and colluded with each other" to determine "who had the authority and power to control and indeed market the image of the Indian."[2] Indian perspectives on the fair are almost always consigned to their reaction to this contestation of their presentation.

While Indian efforts to use the fair to shape their place in contemporary America were an important facet of their experiences, that endeavor extended beyond the intellectual and social definitions to the economic roles that they could play. Indians and other indigenous peoples wanted to delineate their place in a *modernizing* America. This can be viewed as a continuation of a long struggle by Indians to create a place for themselves in the face of an ever-expanding and encroaching American colonialism. As historian Jacki Rand has observed, "Indigenous economies are destroyed and new indigenous economic patterns arise."[3]

As part of the process of economic adaptation, American Indians began to imagine their place in a globalizing world. They had long acted in a transnational context based on their interrelations with other tribal nations and groups. National boundaries were inadequate to contain their economic and cultural needs. At the end of the nineteenth century they also lived lives that defied the simplistic characterizations of them.

Literature that defines Indians solely or even primarily in terms of victimization do a disservice to their experiences. Scholars are beginning to recognize this. Carter Jones Meyer and Diana Royer have written that "cultural imperialism is made more complex when we consider such critical issues as economic need in combination with the need for cultural integrity and self-determination."[4] American Indians who came to Chicago in 1893 had to balance all of these things in an environment that discouraged them from doing so.

Indians who worked for Buffalo Bill Cody in the 1870s and 1880s likely did so, as Louis Warren has observed, because they could earn a living playing out traditional cultural roles, or a version of them, to national and international audiences.[5] And Indians had long traveled to the capitals of empire such as Washington or London to advocate for a place at the center rather than the periphery of it.[6]

In *Writing History in the Global Era*, Lynn Hunt observes that "globalization means interdependence (a two-way relationship), not simply the absorption of Western values (a one-way process)." In other words, peoples such as American Indians do more than simply react to globalizing trends; they help shape them. "The West did not globalize the world on its own; adventurous and enterprising people across the world brought their various locales into greater interconnection and interdependence with each other."[7] And, in relation to Chicago, Carolyn Schiller Johnson has observed that "global relations have affected and influenced even the most apparently local performance interactions in the city."[8] At least some American Indians who participated in the Chicago exposition understood this, in part because they had long participated in vast geographical economic enterprises.

Beginning with the pre-Columbian interhemispheric trade system, Indians had been aware of the economic importance of distant markets. But the advent of the European fur trade found them in an increasingly weak position, on the outside looking in. Material culture trade followed the exploitive pattern of colonial actions that marginalized Native peoples while at the same time extracting their resources with minimal compensation. Nonetheless, their adaptive responses to the drastic changes that came to a head in the late nineteenth century show attempts on the part of individual Indians to gain greater control of the profits of their own labor and production in an increasingly capitalist world.

This book is an attempt to analyze the various ways in which Indians used the fair to infuse their lives into the larger American cultural landscape and its globalizing economy through economic means. Anthropology played a larger role at this fair than at any other before or after, and Indians were a key focal point of the anthropological displays. The anthropology project paved the way for other entrees into the life of the fair for indigenous peoples. And so they also took part in numerous other displays. In nearly all cases Indians were portrayed as a remembrance of the past. In reality, however, many of those Indians who participated were carving out new economic pathways into the future. In fact, hundreds of Indians worked on and off the grounds in connection with the fair. Not only has the Indian work experience been ignored, but according to David Silkenat, no comprehensive study at all has been made of the fair's 25,000 workers.[9]

Indigenous people's labor for and at the fair was wide-ranging. Indians played an astonishingly broad part in both the collection of materials in advance of the fair and in a variety of roles during the months that the fair was open. All of these experiences, whether entrepreneurial or work as hired hands, were part of the newly evolving economies reshaping Indian country and Indian relations to the American society in the late nineteenth century. As the heavy hand of the federal Office of Indian Affairs (OIA) stymied economic development in tribal communities, individual tribal members found new ways to make a living by participating in the cash economy.[10] Scholars have recently begun to explore these experiences. Historians including Alexandra Harmon, William Bauer, Jacki Rand, Louis Warren, and Paige Raibmon have paid attention to Indian labor and economic change, but the field at large is only beginning to recognize the agency of Indians and the development of a changing economy.[11] Aside from two valuable chapters in Raibmon's *Authentic Indians* and sections of Jim Zwick's *Inuit Entertainers*, both of which focus on specific Native groups, this book is the first to explore the changes in Native American labor and economies enabled and created by the 1893 fair.[12] As such it is part of the literature expanding the focus on the place of American Indians in U.S. society at the end of the nineteenth century.

World's Fairs in the United States, beginning with the Centennial Exposition held in Philadelphia in 1876 and extending for the next forty years, helped shape Americans' understandings of their culture and their place within it. They drew some 100 million visitors in that four-decade span.[13] More than a quarter of those attended the Chicago fair.[14] Historian James Gilbert believes that these fairs "are among the most extravagant cultural events staged in modern history." Robert Rydell argues that they were constructed and celebrated as part of a comprehensive and well-planned effort "to make the social world comprehensible" and to define the nation's moral hegemony "precisely because they propagated the ideas and values of the country's political, financial, corporate, and intellectual leaders and offered these ideas as the proper interpretation of social and political reality."[15]

The United States was itself a rapidly changing society of immigrants and industry, its economic landscape in the process of shifting from an agricultural to an urban base. Chicagoans viewed their city as central to this process, and indeed, it stands out in the late nineteenth century among urban areas as reflective of the meeting place of western and eastern American cultures. In an authorized history of the fair, Rossiter Johnson wrote, "the growth of Chicago from a frontier camp to an active city of more than a million inhabitants, with a corresponding advance in commercial, industrial, and intellectual activities, best typifies the giant young nation that occupies the fairest portion of the New World whose discovery the projected fair is to commemorate."[16] In more visceral terms, Chicago, in Carl Sandburg's words, encompassed "the stormy, husky, brawling laughter of Youth, half-naked, sweating, proud to be Hog Butcher, Tool Maker, Stacker of Wheat, Player with Railroads and Freight Handler to the Nation."[17] When Nelson Algren referred to Chicago as the "City on the Make" in 1951, he intended that epithet to refer to the city back to the time of its roots.[18]

Chicagoans who lobbied so hard to bring the Columbian fair to their city wanted to show the world that they were a key ingredient in the great modernizing cauldron of America's exuberant growth. Chicago won a heated congressional battle with New York for the privilege of hosting the exposition. "Nothing that could influence the decision of Congress was left undone," according to a publication authorized by the fair's Board of Control. The authors of the publication loftily opined that when President Grover Cleveland pushed the button to switch on the electric lights on May 1, 1893, "it marked the beginning of another epoch in the life of man,—the planting of civilization's center within the interior of America."[19]

The Columbian Exposition was the culmination of several years' efforts by Chicago's civic leaders to present their city as modern, in the wake of the 1871 great Chicago fire and in contrast to the city's reputation as a frontier-like outlier divorced from modernity and culture. Daniel Burnham designed the fair's layout on Chicago's south side. Through tireless work he led the charge to bring the "white city" to a stunning existence that was as much mirage as reality.[20] Nearly all of the buildings were temporary, built to last only through the summer months. Nonetheless, they were erected on a grand scale that was the result of several years' planning and an intense effort in the months leading up to the May opening.

The fair was built in Jackson Park on Chicago's South Side. A book published in 1893 described the site in florid prose:

Now as to Jackson Park itself, this is the setting of the magnificent architectural jewels, shining in splendor before the astonished sight of mankind. Beneath that surface of undulating green and variegated foliage lies a tremulous pestilential swamp. To-day it is the Venice of the Western World, and when myriads of electric lights pierce night's sable mantle and shed their opalescent rays upon the sapphire waters of the lagoons, it presents a fairy scene of inexpressible splendor, reminding one of the gorgeous descriptions in the Arabian nights.[21]

Local politics and hyperbole aside, on a broader scale, the fairs of the nineteenth and early twentieth centuries, which began with the Great Exhibition at the Crystal Palace in Hyde Park, London, in 1851, reified imperial self-definition. Historian Peter Hoffenberg has aptly observed that they "revealed the tensions and ironies inherent" in "imperial and national" notions of "intellectual and social order."[22] Indeed, even as the exhibition authorities and organizers defined the relationship of the colonizer to the colonized, the latter often upset the status quo by acting independently in their own self-interests.

Rydell has argued that the American fairs reinforced notions of progress and white supremacy as linked, providing a rationalization for both continued expansion of American influence around the world and restrictions on immigration.[23] American hegemony had been accomplished at home; now it was justified in overseas expansion. The American Indian displays at the Chicago fair, especially those organized by anthropologists and by entrepreneurs, reinforced this notion.

The roles defined for American Indians at the Columbian Exposition support Rydell's thesis, but organizers failed to account for the ways that Indians would use the fair, both to fulfill their own needs and to define their own unique place in the modern world. Scholars, entrepreneurs, reformers, and Indians themselves all contested each other for the right to define Indians to the public at large.

In 1893, when Turner declared the closing of the American frontier, American Indians were popularly perceived as the last living vestiges of a vanishing race. White reformers and federal policy makers hoped to provide a place for Indians in the modern United States by bringing Indian individuals into a western lifestyle based on both a severance from their tribal past and an embracing of western economic, political and social ideals. The American policy is perhaps most succinctly described in Gen. Richard Henry Pratt's boarding school motto, to "kill the Indian and save the man." Policy makers intended to accomplish this through assimilation. American Indians too desired to find their place in the modern world, although for them the issue was far more complex. Most did not want to discard their cultural heritage entirely even as they desired to make and find a place in American society.

The very venue where Turner unveiled his thesis brought Indian people and tribes to the forefront of American popular culture and brought American popular culture into Indian communities across the nation. In both the preparations for the great fair, an undertaking of immense proportions, and the actual enactment of the fair itself, Indians participated in many ways that underscore the complexity of the choices they had begun to make and the obstacles they faced as they inexorably became enmeshed in American life and a globalizing world beyond the borders of their shrunken homelands.

Dennis Trujillo argues that this role reflects cultural commodification that had its origins in the 1883 Tertio-Millennial Exposition in Santa Fe.[24] The Indian curios market had long been popular, but it virtually exploded in the late nineteenth century. Indians were desperate to develop new economies in their home communities. Anthropologist Ruth B. Phillips observes, "With the disappearance of land and game, commodity productions closely tied to the expanding tourist trade had become essential to many local [tribal] economies."[25] The impetus for this meshed with the romanticized perception of Indians as living representatives of a dying race. This made Wild West shows, sales of Indian art, artifacts and trinkets, and displays of living Indians in "primitive" conditions both popular and profitable.

But more than this, American Indians were beginning to participate in the cash economy in significant numbers across the United States and Canada. The entry of Indians into the wage labor market and cash trade goods economy did not, however, signify an effort to abandon tribal ways. Rather, it was a recognition of the necessity of adapting to their changing world. As traditional economies lay in waste, Indians needed new ways to support themselves and their families.

They began to identify those ways in the decades before the fair. Historian Jacki Rand has provided an analysis of this in the Kiowa community in what is now Oklahoma beginning in about 1870. As with many tribal communities, Kiowa people suffered great hardship under a system of meager annuity payments and unworkable allotments that they had received in exchange for significant amounts of land and resources. With the destruction of the bison, which had provided not only food but housing, clothing, and a broad variety of other material wealth, families needed to find new ways to feed their children and elders.[26]

As hunting opportunities disappeared, American-induced farming spectacularly failed to fill the void. Kiowa men conducted some trade in cattle hides and went into the freighting business. Women too began to earn cash to purchase food and other necessities. They did so by utilizing the domestic skills and products that had long been part of the Kiowa economy and culture. They supplied local traders with both elaborate and inexpensive artistry and curios. These items became part of museum collections or goods for the tourist trade. They included labor-intensive pieces made for family use that could be sold on commission or hocked in hard times, and as well as quickly made beaded items such as watch fobs, purses, and dolls.[27] These materials also made their way to sale booths at expositions and fairs, and would be among the kind of materials collected for the 1893 fair.

Examples of adaptations to new economic conditions abound. These include not simply working in or from the home but travel off-reservation to earn or supplement a living. The Mohawk steel workers who built Canadian bridges beginning in the mid-nineteenth century and later built New York City's skyline did so while working from their home base on the Kahnawà:ke Reserve in Quebec.[28] In California's Round Valley Indian community, William Bauer has shown that tribal members who participated in the wage labor economy were successful because they had strong "social networks, usually family and kinship groups." These relationships gave them the grounding to navigate within the modern world.[29] According to historian Louis Warren, even the Ghost Dance, long viewed by scholars as a reaction against modernization, promoted participation in the cash/wage labor market economy. At the onset of the religious movement's revival by Wovoka (Jack Wilson), such work was an integral part of the Paiute economy, where the prophet resurrected and popularized the movement. "By the time the Ghost Dance emerged, the hunt for game and wild plants had basically given way to the hunt for work—or more accurately, the hunt for dollars," Warren writes.[30]

In creating space for American Indian displays, fair officials came into conflict with the realities of contemporary lives of American Indians, either by consigning them to the past or to a romanticized representation of their lives. Lee Baker has written that anthropologists played a major role in defining what American Indians could and could not authentically do: "Although anthropologists helped to constitute a theory of [American Indian] culture . . . , they often did it by marshaling scientific authority to authenticate particular Indian practices as genuine, while explicitly and implicitly designating those practices they did not certify as fraudulent, broken, or simply not authentic."[31] Neither entrepreneurship nor participation in the modern economy were viewed as authentically Indian by virtually anyone except Indians themselves. Few people aside from Indians viewed tribal cultures as dynamic.

James Mooney of the Bureau of American Ethnology described the anthropological perspective in stark binary terms. He visited the Indian Territory in 1891 just before the land rush. He was conducting research on the Ghost Dance and collecting for the world's fair. He wrote to his colleague Albert Gatschet in July of that year from Cheyenne and Arapaho country. Those tribes had just received payments for massive land losses. Mooney said that the women had new parasols to guard against sunburn, the men had straw hats and fans, and "You see more baby carriages now than Indian cradles." He glumly concluded, "In a few months this country will be opened + then goodby to Indian life."[32] From this declensionist point of view, modern adoption of American material cultural objects into tribal lifeways signified cultural destruction. Every such change would be considered cultural loss instead of adaptation.

Of course, the American goal was to hasten the process of cultural loss for American Indians. The economic destruction of tribal communities provided policy makers with an opportunity to enforce draconian laws in numerous forms: disenfranchising Indian peoples further from their meager land holdings, controlling and in some cases outlawing tribal governments, quashing tribal religions, controlling everyday lives through restrictive travel regulations and removing children from their families, in some cases sending them to far-away boarding schools.

Despite federal efforts, Indians were able to avoid total destruction of their communities and to shape responses to the onslaught within tribal cultural contexts. One important way that they did this was by using new technologies and experiences to continue longtime practices. Tribal peoples in the Americas had been mobile, moving across vast landscapes on foot or by boat long before the introduction of the horse. They were long used to interacting with people from different cultural backgrounds, first other Native people and later Europeans and then Americans. In the late nineteenth century they continued these practices.

Like the horse had, the railroad now played a key role in expanding the mobility of American Indians. The completion of the Union Pacific transcontinental railroad in 1869 ushered in a new era that transformed Indian country. By 1890 numerous railroad lines traversed the trans-Mississippi West. Many went through or ran adjacent to reservation lands. The railroad brought non-Indians to and through Indian country. In the words of historian Richard White, the transcontinental railroads "poured non-indigenous settlers into a vast region that nation-states had earlier merely claimed." Homesteaders and railroad industrialists coveted Indian lands, and the railroads played a key role in the mass slaughter of bison that led to the loss of freedom and the onset of starvation among Plains Indians in the 1860s and 1870s. White has observed that among scholars, the transcontinental railroads "came to epitomize progress, nationalism, and civilization" across western North America.[33]

In addition to their devastating impact on tribal communities, railroads also had significant impact on Indian individuals, who used them in increasing numbers. When tribal leaders sought to protest the loss of their land and the attacks on their resources brought about by the railroads, they used them to travel to Washington DC to meet with the president or members of Congress. When children were taken from their homes and sent to far-flung boarding schools, they traveled by rail. Indian school sports teams and musicians traveled by rail. Boarding school graduates regularly traveled by rail. American Indians who participated in Wild West shows, whether well-respected shows such as the Miller 101 Ranch or Buffalo Bill spectacles, or fly-by-night entities run by shysters, traveled by rail. All of this was the result of expanded opportunities for mobility for tribal members. Where in the past they had traveled by nonmotorized means over vast distances, an increasing number of Indian people could now travel by rail.

Goods were also shipped to and from tribal communities on trains. Natural resources extracted from tribal communities were transported by rail, as were objects gathered by museum collectors. Railroads would play a key role in shipping the objects acquired for display at the World's Columbian Exposition and transporting the people who would visit Chicago.

Historian L. G. Moses has argued that for American Indians, "Seeing or participating in the pageantry of Chicago's White City probably did not change their lives significantly."[34] For the hundreds of Indians who came to Chicago to be displayed or to work at the fair, the impacts doubtless varied widely. However, the fair stands as a representative moment of a significant change that was occurring for American Indian people and communities in terms of participation in the modern economic system of the United States. American Indian lives *were* changing significantly at this time, and the World's Columbian Exposition played a role both in bringing about that change and reflecting it.

Unfair Labor consists of three main parts. Part 1 contextualizes the story of the fair. Both the representation of Indians and the organizing features of the living Native displays were heavily contested. Indians, anthropologists, entrepreneurs, and government officials all vied to show the world what they believed to be authentic Indian culture, whether of the past of present. This is the focus of chapter 1.

Chapter 2 discusses the ways in which organizers envisioned Indian participation. The nascent field of anthropology began to blossom during the fair and in the years leading up to it. Frederic Ward Putnam, the Harvard anthropologist, led the way. He envisioned a purely scientific presentation. His work distorted Indian life in the modern world and came into conflict with the numerous entrepreneurial exhibits that were brought to Chicago. In the preparatory work for the fair, white actors played an outsized role in defining how Native peoples would participate. These chapters reflect that role and provide background and context for the rest of the story.

Part 2 focuses on the role American Indians played in the years leading up to the fair. Putnam was put in charge of the ethnology exhibit at the fair, and the fair organizers provided him space to erect his own building to house the materials. He hired anthropologist Franz Boas, and together they oversaw the collection of material objects and information, as well as the physical anthropological work that went into the ethnology exhibit. By 1891 they were hard at work, sending people across the Western Hemisphere and beyond to collect for and create the displays. On a smaller scale, the Canadian and other foreign governments, the U.S. government, state governments, and private entrepreneurs participated in pre-fair collecting that impacted tribal communities economically.

Chapter 3 focuses on the three Indians and one impostor Putnam brought aboard to do the actual work of collecting and organizing for living human displays at the fair. He valued their knowledge of the communities from which they were collecting. Chapters 4 and 5 focus on individuals within tribal communities who participated directly in the cash economy: making objects for display at the fair, helping with archaeological collection, or selling their own personal items to be shipped to Chicago. These chapters also explore the economic impact of this work on the communities. The collecting impacted a surprisingly large number of Native communities in the Americas. In some cases it occurred where a heavy tourist trade in goods already existed. In other places such trade was relatively new. Part of the importance of this story is recognizing the variety of experiences and impacts of the trade throughout the hemisphere. These chapters reflect that breadth by delving into local experiences.

Part 3 analyzes the opportunities available to tribal members to work while the fair was in progress. Once it began, Native individuals and families were hired to be part of the displays on the grounds outside of the ethnological exhibit. Others were hired by private contractors to be displayed on the Midway Plaisance's avenue of curiosities or brought in by individual states for their exhibits. The Native people who came to Chicago in 1893 came for many reasons. With the exception of schoolchildren and fair visitors, nearly all came as representatives of specific Native groups or communities. Their experiences were shaped by their own cultural heritage, their own personalities and desires in relation to their participation, and the ways in which they were contracted to live and behave. They are presented in as much diversity as possible in order to show the multiplicity of economic outcomes that they experienced. Chapter 8 looks at those individuals who tried to come work at the fair but did not succeed in getting to Chicago.

The actors in this story played a key role in the shift of tribal economies—and individual efforts to make a living—as American Indians began to integrate themselves into a nationalizing U.S. economy that was rapidly shifting from its agricultural foundation. They did so on a world stage under extremely trying circumstances in which they had to continue their ongoing battle to define to the world who they were. They did this in the face of powerful institutional forces, including governmental, academic, and commercial interests that tried to control them even as Native peoples pushed back in their efforts to exert agency.

UN**FAIR LABOR?**

PART 1

Overview

*American Indians and
Ethnology at the Fair*

1

Fair Representation?

In 1893, in the words of scholar Carl Smith, Chicago put on the "most successful of all world's fairs," the World's Columbian Exposition.[1] Nations from across the planet organized extensive displays to show themselves off to the world. They sent their best examples of everything from industry to agriculture to natural resources to the arts. Anywhere from tens of thousands to hundreds of thousands of visitors attended the fair every day to sate their curiosity about the rapidly changing world.[2]

In some ways expositions such as this were the events that began to shrink the world by exposing fairgoers to both broadly diverse ideas and things and to far-flung peoples. Such exposure to exoticism was open to the masses in this best-attended of all fairs. The exotic ran the gamut from what was considered high civilization to what fairgoers and organizers viewed as primitive. American Indians were categorized among the "primitive." Hundreds of American Indians, and numerous other indigenous peoples, came to Chicago in 1893 to participate in the festivities, both on and off of the fairgrounds.

Most American Indians who came to the fair came to work, although a small number visited as tourists or participated in other ways. Most of the literature describing Indians' participation at the fair focuses on either the ways in which they were presented or, to a lesser extent, the observations they made about the fair, Chicago, and Lake Michigan. While much of this book focuses on the economic and labor aspects of their experience, the social meanings and implications of their representation and experiences also provide valuable insights into the American and the Native American psyche of the late nineteenth century. This has been the subject of much of the study of the Indian presence at the fair.[3]

American Indian realities in the late nineteenth century stood in stark contrast to American perceptions of Indians in many ways. As a consequence, representations of Indians at the fair generally failed to give accurate perspectives to the public regarding Indians and their role in the modern American cultural world. Some Indian people actively spoke out against this, while the actions of others remained misunderstood.

The fair's organizers clearly showed their view of Indians with the printing of the exposition's admission tickets. They sold tickets with four images on them: an Indian in headdress, Christopher Columbus, George Washington, and Abraham Lincoln. These were intended to portray "four epochs in the history of our country," according to one contemporary observer. The latter three represented European discovery of North America, the revolutionary break from England, and the end of slavery. The image of the Indian was meant to show "that period when the country was entirely under the dominion of the savage."[4] This perspective unabashedly consigned Indians to the distant American and human past.

The Indians who came did so both to work and be displayed, on the one hand, and as interested visitors themselves, on the other. However, much of the literature regarding their role at the fair focuses on representation. Numerous competing perspectives infused the efforts of those who were displaying Indians. For the most part they did not reflect Indian reality in the late nineteenth century. They did, however, help create and cement American cultural stereotypes about Indians that would both impede their efforts to succeed in modern America and help define the scholarly literature regarding the fair for a long time to come.

Scholarly works on the role of Indians at the fair have largely pursued a binary analysis. Following long-standing interpretations of American Indians, they describe the displays as depicting Indians either as primitivistic or, in relation to the school displays, progressive. This reflects the scholarly descriptions that largely held until the

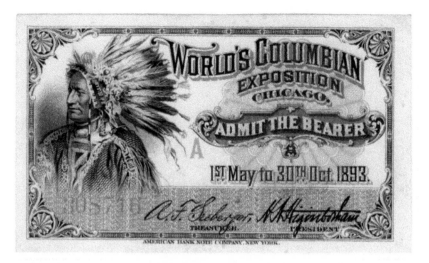

1. Admission ticket representing North America before Columbus's arrival. Courtesy Chicago Public Library, Special Collections, WCE Ephemera, box 4, folder 37.

1980s or 1990s of individual Indians as either traditional or progressive and educated. In part the literature on representation reflects the failure to account for the myriad and broad experiences of Indians who worked at the fair.

In reality, the representations of American Indians at the fair fall into five categories: Indians as they wanted themselves to be known and understood, Indians as objects of science, Indians as assimilating into American society, Indians as romantic images and actors reflecting a bygone era, and Indians as savage or wild representations of America's past. These representations competed with each other in various venues both on and off the fairgrounds throughout the entire run of the exposition.

Indian Efforts at Self-Definition

American Indians made several efforts to control their representations to the public during the fair. They hoped that the public would come to see them as part of modern American society. Perhaps the individual most written about has been the Potawatomi Simon Pokagon. But Henry Standing Bear, as well as tribal governments and other Indian individuals, also tried to show the world who they were.

2. Simon Pokagon. Painting by Elbridge Ayer Burbank. Courtesy Peabody Museum of Archaeology and Ethnology, Harvard University, PM# 2004.29.6369 (digital file# 160480048).

Their efforts collectively stand in stark contrast to the ways in which fair organizers envisioned portraying them.

It was purportedly after a visit to the Midway Plaisance that Pokagon penned "The Red Man's Rebuke," which he retitled "The Red Man's Greeting." In it, he wrote that "we have no spirit to celebrate with you the great Columbian Fair," describing the event as a celebration of "our own funeral, the discovery of America." He poignantly lamented that the trust and aid given by Indians to the white man had led to severe destruction for tribal communities and eradication of hope for future generations. When the publication of this document led to a relationship with Mayor Carter Harrison Sr., Pokagon was invited to celebrate Chicago Day with him. He also met with fair organizers and emphasized the importance of countering the stereotypical views of Indians perpetuated by the Midway displays.[5]

Pokagon had a deeper purpose than simply rebuking the fairgoers who would read his birch bark greeting. His lifelong quest, following the lead of his father, Leopold Pokagon, was to gain recompense for the lands the Potawatomi had sold in 1833 but had not been entirely paid for. The lands included Chicago; in fact, as a child Simon had accompanied his father to the treaty negotiations in what would become Chicago after the land was sold. He developed a friendship with Harrison at the fair, and the mayor promised to help him lobby Washington for remuneration. This never occurred, however, because the mayor was murdered before the fair's end.[6]

Another Indian who came to the fair also did so strictly to advance the interests of his tribe. Terrill Bradby, a Pamunkey Civil War veteran from Virginia, was the uncle of the tribe's chief, C. S. Bradby. He had made pottery objects for the Smithsonian display at the behest of Otis Mason and became a key collaborator with James Mooney. Through Mason, Bradby obtained an introduction from the Office of Indian Affairs, and Harvard anthropologist Frederic Putnam made him an "honorary assistant" in the Department of Ethnology, introducing him as the Pamunkey representative to other Indians on the fairgrounds, including Haudenosaunee and Penobscot leaders.[7]

Bradby made the trip in July with the authorization of the tribe's chief and council, and his agenda was the revitalization of the Pamunkey tribe. Due to outmarriage, their numbers had dwindled to about

3. William Terrill Bradby. Courtesy National Anthropological Archives, Smithsonian Institution BAE GN 00893.

140. Before his trip Bradby met with Virginia's governor and presented him with a peace pipe.[8] He asked for and received a document certifying that the tribe had a reservation and recognition from the commonwealth of Virginia as having title to the land. According to the *Indian Chieftain* of Vinita in the Indian Territory, he hoped to "induce a limited number of young and strong full-blood Indians of good character to settle on the Pamunkey reservation in Virginia and marry Pamunkey maidens." They would be offered good homestead land in exchange. His efforts do not seem to have been successful; when Frank Speck visited the Pamunkey in 1919, he found 90 Indians on the reservation and some 30 others living nearby.[9]

The Pamunkey, like other southeastern tribes, struggled to maintain an identity in a Jim Crow state. They had to constantly prove to the outside world that they were distinct from both their black and white neighbors, walking a perilous tightrope. Sometimes this meant adapting an "Indian" imagery that the white population found acceptable.[10] They were further challenged by their declining numbers. Bradby, like Pokagon, was a visitor to the fair, not a performer or laborer. Viewed together, their efforts in Chicago in 1893 representing their tribes' interests provide a small window into the legal, political, and cultural conditions and challenges faced by Indians in this era of intense assault upon their communities.

Some American Indians who performed and worked at the fair also did so because their work provided them with opportunities to carry forward cultural activities that were under attack, and in some cases even banned, in their homelands. Linda McNenly writes, "When government assimilation policies forbade ceremonies and dances on reservations, patriotic events, holidays, fairs, and Wild West shows provided a context in which warrior songs and dances could hide in plain sight. . . . While Wild West shows were celebrating white society's ultimate victory, Native performers may well have been singing about their own bravery and victories."[11]

Even before the fair opened, Henry Standing Bear, of Pine Ridge, along with several allies protested the roles that it became increasingly evident that Indians would play. He wanted the fair to focus on the assimilation efforts that Indians themselves were making. In an 1891 letter to Commissioner of Indian Affairs Thomas Jefferson Morgan, he proposed that the federal government should pay for tribal elders ("old chiefs") to attend the fair in order to see the value of civilizing influences on Indians. The Columbian Exposition would provide "a grand opportunity to show them why you have taken from them their hunting land and why you are trying to take away from them their paints, feathers and blankets, and make them give up their dances of every kind," he wrote.

But Standing Bear also wanted the public to see Indians as real people, not stereotypes. He told the commissioner, "They want to come as men and not like cattles [*sic*] driving to a show. Before the public they want to bring some impression that they are men and respectable. If they should come to the Fair . . . they do not wish Buffalo-Bills or some government scout or any other that party [*sic*] who will missrepresent [*sic*] our race."[12]

Standing Bear was not the only one who felt this way. A-Te-Ka, a Pawnee man, visited the fairgrounds before the fair opened and was discouraged to learn that Buffalo Bill's Wild West show had secured space nearby. He believed such an exhibit would only reinforce visitors' perceptions that Indians were not part of the modern world. He wanted visitors to see the impact of western education on Indian people. "I have been led to fear that no proper notice of the work being done for our Indians is to appear on those grounds," he wrote, referring to this as a "disgrace." He hoped Indians would have the opportunity to participate in the exposition to counteract the stereotypes that Buffalo Bill presented. "I have hoped delegations from the northern and southern tribes of Indians, some of those grand old Chippeways and those cultivated gentlemen from the Five Nations, would meet at the World's Fair and give the lie to that gross show by their dignified and cultivated bearing."[13]

Putnam also made forceful statements in opposition to Wild West representations of Indians. Standing Bear and his friends wrote to Putnam in 1892 supporting his position:

> In the name of the Nations of the Indian Territory; of the Dakotah Indian Nation; of the Six Nation Indians of New York; and of the Latin-Indian Nations of the North and South, permit us to extend you the assurance of our appreciation of your pub-

lic announcement, that in the reunion of the Nations of the earth at the World's Columbian Exposition, the perpetration of any Wild West show at the expense of the dignity and interest of the Indian Nations will, by you, be neither encouraged nor countenanced.[14]

In late 1892 Emma Sickels reported that an Indian uprising would occur because of dissatisfaction with the Indian exhibits, but the Office of Indian Affairs denied this and no other evidence of it exists.[15] Clearly, though, some Indians were upset with their portrayal at the fair, and Simon Pokagon's articulate rebuke conveyed the disappointment that many tribal members felt. For them, the fair provided a missed opportunity to shape public perceptions of American Indians in the contemporary context.

Other groups of Indians hoped to have their own exhibits at the fair. These included the Five Civilized Tribes (Cherokee, Creek, Chickasaw, Choctaw, and Seminole) of Indian Territory (which would later be incorporated into Oklahoma).[16] A brass band consisting of members of the Santee Sioux tribe of Nebraska asked to be brought to the fair to perform.[17] The Osage tribe of Oklahoma paid the way for thirty students from the Osage Boarding School to be part of the U.S. government education exhibit.[18]

These groups and others hoped to participate in the fair on their own terms, to show the world that they were not prehistoric peoples or Wild West show caricatures. They wanted the fair's visitors to know that they were very much a part of the modern world. Very few succeeded. They had varying motivations and goals. Their statements and efforts signify strong opposition to the representations that would permeate the fairgrounds.

Some Native people, of course, simply wanted to be involved in the fair. One Abenaki woman understood that representation was a key to participation, and she was willing to shape her self-representation to meet whatever expectations fair organizers had. Emma Reeves wrote to federal officials that she had read in the paper "about Indians being wanted for the World's Fair." And she asked for details. "We are Indians from the State of Maine tribe called Abnaki we make fancy baskets and would be very much please to get in the fair if you needed any such Indians. I was in the Buffalo exposition was . . . called the Civilized Indian and showing the improvements of dress and of Indian work of one hundred years ago. I will dress in Indian costume or in citizens dress just as you would like."[19] In the end she succeeded and came as an Iroquois in Putnam's ethnological village.[20]

Matthew Bokovoy has written that "native peoples . . . influenced the conditions and circumstances for the inclusion of their civilizations into regional and national memory" in their exposition work.[21] Although their efforts proved largely ineffectual at impacting white perspectives of Native peoples during the fair, they continued and reinforced Native traditions of insisting on the right of self-definition. Even against great odds and pressures to accommodate, they infused into the documentation of the fair a perspective of their place in it and in American society in the late nineteenth century. They also performed cultural traditions that were meaningful to them and their home communities, unbeknownst to fair organizers or visitors. In this way they subverted the dominant narrative in ways that only they recognized. Careful reading of the evidence gives us the opportunity to reinsert their perspectives into our memory of the fair.

Newspaper accounts of the representatives of the major tribes in the fair's ethnological exhibit occasionally reported on the Indians at the fair as modern peoples. In some cases, they presented them as advanced in western civilization and adapting well to American society, but still maintaining a tribal identity. The Penobscots were described as Roman Catholic, speaking French and English, and being politically and economically independent in Maine based on their long history of interaction with their white neighbors. They worked in lumber camps and farms, leased their riverfront property to lumber barons for timber storage, and used universal suffrage to elect their own governor and lieutenant governor, their own council of chiefs, and a representative to the Maine legislature. They did so at a time when women in the United States were not accorded the right to vote. The Penobscots who came to the fair and set up camp in Putnam's ethnological village were among the tribe's leaders.[22]

The Kwakwaka'wakw were described by a Chicago newspaper shortly after their arrival at the fairgrounds in April 1893 as Methodist or other Protestant rather than Episcopal or Catholic.[23] The men hunted and fished for a living, and the women farmed and gathered berries. Hundreds of women worked the canneries in the summer, according to James Deans, the agent who brought them to the fair. "A more honest people never lived," he told a reporter, "and their love of home and family would put many a civilized nation to the blush." The newspaper article opines, "There is nothing about them that suggests the Indian of the plains save their copper color. Simple in their modes of life, farmers as well as hunters, religious in their tendencies, and trustful of all men as they are themselves honest, they are a strong contrast to the treacherous and wily Sioux and bloodthirsty Apaches."[24] Ironically, newspapers occasionally contrasted Indian groups to each other the way that fair organizers contrasted Indians to white America, to show the differences between "savagism" and "civilization."

The Haudenosaunee (Iroquois) who exhibited themselves at the fair were described as representatives of leading families in their various tribes. Like the Penobscot, they were portrayed as having long interacted politically with their non-Indian neighbors. One New York newspaper poked fun at the efforts to make the Indians seem to be from a past age. "These Indians will live in their original fashion, it is announced, the disinfectants to be supplied by the World's Fair Commission," according to a *New York Herald* story. But the article then went on to say, "The last observation must not be taken literally, of course, as these Indians from New York are really quite tame and very good fellows." The *Herald*'s definition? "They read Bibles and newspapers and like true New Yorkers are ever ready to make sarcastic remarks about Chicago." A Chicago newspaper described the Haudenosaunee evenhandedly upon their arrival, observing, "Civilized and engaged in agricultural and other peaceful pursuits they have retained their native language uncorrupted and have pride in their past achievements."[25]

These stories hardly describe Indians as peoples of a pre-Columbian epoch. A member of the Board of Indian Commissioners told Commissioner Morgan before the fair opened that if full-blooded Indians from among the Haudenosaunee were to be displayed as proposed, it would "seem like an animal exhibition" and be "de-humanizing, so to speak, if unaccompanied by specimens of their industries."[26]

THE PAST LOOKING UPON THE PRESENT

4. Opening day. This image shows how difficult it could be for American Indians to be seen by their contemporaries as modern people. From *Inter Ocean*, 2 May 1893.

Richard Henry Pratt later complained to the secretary of the interior about this: "Whole families of educated Indians were paid to put themselves on exhibition daily in their old tribal garb."[27] In contrast, these newspaper articles describe people and communities that were adapting to the massive upheavals and changes around them. They were participating in the modern economy, and interacting with the non-Indian world around them. Each of the articles also describes features of traditional value systems and practices that still infused the tribal communities.

Even as Indians were presented in a nuanced way in some cases, they were often depicted as peoples of the past rather than the present. When New York planned its exhibit, the organizers reportedly attempted to portray Haudenosaunee "life customs and evolutions as

5. Medicine Horse and Plenty Horses. From *Photographs of the World's Fair*, 347.

a special exhibit at Jackson Park." The purpose? "To demonstrate that the scepter has not departed from the heirs of the Iroquois confederacy, and that [non-Native New Yorkers] remain what nature intended them to be, and what their own strong hands have made them—the Empire State of the Union."[28] In this instance, while New Yorkers were showing Haudenosaunee not only as they were in aboriginal times but also as they were adapting to a changing world, they nonetheless served as foils in white New Yorkers' efforts to center themselves as the epitome of modern progress.

While articles reflective of contemporary Indian conditions were rare, they were not the only indication that Indians' lives differed from the stereotypical images presented at the fair. Some Indians enthusiastically met people at the fair and shared their experiences with them. A book of photos from the fair described Medicine Horse, who came as part of Buffalo Bill's cast, as "different from the average Indian, [he] displays an apparent eagerness to talk. He is very interesting to listen to, and the information he gives regarding his people and the prospects of their civilization becoming more general, is of much interest and value."[29] The records don't show any more than this about what Medicine Horse said, but clearly he wanted fair visitors to have a positive view of the place of American Indians, or at least Lakotas, in modern America. These stories did a better job reflecting the modern reality of the Indians who worked at the fair than did the fair's organizers.

Science and Assimilation

Frederic Putnam was pleased with the division of labor he had worked out with Commissioner Morgan more than a year before the fair's opening. Putnam would oversee the ethnological and anthropological exhibits portraying the Indian of the past, while the federal government would develop a boarding school exhibit with students and instructors to illustrate the American-sponsored path to the Indian future. Putnam hoped to provide "as thorough collections as possible" from the tribes "illustrating their method of life, their customs and manufactures." He wanted these to be "purely Indian in character," and he instructed collectors to acquire objects that showed no European influence.[30] He wanted his display to portray anthropology as a modern science studying and showing cultural purity. This would ignore contemporary Indian community realities in an effort to show fairgoers idealized pre-Columbian lifeways of the peoples of the Americas.

This reflected the focus of Putnam's work at Harvard University in the years leading up to the fair. In describing the roles of the ethnological exhibit and the government school in relation to one another, Putnam said, "the purpose of the Ethnographical Exhibition is for scientific study of the Indian in his primitive life; and that the United States Government undertakes to represent the progress made by the Indian in education and civilization, thus completing their history up to the present time."[31] Any cultural adaptations Indians had already made would blur the contrast. Putnam tried scrupulously to avoid any hints of modernizing influences in his collecting.

The press, U.S. officials, and no doubt the public viewed the contrasting displays in a slightly different way. A Philadelphia newspaper reported, "Professor Putnam will have charge of an ethological [sic] exhibit, next to the school-building, where Indian families will exemplify the condition out of which the Indian schools take their pupils."[32] This depicts a view of the Indian villages as contemporary rather than historic or prehistoric. As a result, it would provide a stronger portrayal of both the necessity of government-sponsored schools and the contrast between savagism and civilization in the popular imagination. Though this contrast did not reflect Indian reality or Putnam's knowledge of late nineteenth-century Indian life, it did reflect his overall plans.

Putnam intended that his ethnological village in conjunction with the displays on physical anthropology and archaeology in the Anthropology Building would provide a baseline to contrast science and progress. While the archaeological materials collected from across the hemisphere and the models made of Mayan ruins and the Cave Dwellers exhibit spoke of a prehistoric past, Putnam intended his ethnological village to reinforce that. Putnam was very conscious of the meaning and his use of the term *prehistoric* as predating Columbus's arrival in the hemisphere.[33] He thought the Columbian Exposition would be an ideal venue to contrast the pre-Columbian with the modern world. His planning and collecting focused on representative pre-Columbian dwellings, tools, clothing, and artisan materials.

Putnam and others spoke and wrote often of the scientific value of his displays. He hoped for scientists from across the world to visit Department M, the Department of Ethnology and Archaeology, and indeed he had amassed the largest extant American-focused archaeological exhibition. The Anthropological Congress held in conjunction with the fair in late August and early September 1893 included a program that heavily featured papers by ethnologists, folklorists, archaeologists, and linguists who studied the ancient Americas.[34]

Some of the Indians who worked to collect materials for the fair also did so in order to help present Indians from a scientific perspective. The Tuscarora military man Capt. Cornelius Cusick hailed from a family that had strong connections to Henry Rowe Schoolcraft, and he viewed himself as an ethnologist. He did collecting work for Putnam. Terrill Bradby, a Pamunkey man who collected for the Smithsonian, viewed this work as scientific in basis. And George Hunt, the Kwakwaka'wakw cultural mediator, spent much of his adult life working with Franz Boas, including presenting a scientific paper with him at the 1893 Anthropological Congress.

The Smithsonian Institution developed its exhibits with a focus on science as well, although it did not use living Indians as part of the exhibit. Curator of ethnology Otis Mason succinctly summarized his hopes early on: "A plan is proposed as follows: To show at Chicago, as accurately as possible the aboriginal life of North America at the time the natives were first viewed by the Whites and before they were changed by contact with our civilization. Such an exhibit has never been attempted for any continent before because the means were not at hand to carry it out."[35]

Mason organized his exhibit around John Wesley Powell's newly developed linguistic classification system, selecting eleven language groups from across the country. He and his crew did this with life-sized casts of Indian people from different tribes, clothing them appropriately and surrounding them with material objects collected from those tribal communities. These exhibits would then be returned to Washington DC after the fair and put on display in the national museum.[36] Mason's efforts to organize his displays based on "culture-

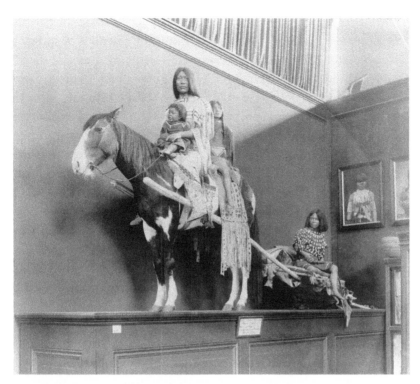

6. Plains Indian travois, Smithsonian Institution exhibit. Courtesy Library of Congress. Photo number 3c07333u.

area" and "life-group" represented "innovations" that would form the basis of future museum displays not only at the Smithsonian but in natural history museums more generally.[37]

Despite this stated purpose, Smithsonian exhibits featured European impacts on Indian cultures in ways that fairgoers might not even have recognized. The Plains Indian display included a horse travois and Navajo Indians were depicted weaving a woolen blanket. These were already archetypal images of Indians popularized in the American imagination. Smithsonian scientists presented them as precontact, although they actually represented significant cultural adaptation with the use of European domesticated animals.[38]

The U.S. government's American Indian schoolhouse stood in close proximity to the ethnological village, an intended juxtaposition of imagery.[39] The school was intended to portray the federal government's heroic efforts to assimilate children. The Canadian government created a similar school exhibit with the purpose of showing the successful efforts of both missionaries and government officials in their assimilation work. With this U.S. government exhibit, Commissioner Morgan desired to contrast the so-called primitive with the civilized. He wrote that nearby "will be the ethnological exhibit . . . where Indian families, dressed in native costume, living in native dwellings and engaged in primitive occupations, will exemplify the conditions out of which the Indian schools are taking and transforming their pupils. The entire picture of barbarous and civilized life will thus be concretely presented."[40] In contrast to Putnam's intention, Morgan viewed the ethnological village as a representation of contemporary Indian life.

Morgan had hoped to develop all of the fair's Indian exhibits, but he soon discovered that budgetary restrictions would prevent this from occurring. The resolution to this problem was for the OIA to focus its exhibit on schoolchildren and turn over the exhibition of aboriginal Indian life to Putnam. Morgan told the secretary of the interior that he was pleased to divide the work with Putnam, as "the curiosity of people to see Indians in their native habitations will be satisfied and the efforts of the Government for the bringing of them into civilized life concretely presented."[41]

The U.S. exhibit brought groups of thirty children from government and private schools for three weeks at a time, with the schools rotating in attendance. The children did school work, probably not very effectively, while visitors crowded around them in the cramped space of the school building. One visitor described seeing children from the Albuquerque Indian School. The girls sewed dresses by hand and machine, while the boys made harnesses and shoes and learned carpentry. Another visitor described seeing a wagon built by an Indian boy.[42]

The most famous boarding school operator of the time, Capt. Richard Henry Pratt, refused to participate in the government school exhibit and went directly to the commissioner of Indian affairs for permission to bring students from Carlisle Indian Industrial School to the fairgrounds to drill, parade, and play music. A contingent of five companies of Carlisle's students had participated in the dedicatory ceremonies in October 1892.[43] A year later he gained permission from

7. Sarah Archiquette. From *Chicago Tribune*, 26 April 1893.

the fair's authorities, on recommendation from the commissioner, to bring 450 Carlisle students to the fair for a week. The military-style training of Carlisle's students drew the enthusiastic support of the fair's leadership.[44] Pratt also mounted a static display in the Manufactures and Liberal Arts Building that critics panned. This showed off examples of student work and photographs of the students, including Jennie Thunder Bull (Sioux), Delia Randall (Bannock), Nellie Fremont (Omaha), and Sarah Archiquette (Oneida).[45]

Anthropologist George Dorsey also viewed the fair as an opportunity to provide this same contrast. The contrast for him, however, was not only a contrast among Indians but also between races. Indians represented the human past, Caucasians the modern world. He described the traditional manufacture work that living Indians would produce at the fair and noted its distinction from modernization. "Their work will afford a very striking contrast to the work shown in the government Indian school, which will be in full operation close by. The illustration of primitive life will make more apparent the material progress made in America during the past four hundred years."[46] Unlike Putnam, Dorsey viewed the living ethnological display as a representation of modern Indian life. Like casual observers, much of the anthropological community insisted on viewing contemporary Indians as peoples of the past and as anachronistic in modern America. In this way, Indians were best viewed juxtaposed to modernism, the opposite of what many Indians themselves believed or wanted the public to see.

World's Columbian Exposition Illustrated, a popular magazine that claimed a monthly readership of 1.5 million, reinforced this perspective. "Almost under the eaves of the [U.S. government Indian] school the red man will be living in his tepee and in his hogan or hut, pursuing his native labors and pastimes," one article observed. "That is to say, the squaws will do the work while the bucks will look after the pastimes, clad in the fashion of the forest before government blankets came into use among them."[47] The Indian village was to provide a foil to contrast not only the development of modern America but also the work of missionaries and government school educators. Indian children were shown off as the fruits of assimilation efforts.

Romanticization and Savage Imagery

While Putnam and the U.S. Indian Service portrayed Indians from scientific and assimilative perspectives, Buffalo Bill Cody romanticized them. His Wild West program was far and away the venue where most fairgoers saw Indians, even if it was located outside the fairgrounds. A vast literature has addressed Buffalo Bill's life and the role of Indians in his popular extravaganas.[48] The seventy-three Lakota Indians from Pine Ridge who participated in the Wild West program in Chicago portrayed themselves as defending their homelands against the inevitable advancement of American civilization, but then making peace with their conquerors.

COL CODY AND SOME OF THE NATIVES.

8. Buffalo Bill and some of his Lakota contingent at the Nebraska Day celebrations. From "Nebraska's Day of Joy," *Chicago Times,* 8 June 1893.

As historian L. G. Moses describes it, "In telling his story of the triumph of civilization over savagery," Cody "reminded his audiences that, where once Euro-Americans and American Indians had met as enemies, challenging each other for mastery of a continental empire, they must now live together as friends." His show presented Indians as valiant, but unsuccessful, protectors of homelands who could stoically accept defeat. One young attendee wrote succinctly of this part of the program that the military "had a sham fight with the Indians." Cody presented Indians in this way to portray to the public "his self-proclaimed mission to 'bring the white and red races closer together.'"[49] Cody put on more than 660 shows during the fair and often sent his Indian performers to represent the romantic past at events across the fairgrounds.

The Indians who worked for Buffalo Bill were easily the most visible at the exposition, despite the fact that they camped and performed outside the fairgrounds. Because of this they played an important role in shaping the public's perceptions of who Indian people were. Most of the visitors who attended the fair had never seen any Indians in the flesh. The Lakota who worked for Buffalo Bill regularly wore their regalia in public, whether in the Wild West show itself, in their camp, which was regularly opened to visitors, or when attending special events. Cody viewed their visibility as an opportunity for free advertising. Since with a few exceptions the Lakota were not gregarious in their relations with outsiders, they gave fairgoers an image of stoic passivity. Together with their energetic antics during the show, and the encampment tipis and campfires, they left most who saw them with the impression that they had seen "real" or representative Indians. Already Plains Indians were viewed by the public as prototypical Indians, and those who worked for Buffalo Bill reinforced this perception.

One of Cody's employees, Short Bull, even served as a model for a statue depicting a Potawatomi man, crafted by the famed sculptor Carl Rohl-Smith, to be erected in Chicago. Rohl-Smith did not seem to think the Potawatomis looked Indian enough for public display.[50] This perception was widespread. In hyping their own city's fair two years later, the *Atlanta Constitution* reported, "'At Chicago,' . . . Buffalo Bill's show had been 'accepted as the key to all' and was voted the most genuine of ethnological exhibits.'"[51]

In contrast to Cody's romanticized focus, the exhibits on the Midway titillated audiences by portraying Indians in a way that would frighten the audience—or at least make fairgoers shudder at the recent western American past. The American Indians and other Native peoples exhibited by entrepreneurs and business interests on the Midway Plaisance reflect yet another representation, that of barbaric, wild, untamed savagery. Drawings in *World's Fair Puck* present grotesque caricatures of the Native peoples exhibited on the Midway, including American Indians, South Sea Islanders, Arabs, and Africans.[52] The Indians on display on the Midway included Lakota individuals at Sitting Bull's cabin, a group of some sixty Ho-Chunk (Winnebago), Potawatomi, and Sioux, and a purported village of Aztecs from Mexico.[53]

The "Esquimau Village," a display of nine to twelve Inuit families from Greenland, while located separately from the Midway, was

9. Caricatures of ethnic groups on Midway Plaisance. From *World's Fair Puck*, 30 October 1893, 306–7.

referred to as a Midway exhibit in some histories. One, a contemporary volume written by former Virginia governor William Cameron, referred to the "Squalid Esquimaux" as "the quintessence of the great unwashed." Referring to the inhabitants of this display, he writes, "In their race characteristics they are a decided novelty. They occupy a class all alone. Indeed, they mark the boundary of the human growth in the North just as the stunted pines do at timber line."[54] The Native people of the Midway were presented to fairgoers as examples of primitive savagery. Most visitors probably did not make distinctions among various Native groups throughout and in proximity to the fairgrounds. Most simply viewed Indians generically, as Indians, not as distinctive cultural groups, despite Putnam's or Indians' own efforts.

It is worth noting that American Indians were not the only people disturbed by the way they were represented at the fair. Humorist Julian Hawthorne, in writing about what he considered the unbecoming Transportation Building, disparaged its sculptures, including those of an Indian and a cowboy on mustangs: "It is impossible to say in becoming language how atrociously bad these groups are," he wrote.

10. Eskimo village. From Bancroft, *The Book of the Fair*, 2 of 2:633.

"Indeed, a cowboy having strayed to this point from Buffalo Bill's Show-grounds, was so outraged at the sight of the alleged portrait of his guild, that he called together a squad of his fellows, armed with crowbars, and prepared, amidst much vigorous language, to upset the wretched thing into the Lake. Only the timely appearance of Buffalo Bill himself prevented the consummation of their purpose, which was a pity."[55]

It should also be noted that some exhibits on the Midway attracted far more visitors than the American Indian exhibits on the fairgrounds. One contemporary history of the fair devoted but one sentence to the Indian village in forty-eight pages about the Midway.[56] This likely reflected the attitudes of many fair visitors. The author of a book of photographs of the fair observed, "The foreign elements at the Fair undoubtedly attract the greater part of the visitors' attention and it is a somewhat lamentable fact that the aborigines of this country are almost neglected."[57] Buffalo Bill's show outside of the fairgrounds drew massive crowds, however.

At one point in June, the "Streets of Cairo" exhibit drew 14,000 visitors a day.[58] Indeed, that display brought in more than twenty-four

PART V.
With one loud whoop, with one fell swoop,
They swarm down on the stand ;
The sons of Ham in the foremost jam,
With a big slice in each hand.

11. "Darkies' Day at the Fair." From *World's Fair Puck*, 21 August 1893, 186–87.

times as much money as the Midway's Indian Village. The Eskimo Village, despite its out-of-the-way location off the Midway, outpaced the American Indian Village by nearly six times. Few exhibits brought in as little money as the American Indian Village.[59] Thomas R. Roddy, who oversaw the village, protested that he was too far from the street to attract many visitors.[60] All of these were dwarfed by Buffalo Bill's profits.

Disparagement of people of color displayed on the Midway from places across the globe was widespread among observers and critics of the fair. This included not only Native Americans but more prominently South Sea Islanders, Far Easterners, and nearly all non-Europeans who were displayed at the fair. Special derision and condemnation was reserved for the members of the Dahomey Village, who were almost universally represented as savage, brutal, and subhuman.[61] By comparison, depictions of American Indians in the popular press, while often demeaning, were far less virulent. One observer wrote in the *Chicago Tribune* about the Dahomeyans, "The wild dances, wilder songs, and yet wilder music of these black people exceed in savage intensity the most warlike ceremonies of any tribe of blanket Indians in America. The ferocity pictured on the faces of the warlike subjects of the Dahoman King when their passions are wrought up over their songs and incantations suggest the savage beast more than the human being."[62] Images published in popular magazines such as *Puck* depicted Africans on the Midway in crude caricatures of barbarity. This even extended to images of African Americans drawn to commemorate what *Puck* called "Darkies' Day at the Fair."[63]

The competition for representation of Indians was won by several parties—including Putnam, Cody, the U.S. Indian Service, and the Smithsonian—but not by Indians themselves. Indians were viewed at the fair, and would be for a long time into the future, in various binary forms: romantic or savage, primitive or progressive, backward or educated. They were not viewed on their own terms, striving to make their way in the modern world while maintaining traditional values.

Although the Wild West show and the Indian villages strengthened popular misconceptions of Indians, the ethnological focus of the fair's organizers laid the groundwork for much of the portrayal of Indians at the fair. It therefore also provided the means by which Indians, even many of those affiliated with Buffalo Bill's Wild West, would experience the fair.

2

Evolution of the American
Indian Displays at the Fair

Indigenous peoples had been put on official display at world's fairs before the Columbian Exposition. Both the Dutch government in 1883 and the French in 1889 organized displays of their colonized peoples at their own sponsored expositions. And unofficial displays of exotic peoples had been made outside of fairgrounds before that.[1] The 1893 Chicago fair was both the first with an officially sponsored live American Indian exhibit in the United States and the first to sponsor a variety of Indian displays that brought hundreds of Native individuals to the venue. In addition, the fair exhibited a massive display of Indian-made objects collected from across the hemisphere.

As with other fairs, officials intended that these displays would be educational and that they would portray American benevolence in a way that justified imperialistic colonization. The colonial subjects—in this case American Indians—rebelled against this portrayal of them, sometimes overtly, sometimes covertly. Although organizers attempted to thwart or dampen their efforts at self-definition, Native participants pushed back. The system that they pushed back against was built with strength. Powerful institutional representatives—governmental, academic, and commercial—all aligned themselves in this effort. In Chicago, they were led by the scientific work under the leadership of the inimitable Frederic Ward Putnam, whom Alfred Tozzer called "the prime force in anthropology for almost fifty years."[2] Like Franz Boas and Daniel Brinton, he is credited with catalyzing the shift in the field of anthropology from an avocation reliant on patrons to a professional science buttressed by university reputations and authority.[3]

The bulk of the effort in developing these exhibits tilted toward the display of objects. This meant that a massive collection project had to be undertaken in tribal communities in the years before the fair. It is not possible to understand the scope of work relating to the American Indians and other indigenous people brought to be on display and work at the fair without an analysis of the work of Putnam and his vision for both the static and the living ethnological exhibits. Though his original plan deviated significantly from what actually happened at the fair, his conceptualization of it impacted nearly every feature of the Native displays.

Putnam's efforts convinced fair officials to deny Buffalo Bill Cody a place on the fairgrounds, pushing the most popular programming that included Indians to a nearby venue. Even though he lost control of the Midway Plaisance, Putnam still retained the right of approval of its contracts, and he maintained some oversight of the Indian people displayed and working there. And of course, his own anthropology building and the nearby ethnological village were entirely under his purview. When delving into the story of the fair itself, therefore, it is necessary to examine the planning for the anthropological and the living ethnological displays in Chicago. The collecting and organizing in the years leading up to the fair paved the way for the possibility of participation for Native peoples in Chicago. It also defined the ways in which fair organizers expected them to participate. An understanding of this will help to clarify the vastly different goals of fair organizers and tribal members—both at home and on the fairgrounds—in creating the displays. It all began with Putnam.

Anthropologist Stanley Freed has called the ethnological exhibit at the 1893 fair "the greatest anthropological exhibition ever assembled."[4] The significance of the fair to the field of anthropology is finally getting its due recognition with the publication of *Coming of Age in Chicago*, an edited volume on the relationship of the field's early luminaries to the fair.[5] Raymond Fogelson has written, "The prominence of anthropology was greater in Chicago than at any previous or subsequent world's fair."[6] Indeed, this was Putnam's aim. He seized the opportunity to do a work that he often felt to be overwhelming in order to show to the millions of fair visitors, and define for the world, the modern state of the nascent field of anthropology.

The massive collections that Putnam, Franz Boas, and an army of collectors gathered for the anthropology building would become, in part, the founding collections of Chicago's Field Museum of Natural History. This was one of the great natural history museums established in the United States in the late nineteenth century. These collections and others like them would bring anthropology to the broader public, although it also purportedly brought educational opportunities for this public to learn about premodern peoples.

Commissioner of Indian Affairs Thomas Morgan explained the relation of the government's school exhibit to Putnam's ethnological exhibit. "This exhibit of Indians in civilized conditions ought to have for its background a setting forth of the Indian in primitive conditions."[7] The latter would be Putnam's job and his platform to promote anthropology as a science. Tentative agreement over relative roles between Putnam, Morgan, and anthropologist Alice Fletcher was reached in January 1892.

Morgan decided that his office would oversee the Indian school "and exhibit its system of educating and civilizing the Indian." Putnam, who already had charge of the nonliving anthropology exhibits, would be in charge of the living exhibit, but would work through the OIA for display and participation of any Indian groups under the authority of the U.S. government and even those from foreign nations. Morgan said in the meeting that the exhibit would be considered a "government exhibit," since the OIA would vet Indian participants. He added, "It could be said that these are Indian Office Indians but they belong to the scientific exhibit." There was no sense from a federal or scientific perspective that the Indian people themselves had any agency or right of self-actualization in their participation. Putnam also gained the right to dole out and oversee the concessions related to the tribes.[8] These living exhibits would supplement the vast archaeological collections and physical anthropology displays in Putnam's building.

Frederic Ward Putnam

After meeting with Morgan and Fletcher, Putnam wrote exuberantly to his wife, Esther, "I am chief of the Natives as I intended to be, but there have been many squalls that I had to guide my ship through although I have said very little about them." He also told her, after the meeting in Washington, "Have fixed everything with Interior Department—*the whole Indian matter is in my hands.*"[9] That turned out not to be true. Oversight of the building, the material culture displays, the scientific laboratories, and the living ethnological exhibits scattered across the fairgrounds would prove too much for him to handle.

Putnam attempted to take on this gargantuan task, but shortly after his meeting with Morgan and Fletcher, the fair's managers gave control of the exhibits on the Midway Plaisance to San Francisco entrepreneur Sol Bloom. Historian James Gilbert has written that "Bloom commented that keeping Putnam head of the Midway was like making 'Albert Einstein manager of the Ringling Brothers Barnum and Bailey Circus.'"[10] Nonetheless, Putnam continued to be consulted on the living exhibits, even those not setting up encampments in his space on the lagoon next to the Anthropology Building.

In describing why he took on the work at the fair, Putnam emphasized that it was an extension of his work toward recognition of anthropology as a professional and scientific field. He added, "For 18 years I have worked unceasingly for the development of the [Peabody] Museum, that it should prove to the world that there is such a thing as science in archaeological research."[11] Archaeology had only become treated as a science in the decade before the Columbian Exposition.[12] The focus of the field was entrenched across the Atlantic. Putnam argued for the significance of context at the same time as he pushed for American archaeology to be valued in the same way it was in Europe. Similar to Chicago's goal to showcase America as a modern reflection of the civilized world, Putnam hoped to showcase American science in the archaeological realm.[13]

When he wrote to Harvard president Charles W. Eliot requesting permission to take a year's leave of absence to oversee the fair, Putnam said he had more than one hundred assistants in the field, including twenty-nine Harvard "private and graduate" students. He told Eliot, "Never before in this country have there been so many persons actively engaged in anthropological and ethnological research." He believed this was the greatest opportunity he would have in his lifetime to shape the field of "anthropological research in America."[14] Half a year after Putnam wrote to Eliot, the exposition's Council of

12. Frederic Ward Putnam. Courtesy Frederic Ward Putnam Papers, HUG 1717.2.14, World's Columbian Exposition, Records and Ephemera, box 37, Harvard University Archives.

Administration officially named Putnam's building the Anthropology Building. This was an important step in realizing his goal of bringing anthropology as a scientific field to the public's attention.[15]

At the time, the field of ethnology was at the end of a century-long process of reinventing itself from its origins as a field building collections of curiosities to one with a scientific basis of inquiry grounded in observation. Its focus was largely on those peoples whose lands had been stripped away by European and American colonization and whose knowledge would inevitably be lost to the world, in the view of ethnologists, as they disappeared as unique peoples either through extinction or acculturation. The foundation of the work thus became defined as salvage ethnology. This caused a mad rush to collect and categorize materials and knowledge. Even the Bureau of Ethnology was established on that basis.[16] To the extent that Native peoples' perspectives were incorporated into this project, it was merely on the basis of recording the past rather than defining their place in the contemporary world.

Putnam's vision for the ethnological exhibit was far-reaching, which is clear from examining his larger goals in organizing it. He worked to make anthropology visible to the larger public, hoping to wrest the locus from government archaeologists and ethnologists, such as those at the Smithsonian, and move it to university anthropology. He needed funding for the massive archaeological collections he was building, and the fair provided him with that.

Putnam orchestrated a media blitz through newspapers and journals in 1890 and early 1891 to drum up support for developing an audacious exhibition in 1893. He outlined his ambitious plans for the ethnological building and outdoor exhibits of live people for newspapers in New York, Chicago, and Boston. The stories were picked up in Philadelphia, San Francisco, and small-town newspapers. In part, he played into Chicago's inferiority complex and its fear that it was still considered a frontier backwater town rather than a modern representation of urban sophistication. In January 1891 he told the *Chicago Morning News*, "Something must be done to show that the Exposition is to be more than a gigantic cattle show and horticultural exhibition. Down east that idea largely obtains." He recognized that the fair would provide the greatest show of electricity ever. But he also wanted to appeal to the international scholarly community. He proposed something that he thought would be intellectually cutting-edge but also popular among the broader citizenry. "I think an ethnological display can be got up that will prove a great attraction not only to the scholar but to all other visitors."[17]

Putnam was appointed as the chief of the Department of Ethnology in February 1891.[18] He had difficulty defining his role, which shifted over time when he eventually lost control of the Midway Plaisance. He hoped to use the fair collections as a foundation for a permanent natural history museum in Chicago. He also insisted that he be provided with sufficient funding for the massive hemispheric collecting project that he envisioned. And finally, he wanted to showcase "his engaged, high-caliber students."[19] His true emphasis was archaeology, and his work was heavily influenced by his role in the development of modern natural history museums in the late nineteenth and early twentieth centuries.

The fair was put on during what Curtis M. Hinsley has called "the golden age of museum anthropology," and Putnam ran a museum that "stands actually alone, as an institutional model." The Peabody Museum, Hinsley argues, was the driving force behind the development of the anthropology department at Harvard.[20] Putnam's goal was to extend the place of anthropology much deeper into American consciousness. Building on his hopes to popularize archaeology and anthropology more generally, Putnam would boast near the fair's end, "This is the first time in the history of world's expositions that anthropology has been ranked as one of the great departments and given a departmental building. . . . Never before has so much new material in anthropology been brought together as is now exhibited in this department."[21] He believed that it met his goal of establishing American archaeological work as on a par with that done elsewhere in the world. His work at the fair also "solidified Putnam's pre-eminent position in American anthropology," according to Hinsley.[22]

The Collections

Putnam's exhibits were breathtaking in scope. Putnam oversaw the collection of material objects, and Boas oversaw the physical anthropology collection. They were housed within the Anthropology Build-

13. Franz Boas. Courtesy American Philosophical Society. U.5.1.22 Cabinet Card, Franz Boas Papers, 1860–1942, Mss B.B61.

ing and on the surrounding grounds on a grand and heretofore unheard of scale.

Putnam brought Boas on board to oversee collecting in 1891.[23] An article in the *Boston Post*, based on an interview with Putnam, said that Boas was specifically training students from both Clark University, where he was employed, and Harvard "to take the proper measurements and descriptions of individuals." The article went on to say, "This has never been done for the native peoples of America, and as a matter of research it will be regarded with great interest by all anthropologists."[24]

Boas, who cut his teeth at the Royal Ethnographic Museum of Berlin, held his first anthropology position at Clark. He resigned in 1892 to work full time with Putnam in the development of the ethnology exhibit.[25] After his collecting work on the Northwest Coast, Boas received a full appointment as Putnam's chief assistant in November 1892.[26]

The two main foci of the collecting were thus artifacts for display and physical measurements. The collectors were also charged, in some cases, with arranging for individual tribal members to attend the fair as part of the displays, to do traditional Native work for fairgoers to observe them in their ancient natural surroundings. The preparations proved to be an enormous undertaking. The bulk of the collecting was done under the direction of Putnam and Boas, by ethnologists contracted to travel throughout the hemisphere to do so, or by purchase from private collections. By July 1891 Putnam had some thirty collectors in the field, in North America, and Central and South America.[27] He used more than a hundred before the fair opened. All had at least small expense budgets that would infuse cash into local tribal communities.

Putnam's original plan, as articulated in 1891 and 1892 and scaled back as time went on, called for bringing Native people to display on the fairgrounds from Baffin Bay to the Tierra del Fuego.[28] He also told the *Boston Post* that "many different tribes of North, South and Central America will be represented either by families or small villages, living in their native habitations." He explained, "During the Exposition these people will be engaged in their various characteristic works, as pottery-making, weaving, basket-making, etc. In every case the object will be to furnish a perfect ethnographical study, and nothing whatever resembling a 'Wild West show' will be for an instant thought of, notwithstanding the newspapers have stated that such plans are under contemplation." In addition, cast models of individuals from various Native groups would be on display and later used in the museum to be built in Chicago.[29]

Through his aides, Boas ended up collecting measurements of more than 17,000 "full-blood and half-breed Indians" for his physical anthropology display. His hope was to use these physical measurements to determine racial classifications, but since so many interracial children had already been born, he was not sure he could do it.[30] Putnam kept the commissioner of Indian affairs apprised of these efforts, which carried not only the blessing of the Indian affairs office but also a letter from the commissioner authorizing this work.[31]

Despite the large numbers of measurements collected, which included children from boarding schools, collectors in the field ran into problems getting permission to make measurements from a number of tribal groups, making Boas's work incomplete. Dr. C. L. Hodgkins of Boston, for example, was sent to Oklahoma to take measurements of Indians, using the measuring rods and two sets of calipers issued by Boas.[32] He made two measurements at the Kaw Agency, including one of the tribe's leaders who died almost immediately afterward. According to a newspaper account, "The members of the tribe at once attributed his death to the mysterious measurements made by the doctor, and no amount of persuasion or threats would induce another one of the Kaws to submit to measurement or questioning." The anthropological work seemed nonsensical and dangerous to the Kaws.

At that point Hodgkins departed for the Osage Agency, where the Ghost Dance was being celebrated. A tribal leader there apparently had a vision that government officials in Washington had sent Hodgkins to spy on and measure Indians so they could plan their resistance to an Indian uprising. Nearly everyone at Osage also refused to be measured. Hodgkins finally left and was shot from his horse, walking the last six miles to his camp while bleeding heavily.[33]

Archibald Tisdale, sent to Nova Scotia, had mixed success, writing to Putnam:

At Campbellton I measured as many as I cd by working all day long for a week, permission to measure being necessary from the chief, who was with a party of Americans fishing 25 miles away. Without his consent the people refused. To get it I had to spend two days, five dollars, walk twenty two miles, wade in a river a mile, there being no road, + take a canoe the rest of the way. You see the difficulties are great, whence I expect you [to] understand why I have not a list of 600 or 700 measurements as my sanguine hopes had expected. Cape Breton was a failure.

He blamed that failure on "the inexplicable hostility of the priest + the stupid prejudice of the chief." The chief and other leaders at Cape Breton refused to let him measure the people of the tribe. The priest supported the chief. He was also refused permission to stay overnight on the island, and so he had to sail back and forth to the mainland each day. This did, however, provide him with an opportunity to make one measurement, which he only achieved through bribery, as he reported to Putnam.

> You will be amused at this—on my way to St. Peter's after my last vain appeal to the priest, . . . I measured the Indian who was sailing me. That was the only measurement. You see I had him apart, where I cd reason with him with no adverse comment of the chief or order to desist. He took shelter behind an island and the sail while I measured him in the boat—a ticklish job. When I was half through, he had a change of mind and threatened to break up my whole outfit. He might well have done it, we being some six miles from St. Peter's. I won him over again however at the cost of a promise never to reveal to the rest what he had done. I told him he might make some baskets and rustic seats for the Fair for his pains.[34]

People in tribal communities justifiably viewed outsiders coming to study them with suspicion. Such visits were increasingly common by the 1890s, and too often they worked only to the benefit of those doing the studying. When tribal members found that sharing information with ethnographers could be mutually beneficial, they would participate. Otherwise, they had no incentive to do so.[35] In addition, most of the collectors whom Boas and Putnam sent into the field had little understanding of tribal protocols or tribal belief systems, and they did not know the importance of learning them. Boas was aware of this. Soon after his appointment to oversee the collecting, he wrote to a colleague, "Of course it is somewhat difficult to induce the Indians to submit to measurements but I find that there are always means and ways to get at them."[36]

In some cases the collectors simply did not care how they got materials or data. One of Putnam and Boas's collectors, who identified himself as Antonio, an Apache, wrote to Putnam that he had measured eighty-five Apache women at Fort Wingate. "There is one difficulty and that is getting a lock of their hair. They believe if a person once gets a lock of their hair that they will always be in their power but I will be able to get plenty in the school."[37] He believed that when the children were away from the influences of their family and under the control of school officials, he could easily circumvent tribal protocol. Hair collected from Indians for the fair is now held by the American Museum of Natural History in New York.[38] The ethics of his actions did not concern him.

Grave robbery was also an important method for collection of both human remains and material objects throughout the hemisphere. A history of the fair published in 1893 accurately described the efforts of Putnam's collectors when it said, "North and South America, the torrid and the frigid zones, were ransacked by agents of the [ethnology] department in search of relics and specimens."[39] Almost all collectors were instructed to procure skeletal remains and funerary objects. Putnam wrote to his assistant Leslie Lee, for example, whom he sent to Labrador, "It is also expected that you will secure skeletons and skulls of native peoples, and if possible the complete contents, including skeletons, of one or more graves; and a number of crania, long bones and pelvic bones from a burial-cave, should you be so fortunate to discover one."[40]

Putnam wrote to George Dorsey in Peru, "I suppose you might possibly find one or two more good graves such as the one of which you gave me drawings. These mummies with the false faces will prove a great attraction and I should like to get more of them if we can. I suppose you took all the 'matting and rafters' over the mummy so that you can set it up again in Chicago. We will make it look just as you found it."[41] Apparently, Putnam and Dorsey did just that. One illustrated history of the fair remarked, "There are ridges of gravel and sandy soil, with mummies in all positions, and skulls, bones, and cloth interspersed. . . . There are more than 100 bodies of the Incas and other personages of note."[42]

Putnam urged Dorsey to view this work as a stepping-stone to his future in the field of archaeology. "It is the one great chance of your life," he wrote. "Do not lose it."[43] Dorsey, whom a contemporary called one of Putnam's "expert grave diggers," apparently decided that the way to take advantage of this opportunity was by collecting massive quantities of material by any means possible. This would become his lifelong approach.[44] Dorsey had few, if any, scruples. He later sent these instructions to one of his assistants: "When you go into an Indian's house and you do not find the old man at home and there is something you want, you can do one of three things: go hunt up the old man and keep hunting until you find him; give the old woman such price for it as she may ask for it running the risk that the old man will be offended; or steal it. I tried all three plans and have no choice to recommend."[45]

Putnam believed that excavations, to have scientific validity, needed to be all-inclusive. From the beginning Putnam emphasized the necessity of collecting data and taking good field notes in conjunction with collecting, an uncommon practice at that time.[46] He believed that all associated materials should be collected because "one and all shall show their associations and tell their story as a whole."[47] Dorsey's method of pillaging was directly contradictory to this method, as he raced from one site to another excavating what he thought were the choicest objects.[48] Dorsey was reported to be "quite enthusiastic over digging up mummies and the various objects found with them."[49] Nonetheless Putnam readily accepted and displayed Dorsey's collections. Together they created an exhibit that was lauded by the press.

Much of the archaeological work for the fair included digging up ancient mounds and removing burial sites—and these were not always ancient. Thomas Holgate wrote Putnam from Ontario, where he was collecting for the fair, "I located two, buried about 70 years ago, and obtained a good deal of information respecting the customs and modes of burial of the Indians of this section but could not persuade the old gentleman on whose farm the graves were to allow me to open them as he holds them in great reverence."[50] Putnam was driven in part to prove that valuable archaeological resources existed in the Western Hemisphere, not just elsewhere.

As anthropology became increasingly accepted as science, it took on the role of defining Indian identity, a role it would carry well into the twentieth century. As Lee Baker has observed in his book on anthropology, race, and culture, "Although anthropologists helped to constitute a theory of culture . . . they often did it by marshaling scientific authority to authenticate particular Indian practices as genuine, while explicitly and implicitly designating those practices they did not certify as fraudulent, broken, or simply not authentic."[51] They did this through displays of material culture and casts of people, and they also did this through the human ethnological displays at events such as the Columbian Exposition.

This, of course, ignored Indian realities. Instead it reified backward-looking perceptions of Indian identity. In both archaeological and ethnographic terms of the era, Indians were frozen in time—a time that was already of the past in Indian country. This made it easy for Putnam and Boas to oversee and provide instructions for the looting of Native American gravesites and objects of material culture. This in turn kept the American view of Indians locked in a bygone age, which dehumanized actual living Indians. They struggled hard to portray their own self-definitions to the outside world, but they faced both scientific and popular misconceptions that already existed and were constantly being strengthened.

Outdoor Ethnological Exhibit

Putnam planned to bring Native people to Chicago from tribal communities from one end of the hemisphere to the other. He expected to host and display Indian families from Tierra del Fuego, Patagonia, Venezuela, Bolivia, and Peru in South America, from the Mosquito Coast in Central America, and "several families of Caribs, the lowest of the races of people that met Columbus on our shores." From North America he planned to bring Indian families from among the Mayans of the Yucatan in Mexico, coastal tribes from British Columbia, and various tribal representatives from across the United States. He referred to Tierra del Fuegans as the "lowest of all in the scale of humanity," and added, "In all cases these simple people will bring their own habitations with them."[52]

He explained his plan in even greater detail in a letter to the fair's Committee on Liberal Arts in September 1891, when he urged them to let him establish an idyllic outdoor Indian display on the Wooded Island in the lagoon, an area central to the exposition but rustic and removed from the bustle of the modern buildings. Putnam believed that the outdoor display would be popular and also provide a wonderful contrast to the progress in civilization and the mechanical and practical arts as reflected in other countries' exhibits.

Putnam explicitly stated as much in one of his monthly reports to Director General George Davis. "To properly show what had been done during the last four centuries" to North and South American Indians, he wrote, "it was essential that there should be a background to the picture of intellectual and material development." That background would be provided by Native people living in their traditional houses, "dressed in their native costumes and living and carrying on their native works, as near as possible as they lived at the time of the discovery of America by Columbus."[53]

The outdoor Indian exhibit needed its own space, however:

> It would certainly be in bad taste to put an Indian wigwam by the side of the Machinery building, or a mud house by the side of the Art building, but what could be more appropriate than to have here and there on the Wooded Island, concealed from view by the trees of the shores, a family of Indians living in their tent of skins, and in another spot a family in their native house made of poles covered with birch bark; while, as one walked about the island and passing a group of trees or shrubs, what could add more to the effect of the place than to suddenly come upon an Indian woman weaving a blanket upon a primitive loom, with the beam fastened to a tree and the strings held tight by a strap about her waist. Or, still further on, to come upon a group of Central American potters in front of a house covered with a thatch of palm leaves.

He described Native stone and metal workers, a Venezuelan shoreline village reflective of the Swiss and European past, and Northwest Coast plank houses, "(to us) strange ceremonies, . . . feats of jugglery," and "the strange masks and costumes suggesting remarkable affinities with other and far distant peoples." Models of ruins of Labna from Yucatan and Tihuanaca in Peru would be scattered around the island to "add to the charm of a ramble through the woods and to enforce the great object lesson" of the decline of the "race . . . [of] barbaric splendor" that left these ruins behind.[54]

Putnam's vision was far-reaching and broad. He believed the ethnological display would reflect a part of world history that had faded into the past. His plans were eventually scaled back. In the end the ethnological village consisted of a small handful of tribal groups of Indian people from north to south across the hemisphere who came to work and live at the fair. It was located on the lagoon outside of the Anthropology Building—ironically, near the intramural railroad and in front of the Leather and Shoe Tanning Building.

Putnam's instructions to those he charged with inquiring about bringing Native people to the fair included that they be representative of pre-Columbian life. "All the tribes we represent must be full-blooded individuals," he told one of his assistants.[55] To another, Antonio, he wrote, "You will also secure full sets of garments of men, women and children. These garments should in all cases be such as were used long ago or should be made as they were in old times; old styles entirely, of native material with native decorations; that is red flannel, beads etc., should be discarded and the original methods of decoration used."[56]

In many places this was an untenable aspiration. One of his collectors wrote to him from the St. Regis Mohawk Reservation in New York, "On the Reservations which I have visited, the Indians have been so civilized, and have given up their old customs to such an extent, that it has been impossible for me to get up a good collection of objects."[57] Correspondence like this did not deter Putnam, however.

The aspiration to portray Indians as they lived in the past, and not the present, extended not only to those Putnam sent into the field but to others who contributed to the ethnological village display. New York's Board of General Managers assigned to oversee the state's exhibits conveyed this view to the governor, for example. "The Indians forming this settlement will be composed of representatives from each of the Six Nations," they reported, "selected with a view to their expertness in making canoes, pottery, ornaments, implements of war and utensils of stone and wood, such as were used by their ancestors before the arrival of white men."[58]

The task often proved difficult to bring about. Archibald Tisdale, who was sent to collect among the Micmacs and Abenakis in New Brunswick, wrote of his troubles. Even the most knowledgeable woman

14. Ethnological village with wigwam, Haudenosaunee houses, Penobscot lodges, and in background, Kwakwa̱ka'wakw totem poles. From Bancroft, *The Book of the Fair*, 2 of 2:629.

he contacted at Little Metis would not be able to create pre-Columbian work, he told Putnam. "The Indian woman of whom I wrote at Little Metis regarding the making of Indian clothes knows nothing of the apparel worn by her tribe anterior to the advent of the White Man and his beads + ribbons. No one among them does know," Tisdale said.[59]

Others had similar problems. Putnam asked Antonio to contract for pre-Columbian Navajo clothing. Antonio asked U.S. Army doctor Washington Matthews to help, but Matthews told him that since those clothes were made of yucca fibers, and Navajos had been weaving clothing of wool since the Spanish had introduced sheep to them, that would be an impossible task.[60] In these cases Putnam was not interested in modern or even historic Indian realities, but intended only to collect what he considered prehistoric artifacts. As anthropologist Ira Jacknis said, "Paradoxically, as Boas advocated comprehensive, systematic collections, the actual collecting was a creative act of omission, for Putnam's instructions to his agents amounted to the falsification of a truly representative record of native cultures as they found them."[61] Native communities had long been incorporating European and American material culture into their lives. American scientists, bureaucrats, religious leaders, and politicians, on the other hand, viewed such adaptations as nothing more than culture loss.

Nonetheless, part of Putnam's massive display included living villages of Indians representing several carefully selected culture areas across the United States and Canada. He presented them as representative of the pre-Columbian past. This ethnological village eventually included people from several Haudenosaunee (Iroquois) tribes, Penobscots, Kwakwaka'wakw from Vancouver Island, Navajos, and an Arawak man from South America. The Indians who came to live there were sponsored by various entities, including the states of Colorado, New York, and Maine, the Dominion of Canada, and British Guiana. Other Indians including Dakotas and Lakotas (Sioux), Ho-Chunks (Winnebagoes), Ojibwes (Chippewas), Potawatomis, and St. Regis Mohawks were put on display on the Midway Plaisance by entrepreneurs, and yet others came to work for Buffalo Bill. In addition, both the U.S. and Canadian governments sponsored displays of Indian schoolchildren that were meant to stand in contrast to the primitive past represented by the ethnological exhibits. The various people who brought the different groups of Indians to the fair did so after sometimes intricate negotiations among several parties, including fair and federal officials. .

At least four countries brought exhibits to the fair that included living American Indians—the United States, Canada, Guatemala, and British Guiana. The latter brought the Arawak man; Guatemala brought Mayan Indians to work; the United States and Canada brought Indians to put on display. Numerous Indians from both the United States and Canada participated, but most did so in U.S.-sponsored displays. Like the United States, though, Canada also brought Indian schoolchildren to the fair, in order to show the work they were conducting in "civilizing" them and to provide a contrast to the "wild Indians" at the ethnology exhibit.[62]

Putnam's great strength was in organizing collections and in organizing people to do the collecting. He knew the nature of the task he took on, so he was able to make the arrangements for the collecting well enough in advance to successfully thrust anthropology into the American imagination. His building was not completed until after

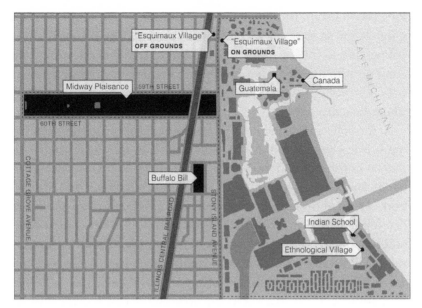

Map 1. Exposition grounds. Courtesy Lucien Liz-Lepiorz.

the fair began, due at least in part to his failure in navigating local politics.[63] Putnam experienced severe frustrations with the politics, bureaucracy, and process of organizing the exhibit, even after Sol Bloom was assigned to oversee the Midway.

The novelist Theodore Dreiser, in a thinly fictionalized tale of Chicago's business elite and their control of the city's economy and politics in this era, wrote, "Those who know anything concerning the intricacies of politics, finance, and corporate control, as they were practiced in those palmy days, would never marvel at the wells of subtlety, sinks of misery, and morasses of disaster which they represented."[64] Putnam knew little of this. He was not fit to tangle with Chicago's corporate leaders, who also played a key role in organizing and overseeing the fair.

But Putnam's displays, wide-ranging and including both human and material cultural components, as well as scientific laboratories, were ready as soon as the building was in shape to take them. He corresponded at great length with the men and women he hired to go into the field from 1891 to 1893. Some of the collecting was archaeological, some ethnographic. Some who went into Native lands had long relationships with the communities from which they collected. Others were students or colleagues of Putnam's who had little or no connection to Indian country. Several were Indians collecting from communities to which they had strong connections, while another was an impostor whom Putnam believed to be from the community where he collected.

As the collectors fanned out across the hemisphere in the years and months leading up to the opening of the fair, they interacted with people in tribal communities in a very modern way. They purchased goods and services with cash. Though the collections and displays were intended to represent the Americas' pre-Columbian past, their development occurred using contemporary means. The commodities and knowledge were purchased with money based on their market values. This came as a surprise to collectors in some instances, but was readily anticipated by those with previous experiences in Indian communities. Taken as a whole, the processes of building the displays in Chicago shed light on the changing economics in Indian communities in the late nineteenth century.

PART 2

Before the Fair

Making Money at Home

3

Native People Collecting for the Fair

Collectors scoured Indian country, in the United States and through-out the hemisphere, to develop the collections for Putnam's anthro-pology exhibit as well as official U.S. and Canadian governmental exhibits. They began their work in 1891 and expanded it dramatically in 1892. Nearly all of the collectors were non-Indian. They included Putnam and Boas's students, Indian agents in Canada and the United States, military personnel, Smithsonian Institution employees, and private collectors. Some were paid for their work, and some were not. All of them infused cash into tribal communities through their pur-chases and hiring. Surprisingly, Putnam and Boas included Indian collectors in this work.

Putnam and Boas brought at least four people they believed to be Indian in to do the actual work of collecting and organizing for both their anthropological and human displays at the fair. One, Cornelius C. Cusick, was a commissioned army officer who had eth-nological training and a family history of leadership within the Tus-carora tribe as well as a family history of aiding ethnological work. A second, George Hunt, was also a member of a leading family in his tribe's community in Fort Rupert, British Columbia. A third, Odille Morison, was a Tsimshian woman from Skeena River whose husband was a Scottish trader. Finally a man simply called Antonio has a more complicated story; he claimed to be an Apache raised on the East Coast. He parlayed his connections to gain employment in the fair's preparation. Cusick, Hunt, and Morison had valuable connections to and insights into the communities where they collected. Antonio had no special connections. Other, small-scale Indian collectors were deeply entrenched in their communities. All of them contributed to the economic base of the communities where they collected, to a greater or lesser extent. All of their experiences provide insights into the role American Indians could play in the collecting and organizing process.

Cornelius C. Cusick (Tuscarora)

Born in 1835 into a prominent Tuscarora family, Cornelius Cusick would take on several long-standing familial roles over the course of his life. His maternal grandfather had served as a captain in the British army, while his paternal grandfather, Nicholas Cusick, had served as an officer with both George Washington and the Marquis de Lafayette. Cornelius's father, James Nicholas Cusick, had been "the associate and companion of [Henry Rowe] Schoolcraft, the Indian historian, contributing largely to his work concerning the subject of 'the myths of the New World.'" In addition, John James Audubon was a regular visitor to his father's home. Cornelius, a "hereditary official of the ancient Iroquois Confederacy," was appointed as Sachem in 1860. He resigned that position in 1866 when President Andrew Johnson appointed him to the U.S. Army, where he became a captain.[1]

This combination of both a military background and an interest in ethnology would provide a dual focus for much of Cornelius Cusick's life. In the words of historian Laurence Hauptman, Cusick "spoke eight Indian languages and was recognized in the non-Indian world as an authority on Iroquoian culture." With all of this in his background, "Cusick was a mediator between cultures. He was a member of the educated elite leadership that has been part of Iroquoian society since the seventeenth century and that has served as liaison and broker between the Indian and non-Indian worlds."[2] Cusick publicly identified himself as "Chief of the Tuscaroras of New York and Lieutenant 22nd Regiment Infantry, United States Army," although he later became a captain.[3]

In early 1891, after nearly twenty-five years in the military, Cusick began an assertive campaign to gain an official assignment working with the ethnology department at the fair. The accomplishment of this goal was complicated by the bureaucracy involved in developing

15. Cornelius C. Cusick. Courtesy National Archives and Records Administration, folder 1, 4653 ACP 1888 (Cornelius C. Cusick), entry 297, Letters Received by the Appointments, Commissions, and Personal Branch Document File, Records of the Adjutant General's Office, RG 94 War Department Records, NARA-DC.

a cooperative relationship between the military and the fair's leadership, as well as the role played by the civilian government through the Office of Indian Affairs. It took more than six months of wrangling, but in late September 1891 Cusick was assigned to work for Putnam.[4]

Cusick wrote first to the adjutant general of the U.S. Army asking to be assigned to the world's fair "if it is contemplated to detail an Army Officer to represent the Indian department in matters appertaining to American Ethnology" there. When that avenue failed, he contacted the fair's director general, George Davis, and finally Putnam himself, requesting an assignment as an assistant. He offered to work without being paid, since he retained a military salary, "and the money should go to the exhibitions." He told Putnam that he was fluent in several Iroquois languages and had good connections among the leadership of several Haudenosaunee (Iroquois) tribes.[5] He also wrote to the Bureau of Ethnology at the Smithsonian looking for work, but they forwarded his documents to Davis, with a note that they were not planning on seeking any military details to help with their work.[6]

Putnam worked through the summer attempting to navigate bureaucratic channels to have Cusick assigned to him. He told the secretary of war, "I believe it will be better to deal with many Indian tribes through one of their own blood than in any other way."[7] Early on Putnam warned Cusick to be circumspect in telling Davis what he would be doing for the fair. "I have a very broad scheme on foot," Putnam wrote, the details of which "nobody knows but myself."[8] That scheme was to hire an American Indian assistant, Cusick, to oversee the Indian focus of his exhibits. Putnam would give up on this idea, but he did seem to understand that his work would be more effective if he could employ Indian people who understood their communities and cultures from the inside to oversee the collecting and organization of materials and peoples for the fair. But both the legal and bureaucratic hurdles proved to be daunting, and he scaled back his plans for Cusick.

Correspondence shuffled between the War Department, the Interior Department, the president of the United States, Putnam, Cusick, Davis, and various federal representatives to the fair as the legality of the appointment was considered. At one point Putnam wrote to

Cusick in exasperation, "It seems almost impossible to make the War Department understand that your detail is asked for in connection with the Ethnological Department of the World's Columbian Exposition, and not in connection with the Indian Department of the Government." In fact, George Davis petitioned President Benjamin Harrison directly.[9] Both the secretary of war and the secretary of the interior proposed a plan to effect the detail, but the law would not support it.[10]

In July 1891 the Army granted Cusick a furlough both for personal time and to do the work, which was extended for four months on September 23. Two days later Putnam informed Cusick that he had been appointed as an "honorary assistant."[11] Cusick retired from active service in the army in January 1892.[12] Although Cusick was made an "honorary assistant" in Putnam's department, the military did not authorize him to be detailed there, which is why he had to take leave from his job to do the work. He was not told why, and Putnam never understood the reasons either, but the adjutant general's office reported to the War Department that unless Congress passed specific legislation permitting Cusick to do such work, he could not be assigned to it. Cusick viewed his title as "an empty capacity," since the military did not let him work directly for the fair.[13]

Because of Cusick's strong background in ethnological work, Putnam initially envisioned a broader role for him to work with all tribes. In June 1891 Putnam told Davis that he had "decided that Capt. Cusick is the best man for the position of Special Assistant to take special charge of Indian matters."[14] Due to the difficulty caused by laws relating to the military, Cusick's assignment was diminished to work specifically with the Haudenosaunee tribes.[15] As with other collectors for the ethnology exhibit, Cusick was assigned a triple role: to collect pre-Columbian style objects of material culture for display, to make physical measurements of individual Indians, and to locate representative tribal members who could attend the fair, building and living in typical housing and carrying on typical pre-Columbian domestic activities as living cultural displays in diorama style. He began his work in late September 1891.

Cusick identified the Canadian Cayuga and Onondaga as well as the western New York Seneca as "still practicing pagan rites." On the other hand, the Tuscarora were "very progressive," even sponsoring "a fine brass band" that would be unsuitable for the fair. The Tuscarora included, however, "both men and women" who could be considered "splendid types of the Indian race."[16]

Cusick's background both in the army and as a member of a leading Tuscarora family gave him an entree into Haudenosaunee society that others would not have been able to exploit so readily. He understood the importance of both custom and protocol and followed both to develop strong relationships with each of the communities he visited. He spoke before councils, told stories of his military adventures in the West (probably including his service under General Miles in a skirmish with Crazy Horse of the Lakota), and only after gaining a rapport did he explain what he was doing on behalf of Putnam.[17]

With the Senecas at Cattaraugus he was introduced by the brother of Gen. Ely Parker (Seneca), who had been the first American Indian to serve as commissioner of Indian affairs. There he purchased a variety of objects for display at the fair, including table wear that Red Jacket had used during his youth and buttons used in a ceremonial gambling game. He also had hoped to purchase a chestnut-brown gambling bowl of "Bear claw workmanship, wrought with flint and other rude instruments," made of soft maple in Genesee more than a century earlier. It was "in use at the time Gen. Sullivan invaded the Country of the Six nations, Date 1779." The owner agreed to loan the bowl but not to sell it. Cusick unfortunately lacked the authority to make contracts for such loans. He was able to purchase some heritage food products, including beans and corn, that dated to the time of Sullivan's invasion, an important historical time marker. He described these as "very interesting as they are of a kind used by Indians for time immemorial." Cusick observed that since it was not summer when he visited, prices were lower than during tourist season.[18] The balance sheet he submitted showed expenditures of a little more than $100.[19]

Cusick visited representative communities of all six Haudesonee tribes. He described his experience at the two Seneca reservations of Alleghany and Cattaraugus in the summer of 1892 as typical. At a meeting of outgoing tribal council members, he described his efforts to encourage tribal members to come to Chicago. "I addressed in a quiet and deliberate manner the object of my visit. It included the proposition of enlisting the interests of the six nations for an independent exhibit by them concerning their early history, relating to ceremonies and other matters appertaining to the life and customs of the past. I did not omit to say: that, if required, the managers of the World's Fair would extend them a reasonable assistance." The leaders viewed this as "highly complimentary to the Six Nations" and thought they should select appropriate individuals.

Cusick reported that the Haudenosaunee liked the idea of doing an exhibit so long as it included "suitable compensation." They clearly viewed this as an opportunity to work for pay. Since the living Iroquois exhibit would eventually be sponsored by the State of New York and not the ethnology department, Cusick did not follow through with recruitment.[20] Those who eventually came did so without salary. But the seed had been sown during these visits, which no doubt aided the state in putting together its living village.

When Franz Boas asked him to do work for the physical anthropology exhibit—taking measurements of Haudenosaunee people—Cusick said in frustration, "I do not think I will do the required work as I am simply 'Honorary assistant.'"[21] Nonetheless, he did take up Boas's assignment. The measuring process was slow due to the number of measurements required of each individual and the variety of tools. It was also slowed by the lengthy council meetings. Cusick had a letter of introduction from Commissioner of Indian Affairs Thomas Morgan to present to Indian agents, and in the end he sent the results to Boas and Gerald West.[22]

Cornelius Cusick was not paid for his service out of the funds set aside for the fair. He worked exceedingly hard to gain an appointment collecting ethnographic data and perhaps even overseeing the Indian exhibit at the fair. In the end he was forced to use leave time to conduct the work, and he continued after retiring from active service in the army. The work that he was able to do proved to be an essential piece of the larger puzzle that Putnam was constructing. Perhaps not coincidentally, the Iroquois exhibit at the fair proved highly successful. The Haudenosaunee who attended the fair and lived in the ethnological village were respected leaders, both in their communities and to the outside world.[23] Cusick's exhaustive work was the foundation of the success of their visit to the exposition.

Cusick believed wholeheartedly in the value of the ethnographic and anthropological work for the exhibits. He carried on his family's tradition of working with social scientists to provide the outside world with a better understanding of Haudenosaunee societies. Putnam recognized these qualities in him as well as his aptitude for research and collecting. While unable to use Cusick to the full potential of his knowledge and abilities, Putnam opened the door for his work. Though Cusick himself was not compensated for this work, he was able to infuse small amounts of cash into local tribal communities before the fair opened and to lay the foundation for Haudenosaunee people from a variety of tribes to work at the fair.

George Hunt (Fort Rupert)

George Hunt was born to a Scottish father and a Tlingit mother in 1854. He was raised at Fort Rupert among the people then known to the outside world as Kwakiutl, and theirs was his first language.[24] He met Boas at least as early as 1888 and worked for and with him for some forty years, becoming a recognized ethnographer and linguist.[25] He had principal responsibility for collecting the Kwakwa̱ka̱'wakw material culture items both for Boas's indoor exhibit and for the living village.

In his biographical sketch of Hunt, Ira Jacknis wrote, "Throughout his life Hunt's activity can best be seen as that of a collector." This was the way Hunt viewed himself. "Hunt could have chosen other labels to identify himself, such as guide, watchman, trader, hunter and trapper, interpreter, even anthropologist, yet he chose to see himself as a collector." Hunt lived nearly his entire life in Fort Rupert, whose residents "were renowned as middlemen and interpreters, and [his] career should be seen in this light."[26]

Hunt used his contract to bring Northwest Coast Indians along with their representative cultural objects to the fair in part as an opportunity to establish himself in those roles in his work with Boas. The "Chicago Fair was the single most important event in his transformation into a native ethnographer." The fair launched Hunt's career as a collector. "Although Hunt had assisted earlier collectors, the fair represented his first opportunity to make an artifact collection on his own," according to Jacknis.[27]

16. George Hunt. Frederic Ward Putnam Papers, HUG 1717.2.14, World's Columbian Exposition, Records and Ephemera, box 37, Harvard University Archives.

Boas viewed the Kwakwa̲ka̲'wakw as the quintessential Northwest Coast culture. He credited Hunt with organizing the trip made by the Kwakwa̲ka̲'wakw visitors from Fort Rupert to Chicago. They were referred to as Northwest Coast Indians, Quaguhl, or Kwakiutl by the contemporary press and in fair guidebooks. Boas wrote, "It is my belief that the peculiar culture of this whole region has had its origin among the tribes of Fort Rupert, the Kwakiutl. . . . For this reason I also desired to bring a number of representatives of this tribe to Chicago, and I succeeded in doing so through the efforts of Mr. George Hunt."[28] Putnam gained the permission of local Indian agent A. W. Vowell to bring this group to Chicago, although Vowell later said he discouraged the Indians from attending the fair.[29]

Hunt began his collecting work in the fall of 1891. The fair's Council of Administration referred to him as a "special agent."[30] He was one of twenty assistants hired under special agreements with Putnam.[31] Putnam reported to Davis in October that "preliminary arrangements have been made with Mr. George Hunt, a resident at Ft. Rupert, Vancouver's island, to collect all necessary illustrative specimens, and to induce a number of Indians to go to Chicago during the Fair."[32]

By January Hunt had collected a house that would accommodate four families, a series of ceremonial masks, and a variety of dishes and tools.[33] He continued to collect household and daily use materials that fit Putnam's criteria throughout the year. In June, for example, Putnam reported that Hunt had acquired "bone implements; fish hooks and nets; spinning machines; mat baskets; doll images; totem posts; masks; rattles; whistles; neck and head ornaments; etc., etc." He shipped the house to Chicago by Canadian Pacific Railroad in September 1892.[34] By the time the fair opened, he had collected more than 360 items, which were later included in the foundational collections of Chicago's Field Museum of Natural History, which was established at the fair's end.[35]

Though there is little documentation specific to Hunt's collecting activities, the scope of his work was quite broad. The objects he collected formed a key part of the anthropological display at the fair and launched his life's work with Boas. It is not clear how much money he earned doing the work leading up to the fair, although his earnings while working *during* the fair are well documented. This work would strengthen his reputation within his own changing community and cement his value to Boas, who devoted much of his career fieldwork to the Northwest Coast.

Odille Morison (Tsimshian)

Another Northwest Coast Canadian Indian collected for Boas, sending some 140 objects to the fair that would also eventually enter the Field Museum's collection.[36] Odille Morison was born in 1855 to a Tsimshian mother and French Canadian Hudson's Bay Company father at Fort Simpson on the British Columbia coast.[37] Morison learned to write English in boarding school, and she worked at Fort Simpson as an interpreter, translator, and host beginning in the 1870s. By the 1880s she was fulfilling these roles for Anglican clerics, government officials, and academics. She translated the Anglican prayer book into Tsimshian, which was a great boon to the church.[38]

Morison first met Boas around the same time Hunt did, in June 1888 at Port Essington on the Skeena River. Boas specifically sought her out as an interpreter.[39] He put her to work as an ethnographer, and the next year she published a two-page article on Tsimshian proverbs in the *Journal of American Folk-Lore*.[40] Boas respected her work, and so she was a natural choice to collect from the Skeena River region, a place with which Boas was familiar. In June 1891 Boas wrote to Morison that he could pay her $100 to collect Tsimshian "traditions . . . in the original language with translations."[41]

He also provided her with $200 to collect material objects with their provenance and descriptions of meaning included. With the help of her family Morison collected ceremonial objects and commissioned miniature models of big houses. Apparently for a separate price, she commissioned a totem pole with Tsimshian crests.[42] In March 1892 Putnam reported, "Mrs. O. Morison is making a collection on the Skeena and Nass Rivers." The next month he reported that she had "secured two totem posts at Port Essington, BC." She continued collecting throughout the summer and fall. In September Putnam wrote that through her work on the upper Skeena River she had acquired "a large totem pole with full explanation of the same" that had "belonged to one of the chiefs at Metlakahtla." She completed her collecting in November and shipped three boxes of materials and the totem pole to Victoria in December.[43] In all she spent nearly $500. She bought some of her materials from a longtime local trader in the region, Robert Cunningham.[44]

Maureen Atkinson, in a brief biography of Morison, writes, "Although her work for Boas and the Chicago World's Fair of 1893 may have brought her greater exposure, her translations of the selections from the New Testament and the Anglican Prayer Book may have been her greatest personal achievement," despite the fact that she did not get the recognition for this that she believed she deserved.[45] As an experienced cultural intermediary for nearly two decades before she did her work for the fair, Morison was an ideal individual to get the material Boas desired for the fair and to provide the cultural context for it that he and Putnam believed to be so necessary to the scientific value of such collections. She was compensated with a combination of pay for her ethnographic work and expenses for purchasing and commissioning objects, in much the same way that some of the non-Indian collectors were compensated by Putnam and Boas. She was classified in a category of twenty individuals who worked under "special agreements." Morison and Hunt were the only two Indians in this category.[46]

Antonio Apache (Impostor)

Putnam thought he engaged another American Indian to collect among the Apache and Navajo. Although Antonio Apache was exposed as an impostor pretending to be an Indian nearly fifteen years after the fair, he fooled Putnam into believing that he was mentoring a young Native man to collect for him in the Southwest in the years leading up to the fair.[47] Putnam later procured a job for Antonio on the fairgrounds in 1893.[48] Originally known to Putnam simply as "Antonio," the young man quickly ingratiated himself to the professor. He was purported to have been a grandson of Cochise, fluent in English, Spanish, and Apache, who was captured along with other youths by Gen. George Crook. He worked as a leather maker in Boston before Putnam hired him; in years after the fair, he would sit as a model for artists.[49]

Putnam sincerely believed that he had engaged a "genuine Arizona Apache" for the job. He told the Chicago press, "Antonio is a full-blooded Apache," whom he was helping in his goal of attending college.[50] Antonio needed to earn some money, and he thought the fair would provide him with an opportunity to do that. He first wrote to the commissioner of Indian affairs in the fall of 1891, asking if he could sell photographs of Indian life at the fair. He wanted to do so without paying a fee. "I am an Apache," he told the commissioner, hoping that his purported tribal affiliation would exempt him from costs.[51] (In May 1893, when the fair opened, Putnam reported that he had taken the name Antonio Apache.)[52]

Like Cusick, Antonio was not paid for his collecting work, but his expenses were covered.[53] In April 1892 Commissioner Morgan wrote a letter of introduction for Antonio to show to Indian agents, and he forwarded it to Putnam. The letter authorized him to make anthropometric measurements, to collect for the fair, and to identify families to come live on the fairgrounds in 1893.[54] Antonio received training in early 1892 from Boas on how to take measurements and fill out the charts.[55] In mid-May Putnam forwarded Morgan's letter to Antonio with specific instructions. He told Antonio to work with the agency physician, Dr. Washington Matthews, to collect from Apache and Navajo people. In addition to measuring people, Antonio was to collect objects reflecting precontact materials and workmanship, including clothing, tools, and weaponry. He was also instructed to identify families who could visit the fair and live on the grounds.

Antonio went about his work with zeal. By June, although unable to acquire clothing made of yucca, he wrote that he would be able to get some five thousand ancient pottery pieces and six thousand blankets that could be sold at the fair.[56] By July he said he had identified approximately two hundred people willing to come to Chicago for the duration of the fair, despite their fear of homesickness that was based on previous experiences.[57] Putnam warned Antonio that he would be limited to supporting about five Navajos in one or two hogans and asked him to identify people with both silversmithing and blanket weaving skills. "You will see that the Indians who come have all the fixings for the house as well as their loom and material for making their various objects. We want everything as purely Indian as possible," Putnam instructed. He added that more Navajo people were welcome to attend the fair, but "if others come they must come

Souvenir of Friendship
Antonio Apache

17. Antonio Apache. Frederic Ward Putnam Papers, HUG 1717.2.14, World's Columbian Exposition, Records and Ephemera, box 37, Harvard University Archives.

at their own expense." When Antonio suggested purchasing wood for building the hogans in the Chicago area, Putnam responded that he would like to use authentic materials; the homes should be built in Navajo country and disassembled. They could then be rebuilt on the fairgrounds.[58]

Putnam received a permit from Morgan to bring two or three Navajo and Apache families to the fair, but he lacked the funding to do so. Antonio made the arrangements with the families. He told Putnam, "I have got the most reliable one's [sic] who are good workers, they hesitated about going to stay 6 months as they said all of them who had been to Washington was home sick soon and it took a whole day to explain the difference and tell them everything." Eventually the State of Colorado offered to pay the expenses and sponsor the Navajo individuals who came to the fair.[59]

Although Antonio's expenses were high, Putnam believed they were worth paying, because "he has done considerable good work in the way of measuring the Indians, and also in getting up exhibits from them."[60] The total cost of Antonio's expenses were $200; Putnam was forced to provide strict oversight so that he would not go overboard in his expenditures.[61]

Antonio had his expenses paid for his travel but did not earn a salary. Later, at the fair, he turned his relationship to his advantage to procure salaried work from Putnam. He was not so well paid as Hunt there, but he used his self-proclaimed Native heritage to his advantage. Problems of frauds such as Antonio have long plagued Indian communities. He used his cultural and identity appropriations to his professional advantage and eventually his financial benefit. He caused Putnam and others to trust that he was Indian, so that they believed they were supporting an Indian in his professional life. Real Indian people who were not so adept at developing such relationships but who could have provided the same services for Putnam as well as or better than Antonio were excluded from those opportunities. Antonio claimed an Indian identity, but Native communities did not claim him as one of theirs. This is an early reflection of a long-standing pattern in the academic world that continues today.[62] This distinction, however, is often lost to the non-Indian world.

A majority of the money for collecting went to non-Indian collectors such as George Dorsey and Edward Thompson. Fair funds paid Dorsey $50 a month from February 1891 until November 1892, when he came to Chicago to organize the materials he collected and his salary was raised to $75.[63] This adds up to more than $1,500 in salary for his work leading up to the fair. After visiting Cuzco in May 1892, Dorsey shipped some forty-four tons of materials he had dug up in Peru to Chicago.[64] This apparently included some thirteen thousand items he had collected, primarily mummies and objects rifled from graves.[65] At one point Putnam reported that Dorsey needed $2,000 for a part of his collecting in Peru.[66] In total Dorsey received some $4,000 in expense money from 1891 through 1893.[67] This did not include salary.

Thompson received some $10,000 in expenses for his work in Central America.[68] This included not only bringing in artifacts from the field but making exhibits such as the Mayan Quirigua and Labna facsimiles displayed on the fairgrounds. Even assistant molders received $75 per month to make these life-sized displays.[69] There was a sizeable source of funding for the development of anthropological displays, but little of it went to Indian collectors.

Although Putnam used only three Indians in the work of collecting, so far as we know, Cusick, Hunt, and Morison, it is worth noting that two of the most successful and lauded Indian village displays on the fairgrounds were the Haudenosaunee and Northwest Coast displays, for which these three had primary collecting responsibilities. Their strong connections to the communities from which they collected, including both kinship and leadership/liaison roles, provided them with insiders' relationships that other collectors would have lacked.

Although Putnam realized this potential strength—which is why he initially hoped that Cusick could oversee all of the Indian material collection—he failed to take advantage of what seems an obvious opportunity. He simply did not have the connections to do so. The people he knew best were his colleagues and students, and so they conducted most of the work for him. In the end this was a lost opportunity for Cusick and for others with connections similar to Hunt's and Morison's to gain much of a foothold in the field.

More commonly Indians who collected materials did so from home on a much smaller scale. Like Hunt they lived where they collected, but unlike him and Cusick they did not have ambitions to use the collecting as a stepping-stone to participate in the scientific work of the fair. They as well as those from whom they collected made or supplemented a living at home as they helped fair organizers build their collections for Chicago's audiences.

4

The Department of Ethnology
Collecting for the Fair

For two years leading up to the fair, individuals in tribal communities throughout the Americas benefited from new sources of income. More than a hundred emissaries from various entities building collections for Chicago exhibits poured into their homelands, searching for artifacts and hiring people to make replicas of old-style material objects. In some places these collectors found thriving markets already in place; in others they found people in dire poverty desperate to make a little money to supplement their incomes. America's continental expansion had crippled Native economies. U.S. and Canadian policies had handcuffed Indians financially, severely limiting their options to earn a living and support their families. Here and in Latin America, Indians increasingly sold their knowledge and cultural patrimony or their labor to make ends meet. The needs of both tribal members and collectors catalyzed the process of movement of mass amounts of Indian relics and material goods from tribal families and communities to places of public display.

With few exceptions, the individuals collecting material objects, inviting people to participate in the ethnology exhibits, and making body measurements for the physical anthropology exhibit at the fair were non-Indian. Beginning in 1891, cash and material goods from this enterprise trickled into tribal communities, paid to individual tribal members for both services and goods, as these collectors fanned out across the Americas and into the Arctic at the behest of Franz Boas and Frederic Putnam. Boas oversaw much of the collecting in Indian country, although some individuals dealt directly with Putnam, and yet others such as James Mooney collected for the government exhibits sponsored by the Smithsonian Institution and the Bureau of Ethnology. Canadian officials and missionaries collected for the Canadian government as well.[1]

Many of the collectors understood tribal protocols to some extent, although there were some glaring exceptions. In many communities, those protocols would have necessitated gift giving in exchange for help and information, and cash in exchange for guidance, information, and material objects.

Since most tribal communities had entered into the cash economy to some extent by the late nineteenth century, including the sale of both knowledge and goods to collectors, some individuals knew the relative values of what they were selling. On the other hand, they would not know the size of the budget set aside for the fair or the scope of the collection process on a hemispheric basis. In addition, the value of goods and knowledge varied considerably among Native communities.

Cultural mediators in tribal communities took on or continued the roles of interacting with outsiders. To collectors and scholars, these were the most valuable of community members. They could provide them with access to knowledgeable and talented individuals that these outsiders sought. It was primarily three groups of Native people and their families who most benefited from the work of creating the ethnological exhibits for the world's fair: those who still held knowledge of the old ways, those with the skills to create or re-create the old-style material culture, and those who could bring them together with the collectors and interpret both the language and the cultural protocols for them. The breadth of Putnam's vision meant that hundreds of Indians and dozens of tribal communities would be impacted by the collection work.

Financial records specific to individuals are extremely rare, and even records showing the amount of money trickling or flowing into individual communities are hard to come by. However, enough evidence exists to characterize the impact of these cash infusions in broad strokes. At a time when tribal communities were at their most threatened economically, these transactions helped pave the way for broader individual participation in newly developing economic systems in tribal communities. They funneled cash, in large or small amounts, into communities where subsistence or credit economies severely limited individual economic choice and access to resources.

Collecting in Canada and the United States

Putnam's instruction to collectors, who served as physical anthropology body measurers, archaeologists, ethnographers, and ethnographic collectors, was to plan to spend about $50 for ethnological materials in any individual tribal communities they visited.[2] In select places such as the Northwest Coast or at Mayan ruins, far more was spent. By the fall of 1892, Putnam and Boas had sent nearly one hundred collectors into the field.[3] This would have introduced many thousands of dollars into Indian country.

In collection of ethnological materials, as with other displays at the fair, Putnam was consumed by the idea that they needed to represent pre-Columbian contact. He told Maxwell Riddle, who was collecting among the Menominee, "It is the real old native things that I am after. That which relates to the life and customs of the Indians before their art was ruined by contact with the whites."[4] Putnam understood this as his charge, in part due to the agreement he had made with the commissioner of Indian affairs and in part due to the Columbian focus of the fair. This is reflected in much of his instructional correspondence.

Indians had already been selling objects of material culture to museums, private collectors, and tourists, and many had a good idea of the market value of their products, at least in the United States and Canada. This was especially true of the Northwest Coast Indians of Canada who had begun participating in the artifact trade more than a century before the fair. (George Emmons, notably, had already collected some 3,800 Northwest Coast items since the 1880s, a significant portion of which the State of Washington displayed at the fair.)[5] But the pattern held elsewhere as well.

In the Northwest Coast collection process, James Deans hired Haida artisans to make a model of the Skidegate village. As Boas described it, "Mr. James Deans whose familiarity with the customs of the Haida Indians is well known, undertook to have a model of one of the Haida villages prepared for the Anthropological Department

of the World's Columbian Exposition. For this purpose he visited
Queen Charlotte Islands and engaged the services of the members
of all the different families represented in this village. These Indians
made small carvings representing the totem poles and houses which
their families used to inhabit."[6] Deans reportedly employed some
fifty people in this work.[7]

Deans explained that he had to get "a large number of these beautiful models" made on credit. He also had to go early to get the models made before the Haida all went out fishing for the canneries, for
which they earned at least $5 a day. By May 1892 Deans had already
received $750 for collecting, but he had incurred more expenses
including the costs for building the Skidegate model.[8] He collected
several railroad cars full of material, including boats, houses, and
totem poles for the anthropological exhibit.[9]

Deans's collecting, together with that of Boas, George Hunt, and
Odille Morison, added thousands of dollars into the Northwest Coast
tribal economies. This money went both to people who made material objects and those who sold them to the collectors. A few dollars
went to tribal leaders in other ways as well. Charles Morison, Odille's
husband, reported to Putnam that when he shipped Deans's materials to the railroad, they had to go by boat. Since the local tribal
authorities controlled the waterfront, he had to pay them wharfage
fees on top of shipping fees. In explaining the expense, and why he
had no receipts to enclose, Morison wrote, "The wharfage on this
may appear excessive but it includes charges on previous shipments,
the wharf belonging to the Indians the charges are high and they
will furnish no bills."[10] Taking control of the shipping processes from
and through their territories had become increasingly important to
tribal communities by the late nineteenth century.[11]

Other collectors also found that American Indians had entered
the cash economy, selling the types of goods that Putnam and Boas
were purchasing for the fair. T. L. Bolton, who went into the field
as a volunteer for Putnam in Utah and Idaho in 1891, learned this
quickly. In July he wrote from the Shoshone and Bannock reservation
at Fort Hall Idaho that Ghost Dance and other religious clothes were
hard to come by. They "required much work and skill" to create, and
therefore were "quite scarce and held at high prices by those who

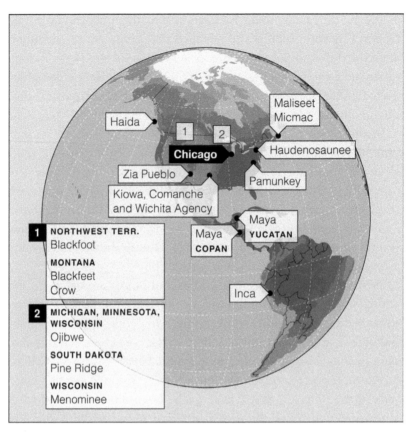

Map 2. Communities visited by collectors. Courtesy Lucien Liz-Lepiorz.

have them."[12] There was a distinction between museum quality and tourist trade work that tribal artisans knew well.

Bolton asked for an increase in allowance for expenses from $50 to $75, which Putnam granted him. Putnam told Bolton, "I simply put the sum $50 as being a safe amount to spend, but I must leave you a certain amount of discretionary power in this matter." He added a comment that reflected a common theme in his correspondence with other collectors. "You know of course that the Indians are very shrewd traders and that they hold things at the highest price they can get, and there is no use buying things where other people have been purchasing and thus led the Indians to think that their work is in great demand."[13]

Of course, the reason that Indians thought that their goods were in "great demand" is because they were. Tourists, private collectors, and museums were already purchasing the same types of materials that Putnam wanted to show at the fair. Bolton learned this when he visited the Uintah Ouray at Fort Duchesne Utah in August. He reported that the Indians there "have been led to ask enormous prices for most of their work by the prices that tourists have paid for some things." Putnam responded that in order to avoid "exorbitant prices" Bolton should refuse to buy until "they find out that you will not be humbugged and you can get things at your own prices."[14] Putnam, of course, needed to stay within his allotted budget, and by choosing to collect from a broad swath of Native communities, he could allot but little funding to most. And Indian people who needed cash were willing to renegotiate based on market conditions.

Maxwell Riddle, collecting among the Menominee and Ojibwe for Putnam, also found prices to be higher than expected. The Menominee were selling beaded sashes, for example, for $10 apiece. Riddle opined that $50 would not make much of a display, and Putnam agreed.[15]

Riddle had better luck when he attended a Menominee Dream Dance religious ceremony. The Dream Dance had been introduced to the Menominee by their neighbors the Potawatomi in the early 1880s and had been incorporated into the traditional Mitāēwin religion.[16] After watching the ceremonies, Riddle bought a number of items of clothing from the dancers. These included leggings that "have been worn in the dance," dancing garters "made by pagan section of the tribe," a pair of moccasins "used for everyday wear and also in dances," and a hat band "made by the Pagan Menomonees" that "was being worn when purchased." Both Putnam and Riddle viewed this as a good purchase. There is no record of specific prices, but Riddle stayed close to his fifty dollar allotment for the Menominee.[17] The Menominee were in the process of building up a commercial logging business on the reservation, and by the 1890s both tribal leaders and most individual tribal members participated in a cash economy that supplemented their agricultural, fishing, hunting, and gathering economy.[18]

Not all Indians were paid for the works they provided for exhibition at the fair. A Quebec middleman collected objects from the Maliseet,

Naskapi, and Montagnais, including a "Wall Pocket" woven hanging described by historian Laurel Thatcher Ulrich as a "Victorian extravaganza." The artist, Agathe Athanase, a Maliseet, adorned it with "forty-five miniature baskets," flowers, snowshoes, and other models of Native artifacts. After being sent to the Peabody in Cambridge on a temporary basis and displayed at the fair, the museum eventually accessioned it into the collections when the collector "failed to return letters." Ulrich concludes that "Athanase was apparently never paid for her work."[19] Her intermediary failed her.

Perhaps this failure was not for lack of trying. In some cases there were multiple intermediaries. Archibald Tisdale corresponded with Putnam after the fair and into 1895 in an effort to finalize compensation for materials he had collected through Père Arnaud that were displayed at the fair. In some cases Indian sellers asked specific prices for objects that were going into the Peabody collections. In one case, Tisdale thought the asking price of $20 for a cloth coat with "beaded collar + wrist band" was too high. In other cases Tisdale recommended that Putnam simply make an offer.[20] Evidently some of the objects were purchased and others returned. Athanese's piece did not fall into either category.

Guides and laborers were crucial contacts for Putnam's collectors, since most were in unfamiliar territory. Tisdale, who collected and made measurements among the Micmac and Maliseet in Nova Scotia and New Brunswick, paid both guides and a sailor to transport him in the interior and across the water to village sites. In the summer of 1892 he reported from St. John, New Brunswick, that he had difficulty measuring Maliseets without the permission of the local chief, who was twenty-five miles from the village site, fishing with Americans. In order to gain permission, he traveled a great distance through difficult terrain and spent $5.[21] The money was likely for a guide, although some of it could have gone to pay the chief.

Tisdale had some success among the Maliseet in Cacouna. There he was able to arrange for several items to be made on consignment, including wooden buckets, toys, knife handles, a basket, and "all the accoutrements of an ancient wigwam." In this case the tribe's leaders trusted him to make objects that could be sold at the fair, and paid for later, with the stipulation that they may try to sell them before the fair or have those items not sold be returned after the fair.[22] The Maliseets took advantage of a thriving tourist market for these goods, so making them on consignment was not much risk.[23] This was an experience that most Indians did not have. At Cape Breton, Tisdale had even more difficulties than he had at St. John.[24]

Tisdale's expenses for the summer of 1892 totaled at least $150.[25] This went to both travel and purchases. In the spring of 1893 Putnam informed him that since the Canadian government was purchasing materials in the same region, and they would be incorporated into Putnam's anthropological display, Putnam would no longer be spending money there.[26]

Emma Sickels, whom Putnam was forced to hire for political reasons to collect in Lakota country, also used some of her funding to pay for guides and translators.[27] She wrote Putnam in October 1891, "Yesterday I acted upon your suggestion of enlisting the interests and services by means of judicious gifts and equipped myself with some articles which experience has shown me, that they appreciate and which can be purchased at half the cost at agency—fur caps, silk handkerchiefs &c. to which they are very partial."[28] She spent $6 on coney hats, "to exchange with Indians for work." She gave one to an interpreter who helped her hire a horse.[29] For another individual, perhaps Henry Standing Bear, she spent $31.40 to buy a ticket to Chicago and to pay for interpreting services in advance of the fair.[30] Sickels reported that she was working with Young Man Afraid, Little Wound, Fast Horse, and Standing Soldier, although she did not specify their respective roles.[31] She clearly knew the cultural importance of gift-giving in such transactions.

Sickels had a better understanding than most collectors of how to build trust based on relationships in tribal communities. At one point she told Putnam, "I have been very careful about my purchases for the Fair, and about my expenses—expending the money so that those I dealt with might feel that I was liberal and generous and be inspired to be the same. That is, I endeavored to manage so that when I spent any money—it was done in that way."[32] The year of the fair 78 percent of Lakota people living on the Rosebud Reservation were reported to subsist on government rations.[33] Even those who were able to work were impoverished, however. The agent reported that although Rosebud "is not adapted to agriculture," he nonetheless required Indians to farm to keep them from being idle. The crops nearly always failed.[34] Freighting and sale of cattle to the government agency brought the Indians some cash. Any cash that Sickels brought in to community members would be welcome.

Dr. D. Scott Moncrieff collected among the Klamath in the Pacific Northwest, and he reported how much he spent. His expense sheet indicated a cost of $24.50 "To guides, Interpreters + for assistance in obtaining measurements." He also spent $1.50 for a day's use of the agency interpreter.[35] The Klamath had entered the cash economy some two decades previously, earning money by logging, freighting, and both temporary and permanent government work including serving as interpreters beginning in the 1870s.[36] Indian police privates earned $10 a month at Klamath in 1893.[37] In 1893 a dollar would purchase almost forty pounds of wheat flour, or nearly eight pounds of fresh beef.[38] Small jobs such as Moncrieff brought provided valuable sources of income for those who were able to get them.

Collecting in Latin America

Putnam sent collectors into Indian country in Latin America, where he authorized spending of ten times the amount that he had in U.S. and Canadian Native communities. The Latin American collectors needed large numbers of laborers for their prodigious collecting. Much of the expense in Latin America went to labor-intensive archaeological digs. Some direct and indirect purchases of Native-made artifacts also occurred. Documentation of cash spent in Native communities is spottier in these cases than in the United States and Canada, but some does exist.

George Dorsey hired American Indians on occasion in his collecting and grave-robbing work in South America, for example. He indicated that he hired "Cholos or half breeds" to dig up graves for him, although he did not indicate the amount that he paid them.[39] It doubtless reflected a minuscule amount of his expenses. But it would have provided paid work for those he hired.[40] Indians in South America long before had entered the cash economy by working in mines and selling material goods to collectors.

Indians were reticent to work for Dorsey, but he eventually found paid help. According to one newspaper report, "Mr. Dorsey secured, after much trouble, an escort of six natives, lineal descendents of the Peruvians whose bodies rest in the tombs." These workers did their best to honor the dead when they rifled through their graves. Before beginning their collecting work they conducted a ceremony in which they "called upon their dead to remember that the work they were about to do was not of their own volition." They also made an offering of food and drink to their ancestors before they approached the graves.[41] There is no evidence regarding how others in their community felt about the work they were doing for Dorsey.

The collecting at Copan is better documented. In the fall of 1891 Putnam sent his first crew from Harvard's Peabody Museum to Honduras to excavate the Copan ruins. In July the Peabody had acquired all rights to the ruins in Honduras for ten years from the Honduran government. These rights gave "the Museum not only the charge of the antiquities in the country, but also the exclusive right of exploration and the permission to take away one half of all the objects found during the excavations."[42]

The work conducted at Copan involved reclaiming the ancient site from a millennium of rain forest overgrowth. It could not be done without the help of locals. Hiram Price was initially charged with hiring them. He worked through both the Honduran minister of interior relations and the local district jefe. The hiring process began in spurts. The work crew members stayed with their families on holidays and feast days.[43] They also showed little enthusiasm for doing the hard work of cutting brush and digging when they considered the wages to be too low. The sponsor of the expedition, Charles Bowditch, the Boston industrialist and a founder of the American Anthropological Association, warned in a sharply worded letter that the Indian people were to be treated with respect. "All their transactions with these people should be scrupulously just + exact," he wrote to Putnam. "No infringement on their rights should be allowed, whether in Excavating outside of the 2 caballerias [a unit of measurement] belonging to the Gov't, in buying provisions, in paying for their work, +c." He added that in cases of "Excavation injuries [to] the crops of any one, even in the 2 caballerias, recompense should be made." He seemed especially concerned that the Peabody Museum crew would be welcomed back in the future.[44] Early on, at least, there is not much evidence that Price followed Bowditch's edict. But as work crews went unfilled, at least some adjustments were made.

The laborers came in two groups, those assigned by the local official and "volunteers" who came of their own accord. They were paid on the same scale. The expedition leaders were bound by the vagaries of the work crews. To an extent the trabajadores or laborers were able to negotiate the terms of work or at least the pay scale. If the pay was too low, they simply did not show up to work. They were able to do this because the demand for labor was higher than the number of workers provided by local officials. The laborers did the bulk of the clearing and excavation. Most of the workers in this category of unskilled labor were likely Native American, from among the local Maya and those who had been displaced from Guatemala. The officially assigned workers were drawn from at least eight local villages, with two to four workers coming from each.[45]

The laborers did not receive board; they paid for their own food. They slept in a "mere shed" on the grounds. In mid-December Price agreed to pay the workers 2½ reals per day. A real was equivalent to approximately 12½ cents American money. He wrote that "the full supply of men asked for will arrive tomorrow or next day." It was not to be. By the new year he had only nine assigned men and six or seven volunteers. Many had stayed home to celebrate the holidays. So he raised the pay rate to 3 reals per man, but kept it at 2½ for boys, or even 1½ for small boys.[46]

That still failed to do the trick. By the end of January another expedition leader reported to Putnam that "we have been very hard pressed for laborers."[47] At that point they raised the pay to 4 reals. By February they had more than fifty workers, which they considered sufficient.[48] In fact, the president of Honduras and Minister of Foreign Affairs Jeronimo Zelaya insisted that 4 reals was the appropriate pay rate.[49]

Few women worked in the camp, but they were paid less. The expedition paid the camp cook $8 a month, which works out to approximately 2 reals a day. The tortilla maker earned $3 to $4, about 10 cents a day.[50] Presumably they worked seven days a week. One in the

1892–93 season, a woman named Josefina, lasted only two days but was paid $1.40. She appears to have been replaced by Francisca Montenegra, who was paid $4 per month.[51] By that next season prices had apparently increased for labor. The expedition refused to hire workers for $1 a day to work at nearby Quiriguá, although the banana plantations were paying that amount. Even at that rate, the plantations were short of labor.[52] The work at Copan was backbreaking, and the pay was low. But the Honduran government had guaranteed workers to the expeditionary crew.[53]

Once the pay rate was established at what was considered a fair level by the Honduran government and apparently by the workers themselves, the work commenced apace. Putnam viewed the work as "the grandest effort yet made for archaeological research in America."[54]

Although the materials gathered played an important part in the collection of objects and molds for the world's fair, Putnam and Bowditch viewed the task in Honduras as a long-term coup for the Peabody Museum. The collection process continued long after the fair ended and created the foundation for the museum's Central American displays, which are still an important feature of the museum collections and displays today.

Thus the treatment of local Maya villagers was foremost in Bowditch's mind, if for no other reason than the site would be protected during the off-season and Peabody collectors would be welcome in the future. Price received permission to purchase extra medicine and to treat people for lingering cuts and injuries.[55] The team also leased out land on the site for local Mayan farmers to plant their milpas, or maize fields. They did so in exchange for a share of the crops, but the farmers "seem quite satisfied with this, as they were afraid we should claim the land exclusively for our own use."[56] After all, Native people's lands in the region had been confiscated without recompense for centuries.

Both inside and outside of the work of the expedition, local community members were incorporated into the lives and work of the collectors. But aside from hiring and finances, the documents show little recognition of the role or conditions of the labor force. In fact, John Owens and Marshall Saville reported their work as if they did it alone with no help from local laborers. Saville wrote to Putnam, for example, that "Mr. Owens has finished M[oun]d 36," and this is typical of the correspondence.[57]

Needless to say, the archaeological work could not have been accomplished without the majority of it being done by Native trabajadores. They worked within a long-developed context of balance between work and home life. Though they lived in deep poverty, they refused to work for below market wages, low as market wages were. They only worked for what they considered fair, if meager, wages.

Several of the people who collected for Putnam in Latin America were military personnel. As with the Northwest Coast, their budgets were significantly higher than those in most U.S. Native communities. Roger Welles, a navy lieutenant, collected in Venezuela. He traveled the Orinoco River, spending $128.40, making some of his purchases with cash and some in trade. He spent more on goods to trade than he spent for actual purchases, telling Putnam that a list of items was not bought "with money; but the articles were bartered with uncivilized and wild natives, belonging to the different Indian tribes on the Upper Orinoco and its tributaries, for what is generally known as 'Trade Goods.'" He bought calico, beads, hollands (heavy cloths), knives, and spear heads for trade. Welles also spent $20 on a hammock and $5 on a feather basket.[58] For the Native people of the Orinoco, trade goods had more value than cash. Some communities were slower than those in the United States and Canada to move from barter to cash exchanges, since goods remained more valuable than money there.

William E. Safford, also a navy lieutenant, reported separate purchases of more than $1,000 in Bolivia in 1891. This included more than $400 in a single inventory of items purchased from the Aymara.[59] He also purchased three "Jíbaros" and two "Zaparros" ceremonial dresses that "were not made to sell but for use." He bought these under the auspices of the Latin American division of the fair, although they were apparently provided to Putnam under an agreement between the two divisions. He also hoped "to use my $500 for such things as dresses of the Michnas and Aymara Indians, native plows, boats, musical instruments & the like." It was not clear the extent to which he was purchasing these directly from Indian people or from traders or collectors or middlemen who had already bought them.[60]

After the fair a significant portion of material objects from the anthropological exhibits was turned over to the newly established Field Museum. Lot sizes ranged from a small handful to more than one hundred. The cost of purchase for museum collections is indicated in many of the Department of Anthropology accession records. In some cases the collection costs are included in the documentation. Very rarely are labor costs included, although in one case $45 was spent on "peons and per diem" over a nine-day period of collecting Salamanca Indian materials in Costa Rica in 1891. Even this collection, as with others, includes no indication of whether objects were purchased directly from Indians or through intermediaries.[61]

The economic impacts of Putnam and Boas's collectors varied significantly from community to community. In communities where there were already long-standing practices of selling material goods and information to outsiders, there were networks of individuals who knew the value of what they sold and were able to take advantage of the opportunities the fair provided. In those cases, Putnam had to decide how much of his budget he was willing to commit. In other communities, where the commercial ventures were not well established, the money went farther in terms of supporting the anthropological display. In cases where people were desperate for cash, they sold valuable items for low prices. Putnam knew the tricks of the trade in terms of driving down prices; in some cases he was very successful, while in others where people had multiple options for selling their goods and services, he had to accept the prices asked or leave the goods for others to collect.

The benefit was heavily weighted to the non-Indian participants in the development of the fields of anthropology, archaeology, and history and in the development of natural history museums across the United States. For instance, Dr. Daniel Bertolette received $125 for Paraguayan Indian "implements, ornaments, weapons, etc." that he made himself.[62] E. H. Thompson received more than $10,000 for collecting and having made replicas of Maya ruins from the Yucatan. He, Dorsey, and Boas together received more than $25,000 from the budget, most of which did *not* go to tribal members.

In most places where Putnam and Boas's collectors infused cash into the local economy, the impacts were short term. And in those places where collectors stayed close to the $50 limit, only a few people benefited. In other places, where more money was spent, a broader sector within local Native communities felt the impact. Dozens of people found work in Copan in a project that would extend beyond 1893. At Queen Charlotte Island in British Columbia, numerous people found employment in preparation for the fair preparation work. This region had become an area well attuned to the tourist and museum trade.

Most places in the United States, and many in Canada and Latin America, though, saw small infusions of cash to a limited number of individuals in what was becoming a minor but important fixture of tribal economies—providing old and new materials, both physical objects and knowledge, to collectors and ethnographers. Small amounts of cash could be the difference between survival and starvation in desperate times. And of course, there were others collecting and buying in Native communities, including others collecting for the fair.

5

Government Agencies
Collecting for the Fair

Putnam and Boas were not the only ones sending collectors into Indian country in the early 1890s. The Columbian Exposition occurred during the early stages of the scramble for artifacts that sent museum collectors across America scouring Native communities to build their assemblages of material culture.[1] This would eventually cause the dispossession of Native objects, both sacred and secular, from tribal communities and their removal to non-Indian controlled cultural and educational institutions. In addition to Putnam and Boas, both the Smithsonian Institution and the Canadian government abetted in this process in building their displays for the fair.

The Smithsonian's Natural History Museum employees had been traveling across the United States to build what would become massive ethnological collections since the 1870s. The Smithsonian efforts, particularly in the Southwest, had begun on the basis of barter but evolved to exchange for cash.[2] The Smithsonian used funds from its budget for collecting in the years leading to the fair, with the plan to create displays that could be incorporated into the National Museum's exhibits. So although its display was a U.S. government one, it was not affiliated with Putnam's anthropology building or ethnological village.

Canadian government officials also decided to include representation of Native peoples of Canada in their national display. Ottawa sent instructions to local and regional Indian agents to collect material culture objects for this and set aside a modest budget to do so. The efforts of these two entities were not nearly as far-reaching as those of Putnam and Boas. They worked with small amounts of money, but nonetheless impacted local Native communities, at times in significant ways.

Collecting for the Smithsonian Institution

Anthropologist Nancy Parezo has credited the Smithsonian Institution with playing a key role in defining the collection of material objects as a scientific endeavor. Beginning in the 1870s, and particularly from 1879 to 1884, the Bureau of Ethnology sent collectors primarily to the southwestern United States to gather materials for the National Museum. A major purpose of this work was to record the meaning and role of the collected objects in the societies from which they originated. While the bureau used funds from its own budgets to sponsor such trips, it was able to bolster those funds when collecting for world's fairs.[3] As it had in the past, beginning with the 1876 Centennial Exposition in Philadelphia, the Smithsonian used the Chicago fair as an opportunity to obtain funds to significantly build its collections. In preparation for the U.S. government display, the U.S. Bureau of Ethnology sent agents to purchase or borrow materials for exhibit at the exposition. The Smithsonian budgeted $10,000 for the fair, but apparently augmented that by assigning agents already on staff or in the field to collect for the exhibit.[4]

Otis Mason oversaw the Smithsonian's development of an ethnological exhibit at the fair. He sent James Mooney into the field to collect, and Mooney purchased more than 370 objects in Oklahoma.[5] He also instructed Walter James Hoffman, who was already in the field, to buy for the fair in the Midwest. Henry Henshaw made collections in California, and other agents collected in communities where they already had connections. In addition, Mason purchased several items from a Pamunkey Indian man from Virginia, Terrill Bradby. The Smithsonian also used some of the same connections as Putnam in the United States and Latin America to fill its collections.

Smithsonian collectors, though few, were given a budget and relatively free rein in decision making regarding what to purchase and ship to Chicago or the museum. James Mooney was provided $4,700 for three collecting trips totaling ten months' time; Walter Hoffman was given a budget of $2,300 for two and a half months' work.

The funds were meant to pay salary and transportation costs, and to include purchase of materials for the Smithsonian's mannequin display cases from either tribal members who had them to sell or from private collectors. Both kinds of purchases were made. Both men's salary were $116.67 per month. Expenses also included "interpreter fees and such other assistance as may be necessary in collecting and transportation," including purchase of gifts for distinguished tribal members, as well as local guide fees.[6] With their previous experience in the field, these collectors knew that gift giving was appropriate protocol for working with tribes and Indian people. They also knew that cash would be necessary to consummate purchases.

James Mooney worked for the Bureau of American Ethnology, a branch of the Smithsonian Institution. William Henry Holmes, who was in charge of developing the bureau's displays for the world's fair, sent Mooney to the Southwest "to collect Navajo and Hopi costumes, foodstuffs, and native crafts," according to historian L. G. Moses.[7] Nonetheless most of his collecting for the fair was done at the Kiowa, Comanche, and Wichita Agency and the Cheyenne and Arapaho Agency in Indian Territory. A letter from George Brown Goode, the assistant secretary in charge of the U.S. National Museum, instructed Mooney that "special attention should be given to obtaining materials illustrating the Ghost-Dance, a warriors [sic] complete outfit, the paraphernalia of the medicine men, and other characteristic tribal ceremonies."[8] Much of Mooney's budget went to tribal members. One series of vouchers he submitted from Indian Territory in June 1891 included $119.20 for "services" and a total of $508.65 for "specimens."[9]

At this time some forty Indians at the Kiowa, Comanche, and Wichita Agency worked as government employees, earning from $10 to $20 per month. Their jobs included blacksmithing, carpentry, and law enforcement, both as judges and Indian police. The latter earned $20 per month. The Comanche leader Quanah Parker, who served as a judge, earned $10 a month for those duties.[10] The agent there reported that annuity goods arrived late in the winter, later than scheduled. In addition, the Indians' payments for grazing fees came in late, and they were negotiating new grazing compacts. Most tribal members made a meager living from agriculture and raising stock.[11] Supplemental income would be important for all of them.

The agent at the Cheyenne and Arapaho Agency reported that Canadian County was preparing to assess Indian allotments for taxes, although he resisted the efforts.[12] This practice would later lead to enormous land losses for Indians across the United States.[13] Even for those who held paying jobs, the money that Mooney spent would represent a windfall.

Mooney often spent his funds before he received them and was constantly writing to Washington for reimbursement. Indians simply needed the money. He eventually became disenchanted with collecting for the fair because of the slow pace of bureaucracy involved in filling out forms and getting reimbursed. He could not buy on credit from Indians; they needed cash for their sales. In June 1891 he telegraphed his boss, "Money nearly all spent or contracted for and will take three hundred more for proposed work shall I draw on next fiscal year now or not going back to camp depends on answer please answer at once no receipts yet from vouchers."[14] In a follow-up letter he wrote,

> I have spent $500 cash of my own. I have paper + contracts out for about $400 more. There is more to be done to make it complete. I have spent the last two weeks in a dirty teepee, sleeping on the ground + living on crackers + coffee, because I wouldnt [*sic*] eat a sick colt. I come back to find my vouchers returned + no money + to dodge the traders + stand off a mob of wild Indians. In the morning I go back to camp again. When I return I must have money + if vouchers are not in shape I must have money anyhow from some source + after that I can sit down + make vouchers to suit all the red tape requirements of the treasury.

He was told the institution "regrets very much the embarrassment caused you and is very anxious that no further delay should ensue."[15]

By July Mooney complained to a friend, "It is too long a story to tell now, but the amount of it is that I am thoroughly sick + disgusted with my experience with the World's Fair."[16] Bureaucratic red tape involving funds impeded his efforts to make purchases in Indian country as effectively as he would have liked.

Mooney had a slightly easier time buying from traders than from Indians. Traders were willing to work on a credit basis, trusting that

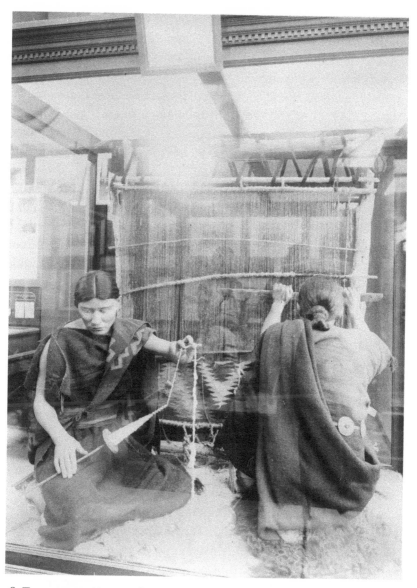

18. Two mannequins weaving, Smithsonian Institution exhibit. Courtesy Library of Congress. Photo number LOC 3c09761u.

the federal government eventually would be good for payment. They also had fewer cash flow problems than desperate Indian people. Mooney also purchased from private collectors, most notably Reverend Henry Voth. Voth sold Mooney a collection of Cheyenne and Arapaho materials for $750. Voth had purchased these items over his years at the agency, and according to Mooney, he had "history noted down" on all the pieces, an important consideration for Smithsonian collections.[17] While this purchase did not provide cash for Cheyenne or Arapaho people, the previous purchases by Voth and others had helped establish the cash economy at the agency.

Walter J. Hoffman also collected heavily for the Smithsonian exhibit. His first assignment was to collect from the Ojibwe and Menominee in Michigan, Minnesota, and Wisconsin. He was budgeted $800 for three months' salary, travel expenses, and collection purchasing in July 1891.[18] He was already in the midst of an in-depth study of Menominee religious and cultural practices for the Bureau of Ethnology that would result in a major publication.[19] He was the first ethnographer to visit the tribe in more than sixty years.[20] He spent $75 for "fees for interpreters; to 'Medicine Men'; for feasts at Mīdē [Mitāēwin] Society and for Indian records and charts, horse hire, etc. etc."[21] Hoffman not only paid tribal members for services but also sponsored a feast at a religious ceremony, which would have shown tribal members that he had some knowledge of appropriate protocol.

In May 1892 he was sent back and then sent farther west to collect from the Crows in Montana and tribes in the Dakotas as well, with a budget of $1,500 for six weeks.[22] In June he spent $424.75 on direct purchases from Crow and Chippewa tribal members. He seems to have visited the Crow Reservation early in the month where he spent $392.25 on direct purchases, and then he returned back east at the end of June. His purchases from Crows varied from 25 cents spent on various objects, including a pair of children's moccasins and a horse whip, to $90 for "Chief's war garments,—suit consisting of buckskin fringed with ermine; one pair of fur and beaded trimmed leggings; pouch and knife sheath." He also spent $20 on a fully beaded youth's coat, $12 on a woman's saddle that was covered in beaded buckskin, and $15 on beaded war leggings. He purchased clothing, ornamentation, tools, and decorative and utilitarian objects of everyday usage.

All of these objects were purchased for display at the fair and eventually accessioned into the Smithsonian's collections.[23]

According to their agency superintendent, the Crows were not suffering as much as other tribes that summer. They were mostly farmers and ranchers, with many living on or claiming individual allotments. A handful of Crow men worked at the agency. Fourteen policemen earned $10 a month, while two officers earned $15. A few men worked as carpenters and blacksmith's assistants. The best paid tribal employees were two herders, who each received $300 per year.[24] The supplemental cash that Hoffman brought to Crows would nonetheless have been welcome. There were few opportunities to earn an income in eastern Montana beyond subsistence farming, ranching, and the few agency jobs available.

Because of Northwest Coast tribal communities' long history of trade, materials were especially expensive for the Smithsonian to obtain there. James Swan of Port Townsend, Washington, reported accurately to the Smithsonian in 1891 that materials were both scarce and expensive. He wrote hoping to sell a collection he had made of blankets, clothing, and adornments. He said that these things were "now very difficult to procure, since the influx of tourists and visitors to Alaska and western British Columbia, who have gathered up every article of Indian manufacture they could purchase."[25]

Matilda Coxe Stevenson collected masks from Zia Pueblo for the fair, eventually spending $250 for fifty masks. She apparently followed tribal protocol to procure them. She first had to ask the Pueblo's leadership for permission to make the purchases. These purchases needed community, not individual, approval. Then she awaited their answer. A letter from several Pueblo members said, "As you told the party of four pueblo and as you wrote to our priest, we had a meeting of all the people of our place and we talk about the matter in question. Everybody agreed to let you have what you asked from us. There has been no dissention at all on that subject. So you shall come again among us as you say, so we shall have the pleasure to see you and welcome you for few days though."[26]

Henry Henshaw purchased baskets from California tribes, including the Maidu, for the fair. "I have about cleaned the Indians out of baskets and their season for making is not yet here. They spend months on a fine one" and charge "from $10 to $20 for it when done and they get it too," he wrote.[27] The baskets he purchased directly from the makers cost from $15 to $30 each and were sold by traders for $40 to $100.[28]

Some of the objects collected by the Smithsonian came from individuals working in Indian country and not from agents sent into the field. A Piegan black steer robe painted with tribal history and purchased from the Blackfeet Reservation in Montana is an example of this. Z. T. Daniel, an "old collector," bought it from the artist, a Piegan man named Sharp, and sold it to the museum for $12. He included a written version of the story that was portrayed on the hide. Mason urged his supervisor, "Please buy the robe for the World's Fair. These things are getting scarce and this is very cheap."[29]

The Piegan were desperate that winter. They lost 10 percent of their cattle with the harsh weather lasting from November through May.[30] People were forced to sell what they had at below market prices. Unlike the Northwest Coast, there was little current demand, especially in the off-season, which explains the bargain price the museum paid for this piece of art.

Another collector in Santa Fe purchased "idols" for the museum from an Indian who was likely breaking tribal protocol. These were probably protected religious objects. He had thought the man was charging high prices by making false claims that it was dangerous for him to collect and sell them. The collector wrote to Henry Henshaw at the Smithsonian that he was glad to learn from Henshaw that the man's story was accurate. The man was unwilling to sell the objects "for less than $5.00 a piece as he held that he was taking a great many chances for his life etc. the same story over and over again that I told you when here. So on the strength of your letter I gave his story a great deal more credit than I had here to fore done and thought if they were worth anything they certainly were worth that amount under the circumstances."[31] These objects either needed communal approval to be sold or were forbidden entirely to pass into profane hands.

At the same time museum officials feared that these items were easily duplicable for the market and would thus be inauthentic. Henshaw observed, "No doubt many of these idols are genuine perhaps all that are in sight are so; but they are so easily made that just as soon as the Indians find there is a market for them they are sure to counterfeit them for sale."[32] Indians themselves did not always view such duplicates as inauthentic, however. In fact, in some places where individual Indians held ownership rights to designs, they could make multiple copies of objects, and all would be considered original.[33]

Nonetheless, museum officials viewed themselves as acting ethically in this case by paying low prices for what they considered to be valuable materials for their collection. The Indian who sold these to the museum for the fair was apparently collaborating in an illicit trade, at least from a tribal perspective. In both this case and with the Piegan robe, the museum benefited from conditions in remote markets that rewarded duplicity.

Emma Sickels, a Putnam contact whom Mason also used, took a similar approach for the Smithsonian—she underpaid for purchases with the promise of doing return business later. Sickels sent Mason $54 worth of Lakota material objects, primarily from Pine Ridge, for the fair in August 1892. These included two $15 travel bags, one embroidered with porcupine quills, and a $15 baby bonnet decorated the same way. She told Mason, "The prices are if anything less than the prices they charge and as I explained were given in order that I might influence the women to bring forward their goods and in the future enable me to have a wider selection on better terms."[34]

Mason also engaged Terrill Bradby, a Pamunkey man from Virginia, to provide collections for the fair. He purchased twelve items from Bradby, including a dugout canoe, an ax, a war club, a corn cracker, a chisel, arrowheads, and pottery that Bradby made expressly for Mason, all for a total of $15.[35]

William Safford, who collected for Putnam in Bolivia, collected for the Smithsonian as well in Bolivia and Peru, spending hundreds of dollars. His Smithsonian purchases seem to have been made from a collector or middleman, so it is not clear how much of this money flowed into tribal communities. At some point tribal members had presumably been paid for what Safford purchased. Similar to the instructions that collectors received from Putnam, Safford was told by an assistant secretary at the Smithsonian, "The specimens should be limited to ethnological and archaeological objects illustrating the domestic life and simple arts of the primative [*sic*] people."[36] The instructions did not include a directive that they reflect pre-Columbian objects, however. For the Smithsonian, presenting Indians as they currently lived would be enough to relegate them to a status as peoples of the past.

Another Navy lieutenant, Fran Sawyer, sent $398 worth of materials from several tribes in Brazil, including a dress that cost $60 and a set of war weapons for $90.[37] In his case, too, it is unclear if he spent the money in tribal communities or purchased from traders.

Collecting for the Canadian Government

A third entity bringing cash into tribal communities through the purchase of American Indian cultural patrimony for fair displays was the Canadian government. It provided the Indian department with a small budget to develop its display for the fair. Even after increasing funds, Canadian expenditures were significantly less than Putnam's. They were also a smaller amount than the United States spent on its school and Smithsonian displays. The Canadian government collectors, like those from the Smithsonian, did not develop the kind of cutthroat competition that characterized the mad scrambles between the major museums over the next couple of decades, but they did provide opportunities for tribal artisans to earn some money.

Both those tribal members selling wares and those helping collectors profited, funneling small amounts of cash into Native communities. This was an especially difficult venture for Canadian collectors, who were usually government Indian agents, since they were instructed by federal officials to collect on the cheap. And, of course, the infusions of cash were not enough to cut into the intense poverty of reserve communities. On the other hand, even a small amount of cash would be welcome. During the year of the fair, the part-time Indian agent assigned to Christmas Island on Cape Breton reported that the Micmac under his supervision lacked the necessary capital to purchase even the most basic equipment needed to manage their farms.[38]

This was a difficult time for First Nations communities across Canada. The autumn prior to the fair, potato crops failed from Nova Scotia to the Rocky Mountain front. Canadian Indian policy since the 1830s had focused on development of agriculture as a primary

19. Canadian exhibit, including materials gathered from First Nations communities. From Bancroft, *The Book of the Fair*, 1 of 2:243.

foundation of tribal welfare, and in much of Canada this meant a reliance on root vegetables. In most places the northern climate was not conducive to widespread farming.

The general Canadian Indian policy had three prongs—protection, civilization, and assimilation. Farming in sedentary community sites would support all three. Unfortunately, as in the United States, much of the land set aside for Native people to farm was not particularly productive in good years and could bring massive crop failures in bad years. In part, this meant that in order to survive, First Nations individuals would need alternate sources of income. The small infusion of cash into tribal communities in Canada by collectors helped to some degree.

Like the Smithsonian, the Canadian Department of Indian Affairs (DIA) also made a display of Indian manufacture that included traditional works, which were purchased from tribal communities. A DIA circular sent to Indian agents asked them to provide both agricultural products and manufactured products for the display, including "Fancy work or other kinds of native work of any description, baskets, beadwork on leather or cloth, ornamented articles of wearing apparel, birch bark ornaments, &c., &c." Two thousand dollars was originally set aside for the "ethnology" display in the Canadian Pavilion, and the budget eventually increased to at least $6,500.[39] At least some of that money went to tribal communities.

Despite Putnam's efforts at budgeting, his team's efforts pushed prices up for everyone. The massive collecting that Putnam financed could discourage other collectors. The Indian agent at Christmas Island reported to the Canadian Department of Indian Affairs in December 1892 that he would have little success purchasing Indian wares for the government's exhibit because so much had already been collected from the Cape Breton region. A Micmac Indian had already scoured the local Indian communities. This man "was not employed by me to collect rare specimens of the handicraft of the tribe," A. Cameron wrote. "He was employed by an American agent of the government, or of the committee of the world's fair, and was paid not only for everything he selected but also for the time spent in doing so. The Indian did not belong to this agency, but was time and again here, and travelled throughout all the agencies of this Island in quest of whatever was rare or curious or in any way excellent among his tribe."[40] Records do not indicate who this individual was or for whom he was working. Perhaps this was the sailor whom Tisdale had hired in his work for Boas and Putnam.

Nearby, an Abenaki chief, Joseph Laurent, collected directly for the Canadian government. This was rare; nearly all of the materials Canada brought to the fair were procured through agents. Laurent received $75.05 for baskets and other materials. He became known among academics studying the Abenaki language, according to his son. He wrote a text on English and Abenaki languages and a French-Abenaki dictionary. Apparently he had enough control of his territory to do all of the collecting for his tribe.[41] This way, without middlemen gobbling up travel expenses, more money could go directly to the individual doing the collecting. Laurent's role was more similar to Terrill Bradby's than to Cornelius Cusick's or the Northwest Coast collectors who worked for Boas and Putnam. But like Bradby, Cusick, George Hunt, and Odille Morison, he was interested in scientific preservation of his tribe's history and knowledge.

In British Columbia, Indian agent A. W. Vowell tried to return the $500 check he received from the DIA for the purchase of Indian-made goods. The reason? Putnam's agents had already spent more than $4,000 purchasing material goods in the region, and in addition, there was a brisk tourist trade. There was little he could do with $500. Nonetheless, his request to return the money was refused, and he was ordered to purchase what he could "to the best possible advantage" to provide materials for the Canadian exhibit.[42] He eventually bought $495.40 worth of goods from forty-six Indians.[43] All of this pumped significant cash into a small number of local Native families and economies on the British Columbia Northwest Coast.

In fact, the British Columbia response to the DIA request provides valuable insight into the local economy. Despite the fact that the lion's share of collecting for the fair here went to Putnam's collectors, the $500 available to British Columbia brought several suggestions from the Indian agencies within the department regarding how it could be spent.

Vowell, the Indian superintendent for the British Columbia region, requested that the agents under his authority let him know what could be procured. Their responses varied. The agent from the Williams Lake Agency informed him that the Lilwat Indians and those near Clinton could provide arrowheads, bows and arrows, and stone implements for a modest price. He itemized Chilcoton manufactures of such things as a rabbit skin blanket, a woven waterproof basket, and a caribou riata that would total $48 in cost.[44] On the other hand, the agent in charge of the Babine Agency responded that the Indians were not even in his vicinity at the time of the request, and so he could not know what goods they had to sell. He also thought that if they knew the purpose of the sales, they would charge "unexpectedly much." Nonetheless, the Babine agent thought he could procure high-quality toboggans and snowshoes from the "Kit-khauns" and "Hoguel-get" for $4 to $5 apiece.[45]

The agent at the Cowichan Agency suggested the purchase of a cod fishing spinner and spear, dog fish line, halibut hooks and line, reed hats, Indian blankets, cedar hats, and older war clubs, bows and arrows, and spears. All could be had for about $50, but they could not be bought on credit—payment would have to be made at the time of purchase.[46] Indians in his region of Vancouver Island were already integrated into the cash economy, and they well knew the distinction between sales on credit and for cash.

The agent at Alberni suggested a 30 to 32 foot canoe for between $120 and $150 and things such as dancing masks ($5 to $10), whaling and fishing gear ($5 to $25 each), and cedar clothing and blankets and mats ($3 to $8), some made by women. He also said he could procure wood carvings in the $8 to $18 range, but they "would have to be made to order by Atlu alias Doctor of Clayoquot who is the only good carver on this Coast." Carving was not Atlu's only employment, however, as the agent added, "He is at present in Victoria fishing." Fishing could provide a combination of subsistence and cash-in-pocket with the rich natural resources of the region.

Finally, the agent from the Kamloops-Okanagon Agency sent an exhaustive list of potential materials that he could procure. He suggested a variety of animal furs and skins that ranged in price from 15 cents for a muskrat to $60 for a silver fox. He also recommended native plants, minerals, and old-time tools and weapons, as well as manufactured goods such as clothing, fishing equipment, snowshoes, baskets, and models of a canoe, a house, and a fish spear. The cost of the manufactured goods would come to a little more than $85.[47]

All of this means that the various First Nations people of British Columbia, at least those living near the coast, were savvy to the fluctuations of market—they had a clear knowledge that they could charge what the market would bear. That is, there was no innate value to the goods they produced for sale. The value was defined by the market demand. Canadian officials may have considered these Indians uncivilized, but they knew the value of their production in terms of regional, national, and international market conditions. If there was no outside demand for what they produced, they would have to charge less. If there was widespread collecting, this actually drove the prices up. In addition, they would not sell their products on credit. They lived in an economy that was in part cash-based, and they insisted that when they parted with items of their own manufacture or objects that they themselves still used such as fishing gear or winter travel equipment, they would be appropriately compensated for it.

Other First Nations communities in Canada benefited from the collecting for the exposition, although to a lesser extent. The superintendent of the North-West Territories, Hayter Reed, received $800 to purchase objects for display at the fair. Some of that money was spent on the Blackfoot Reserve in what is now southern Alberta, on the plains near the Rocky Mountains, just north of the U.S. border. He purchased a porcupine quill dress that appears to have been made by Red Crow's wife. The dress must have necessitated an extraordinary amount of work; the price was $50.50.[48] Other objects cost less. Reed also asked the Blackfoot to supply drums, shields, and a lodge.

It is unclear what type of hides were used to make the lodge, but they were tanned by the best tanners in the tribe at cut rate prices. The tanners received $2 per hide, tanned on both sides, while the normal price was $3.25 for tanning one side. The local agent Magnus Begg bragged to Reed, "There are only a few Indians here who understand tanning skill, and it takes about a week to tan one hide, so they only make about 35 cents per day." Begg acquired the lodge poles for free instead of the usual $4 to $5. He did so as part of a deal he made with tribal members to go into the mountains to cut wood for their own needs. The lodge was built and painted by Chief Old Sun's wife, the most skillful in the community at this task, for somewhere between $7 and $11. Begg told his superior, "As they say she is the best, the skins cost $2.00 each and she earned the money." It was eventually shipped to Chicago later than the other goods, since Mrs. Old Sun was unable to paint it properly until after the extreme freezing weather in February broke. Crowfoot's daughter also made a porcupine quill dress for the exhibit.[49]

The Blackfoot who made these items for the exposition did not receive fair wages for either their labor or their skills. They were underpaid but probably desperate enough that any work and income kept starvation at bay. The winter of 1892–93 was particularly harsh on the Rocky Mountain front where the Blackfoot lived. (This was the same winter during which their relatives to the south, the Piegan, lost so many cattle to harsh weather.)[50] The previous summer (1892) their root crops had almost entirely failed.[51] They had little control over the price for their labor and few resources to support their families. Unlike the British Columbia Indians, they lived remote

20. Mrs. Old Sun with her husband. Courtesy Provincial Archives of Alberta, B1035.

to other areas where they could earn a living. There was as yet little competition for the purchase of their goods. That made the market value lower in their case. The agricultural policy was failing them, the bison had long disappeared, and the stubborn Canadian federal policy focused on unsuccessful farming, so any cash would have helped. Unfortunately, they had to sell what they made at low prices in order to make the sale at all.

At the Crooked Lake Agency near Regina in Assiniboia (now Saskatchewan), agent A. McDonald purchased tanned hides and had them made into a lodge at the request of the Indian department on credit. This did not sit well with the Cree Indians who sold them. Though the amount was but $28.23, McDonald could not get the department to send him the money. "I wrote . . . informing you I could not get the hides tanned without being paid for," he told the Indian commissioner, "and unless I had understood from your silence on this point, that I might issue vouchers in payment, I would not have had the work done, as the Indians distinctly refused to do the work, unless assured by me that cash payments would ensue." It is not clear whether he received the money in the end, paid from his own pocket, or returned the hides.[52]

However, this example makes clear the importance of cash as payment, even in remote areas. In Canada, as in the United States, Indians needed cash to supplement their incomes and had experience dating back to the early fur trade with credit payments by which they could eventually be cheated out of the fruits of their labor. Another agent wrote in September 1892, "I have no doubt that we shall be able to purchase cheaper, and certainly with more satisfaction when we have the money in hand to pay for the articles."[53] Back east in Nova Scotia, agent Thomas Butler wrote that the Indians at Greenfield and Caledonia Corner "are ever ready and willing to do anything that will bring them fair wages."[54] All of these examples show both the need for some kind of financial prospects and the value of cash for tribal members in pay for their work.

The initial U.S. federal funding for government exhibits was divided among the ten government exhibits, including the Department of the Interior, which had but a $52,500 appropriation to split among its eight bureaus and government territorial exhibits. The department wanted to portray Indian industry such as weaving and pottery work. Its initial solution, never fulfilled, was to have the best Indian artisans make materials for the fair at no cost to the government but with the opportunity to profit from sales. "It is believed, however, that the greater part of the expense may be met by the Indians themselves, who will be permitted and encouraged to dispose of their manufactures for their own profit, under such rules and regulations as the Commissioner of Indian Affairs and the exposition authorities may jointly make," the Department of the Interior's representative Horace A. Taylor wrote to Secretary John W. Noble in September 1891.[55] This certainly would have worked to the benefit of Indian artisans and was a model used at later world's fairs.[56]

Nonetheless, other collections from Indian country were made for the fair. For example, as the fair approached, the U.S. Indian office did not have enough funding to complete and furnish the Indian school exhibit. The office authorized four to six Navajo blankets from the trader Thomas V. Keam at Keam's Canyon in Arizona at $40 total to cover door openings in the school. Keam was paid $44.50 for these blankets, but it is unclear how much he paid the artisans for them.[57] At any rate, the three entities with the most financial impact in tribal communities in the Americas were those run by Putnam and Boas, by the Smithsonian Institution, and by the Canadian government. To a small extent, several U.S. state exhibits and several other foreign government exhibits brought some cash into Native communities within their territorial boundaries as well.

Indirectly, of course, numerous Indian people benefited economically from the fair. They sold objects and guided collectors and shared oral history and music with ethnographers and collectors whose growing interest coincided with the increased popularity of the field of anthropology. Ethnographers who lacked personal wealth often sought wealthy patrons to support their work. The fair's success and the museum world that expanded because of it broadened the public understanding of the nation's past. This collecting frenzy helped countless ethnographers and museum collectors make a living and supported the work of curators and scholars for decades to come—in fact, into the present.

The collecting work helped develop a growing cash economy in reservation communities for decades following the Columbian Exposition. The difference was that while non-Indian scholars and collectors made a comfortable living from the history, culture, and material objects of Native peoples, the Indians benefited primarily by gaining enough cash to avoid more severe starvation than they were already experiencing. These benefits were only short-term for Indians, while entire scholarly careers could be built on collecting work.

This followed a longtime colonial pattern of settler society people benefiting from indigenous people's resources. As with Native lands and natural resources, Native material culture was treated by American and Canadian society at large as fair game for exploitation. Using the excuse of budgetary constraints, those in charge of collecting instructed their employees to purchase as much as they could as cheaply as possible.

The benefits were unevenly distributed. Some Native communities— those with a combination of market demand and market savvy— benefited to a greater extent than others. But all were at a disadvantage due to colonial power structures and relations. Their introduction to the cash economy came at a time of intense tribal political and economic weakness and in conditions where individuals bordered on or lived in desperation. For Native people, new ways of earning a living were critical to survival. While some did so at home, others increasingly traveled, sometimes great distances, to support themselves and their families. When the Chicago fair opened, hundreds of American Indians attended, many as part of various displays for which they received income of varying sorts.

PART 3

During the Fair

Working in Chicago

6

Working the Anthropological and Education Displays

Once the fair opened, American Indians lived and worked in a variety of places, on and off the fairgrounds. Hundreds of Native people came to Chicago to work for the fair. Many were paid for their work, but some were not. Some received what they considered fair compensation. Some who did not protested in a variety of ways for better working conditions and pay. There was no singular experience for Native people working at the exposition in 1893, although non-Indians in most cases earned more. To gain some understanding of the meaning of work for Native participants, we must consider the goals and experiences of people from numerous tribal groups and indigenous communities using the evidence that we can gather.

Shifting plans between 1891 and 1893 created a sprawling and confusing combination of exhibits featuring Native American and other indigenous peoples. The agreement between Frederic Ward Putnam and the Indian bureau cleanly divided the focus of official fair representation of Indians between the past, reflected in anthropological exhibit, and the future, portrayed in the Indian schools. Many Indians, not surprisingly, were more interested in the present. Separate states took responsibility for bringing some living Indian exhibits, but these remained under Putnam's authority. Several foreign governments also brought Indians and Native peoples to the fair, some under Putnam's authority and some not. The Smithsonian Institution created displays of Indian people but included hardly any living people in their work at the fair, instead creating mannequin models that could be moved to the national museum at the fair's end.[1]

The anthropological and government displays were meant by Putnam and U.S. officials to be the showcase exhibits featuring American Indians. Putnam's exhibit was relegated to a distant, rarely visited section of the fairgrounds and would be overshadowed by both the exhibits on the Midway Plaisance and Buffalo Bill's Wild West show. His ethnological village became the home and place of work for Indian people from several tribal communities during the summer. Their homes were open to visitors. They conducted old-time work there, and occasionally in other places on the fairgrounds, for the tourists. Students from seven U.S. government or contract boarding schools came for three to four weeks at a time to perform without pay. The best-known Indian boarding school of the era, Carlisle Indian Industrial School, refused to participate in the government-sponsored program, but brought students to the fair to perform separately.

The performers who lived in Putnam's village were portrayed by fair organizers as representing the past. However, by working on the grounds at least some of them engaged in the very modern role of working for pay, either by contract or by selling articles for the tourist trade. For American Indians in the late nineteenth century this work often meant "playing Indian" for non-Indians. However, in doing so, some found a way to earn wages so that they could participate more fully in the modern economic system. Students in the government school display did not seem to have this opportunity. The Carlisle students, however, apparently used wages earned at school to attend the fair and for spending money when in Chicago. Each group's experiences and hopes were unique, and even individual experiences varied in small and significant ways within each group. But by viewing the breadth of these we can begin to unravel the ways in which Native people were participating in the modern American economic system.

Indian People and the Ethnological Village

Putnam officially oversaw four cultural groups who set up camp outside the anthropology building during the fair. Sixteen Kwakwaka'wakw men, women, and children from the Northwest Coast, sponsored by the Canadian government as part of Putnam's exhibit, built their plank houses for living and ceremonial quarters. Putnam spent far and away the largest portion of his funding for the village on this exhibit. Boas explained, "It was decided to make the tribes of Northern Vancouver Island the central point of interest, and to group all the other collections around them."[2] Maine sponsored a small Penobscot encampment of nine people in their birch bark lodges. Fifteen Haudenosaunee individuals from several tribes of the Iroquois Confederacy lived on the grounds in their longhouses, with the backing of New York State. Five Navajo Indians came and lived in hogans under an agreement with the state of Colorado.

Other tribal groups also set up camp on the anthropological grounds, which was apparently a comfortable and welcoming place to join the Indians already encamped there. An Arawak man brought in by the British Guiana government moved there. A group of Canadian Cree visiting the fair from the Northwest Territories reportedly camped there during their stay. And some of those who were brought to the Midway Plaisance also set up camp in Putnam's village, probably including Ho-Chunks (Winnebagos), Potawatomis, and Sioux.[3]

The most expensive living exhibit that Putnam arranged to be paid from World's Fair funds was the Northwest Coast village display from British Columbia. Boas worked closely with George Hunt to organize the Kwakwaka'wakw visit to Chicago. Hunt recruited the people who would participate from among the leadership of various Kwakwaka'wakw villages.[4] Hunt began his organizing work in the fall of 1892.

Hunt was paid $90 per month as an "ethnographical assistant" for eight months' work, while the other Kwakwaka'wakw earned $20 per month for seven and a half months' work during the fair.[5] Hunt was paid from the time the Kwakwaka'wakw embarked from British Columbia on their trip to Chicago.[6] He reported directly to Boas. Their contract, negotiated solely between Hunt and Putnam and signed by both, included travel and living expenses, and the opportunity to earn extra income from the manufacture of crafts if sales exceeded costs of expenses of bringing the Indians to Chicago and subsisting them there. Children, however, were not paid.[7]

According to historian Paige Raibmon, "The timing of the industrial wage labor cycle conveniently matched the cycle of older migrations for food and resource collection and usually did not interfere with the winter ceremonial season."[8] This was true of the timing of the Chicago fair. Still, for most the trip was a financial sacrifice; they could reportedly earn from $300 to $400 apiece working in the canneries in the summer.[9]

The disorganization that marred the fair's opening also affected the Indian village exhibit. The Kwakwa̱ka̱'wakw arrived after an arduous rail journey in early April and were expected to build their houses, the materials for which had already been shipped to Chicago and lay in waiting in storage on the grounds. But Putnam had trouble getting the materials delivered from the warehouses to the village site. Boas wrote to his parents, "Even my Indians got nowhere because the construction department simply does not supply requisite materials. Then one has to run around all day and is fed nothing. It's been bad."[10]

The Northwest Coast Indians were housed in "three small rooms" in the stock pavilion upon arrival. Putnam ordered a cot for Hunt and "cheap mattresses" to be spread on the floor for the rest of the contingent. He also arranged for three meals a day in a restaurant on the grounds that served employees before the fair opened.[11] They were well fed there, especially enjoying the roast beef, whitefish, cream, and butter, which one newspaper proclaimed they ate "with the recklessness which comes with an appetite unchecked by financial considerations." In fact, they ate so well that when they skipped one of their dinners, one of them later told a waiter, "Too full. Can't eat. Make us sick to eat now. Wait till morning."[12]

When the materials were finally delivered to the site, the construction went quickly.[13] On May 6 the Kwakwa̱ka̱'wakw moved from the stock pavilion to their new homes following the appropriate ceremonial protocol. This included dance and song, a feast featuring fish oil, and ceremonial gift giving. Putnam explained that "these Indians never enter any home without elaborate ceremonies of dancing, feasting, and giving presents."[14]

Once the fair opened, the Kwakwa̱ka̱'wakw entertained visitors with various cultural activities. These included a weekly Thursday evening performance of song and dance. Putnam described it as an "exhibition on one of the floats, when they perform ceremonial songs and dances, as it is our wish to have these Indians appear in a manner purely native."[15] They performed different versions of traditional dances throughout the entire run of the fair.[16] In addition to their regular salary, paid after the exposition ended, the dancers

21. Northwest Coast house. *Left to right:* unidentified, unidentified woman, John Drabble, Mrs. Drabble, unidentified, unidentified girl, unidentified woman (may be Mrs. J. Whonnock), John Whonnock, Chicago Jim, George Hunt, Q!wélelas, unidentified woman, unidentified woman, King Tom, David Hunt, Hais'haxēsaqEmē." Gift of Frederic Ward Putnam. Courtesy Peabody Museum of Archaeology and Ethnology, Harvard University, PM# 93–1-10/100266.1.30 (digital file# 99010048).

received tips from the audience for their performance, which they generally spent on the fairgrounds.[17]

One of the dances, held before an audience numbering some ten thousand in August, caused an international outcry. Prominent visitors and newspapers from Victoria BC to New York to London raised their voices excoriating fair officials for permitting a dramatic reenactment viewed by outsiders as a barbaric cannibalistic performance. The perceptions and descriptions of the performance were both inaccurate.[18] It did, however, necessitate a response from Canadian officials, who simply used the opportunity to attack the Indians.

The fair's executive commissioner for Canada, S. J. Larke, disavowed any responsibility for bringing Hunt to the fair. He said Hunt was

22. King Tom, Kwakwaka'wakw dancer. "Seated is Hais'haxēsaqEmē, next unidentified, next Q!wélelas, Dancing is King Tom, next kneeling is Chicago Jim, last unidentified." Gift of Frederic Ward Putnam. Courtesy Peabody Museum of Archaeology and Ethnology, Harvard University, PM# 93–1-10/100266.1.27 (digital file# 99010045).

"described as an Indian Interpreter, but who is not in the employ of the Dept.," referring to the Canadian Pavilion at the fair. He added that Hunt came "without any authority from this Dept., had previously been instrumental in preventing the enforcement of the law against Potlach [*sic*] and Tamanawas dances in British Columbia."[19] Such activities had been banned under Canadian law and were viewed as undermining Indian policy, which focused on assimilation and Christian civilization initiatives.

Larke wrote to A. W. Vowell, the Indian agent at Cape Mudge, demanding an explanation. Vowell too disavowed any connection. "In reply I beg to state that I knew that Hunt had been commissioned by Dr. Boaz [*sic*] to make a collection of Indian Curios, and also to endeavour to persuade about a dozen Indians to go to the Chicago Fair, as specimens of British Columbia Indians and to illustrate their

23. Q!wélelas, Kwakwaka'wakw dancer, with Leather and Shoe Building in background. "Dancer with 'bow' is Q!wélelas." Gift of Frederic Ward Putnam. Courtesy Peabody Museum of Archaeology and Ethnology, Harvard University, PM# 93–1-10/100266.1.35 (digital file# 99010054).

mode of life, as a large Indian House went with them, but I had no idea that Hunt contemplated engaging them in such a dance as is reported to have taken place." He added that he had thought ill of this trip from the start. "Several Indians who asked my advice in regard to their joining Hunt's party, I strongly advised not to go, as I did not consider it in any way to their advantage."[20]

These efforts by Canadian officials to distance themselves from the controversy and cast aspersions on Hunt buttressed the efforts of Christian religious and government officials who worked to eradicate traditional aspects of Indian culture. Putnam also disavowed any responsibility, telling the commissioner of Indian affairs, "The Indians from Vancouver Island . . . are entirely outside the jurisdiction of the United States."[21] Raibmon persuasively argues that the Kwakwaka'wakw performers at the fair used their public platform to push back against Canadian assimilation policies.[22] Canadian officials seemed to understand this. They fought hard to denigrate the Kwak-waka'wakw and to distance themselves from their activities.

The Kwakwaka'wakw used their fair experience as both a cultural and an economic statement of their place in modernizing Canada. Hunt was initially successful at this. He worked hard to prove himself as an ethnologist in his work, probably looking to the future. When the International Congress of Anthropology held an academic conference in August and September in conjunction with the fair, he presented a paper with Boas, "The Rituals of the Kwakiutl Indians." Other presenters at the conference included luminaries in the rising field of anthropology, such as Frank Cushing, Otis Mason, Alice Fletcher, Daniel Brinton, Matilda Stevenson, and George Dorsey.[23] Ira Jacknis has written, "For Hunt, the Chicago Fair was the single most important event in his transformation into a native ethnographer."[24]

Both Hunt and Johnny Drabble used their earnings from the fair to sponsor potlatches when they returned home. These events were traditional activities that included gift-giving as a signal of leadership ability. Potlatches were banned by the Canadian Indian Act, which like U.S. law was intended to eliminate institutionalized generosity that served to spread wealth within Native societies. Such activities were viewed as inimical to individual economic advancement. They also reflected a continuation of cultural and religious traditions that stood in the way of assimilation into a western-based cultural value system. Northwest Coast tribal leaders continued the practice, however. As Raibmon explains, "George Hunt used his high salary from Chicago to reinforce the position of himself and his son with Kwak-waka'wakw society."[25]

Four Penobscot families, sponsored by the state of Maine, were the next to join the Kwakwaka'wakw in Putnam's ethnographic village. They left their homes in Oldtown, Maine, in late April and set up camp in early May. The families, among them the Sockebeasons, were selected to participate by their Indian agent.[26] They represented leading families in the tribe. For the Penobscots, too, there were delays in getting their living arrangements established. Putnam lamented that when the Penobscots arrived, the exposition's grounds crews had still failed to grade the ground on which their lodges would be

24. Penobscot lodges. From Bancroft, *The Book of the Fair*, 2 of 2:645.

erected. Like the Kwakwa̱ka̱'wakw, they were forced into temporary accommodations until that work was completed. The Penobscots stayed in canvas tents.[27]

They eventually erected their birch bark wigwams near the lagoon and brought their birch bark canoes with them.[28] Despite Putnam's efforts to create a representative pre-Columbian exhibit, the Penobscots were more often portrayed as nineteenth-century Americans. The Chicago *Inter Ocean* referred to them as "industrious," and added, "They are comfortably well off, cleanly and educated."[29] One fair guide represented the Penobscot as modern people in a caption accompanying a photo of their lodges: "They elect a Governor and Lieutenant Governor and are in a measure self-governing."[30] At the fair's end, the Penobscot wigwams and canoes, together with some "curios," were donated to the new Field Museum in Chicago.[31]

Maine apparently did not pay the Penobscots who visited the fair, so they earned money selling arts and crafts, and in occasional other ventures. One visitor reported that the Penobscots were selling articles made of braided sweet grass, though she did not indicate the price.[32] The University of Chicago anthropologist Frederick Starr recorded in his diary, "Lagoon—Penobscot Indians birch bark houses with Indians making baskets of sweet grass + splints." He also did not indicate sale prices.[33] They sold baskets, sweet grass fans, and other articles that they made.[34] The U.S. superintendent of Indian Schools visited the fairgrounds in September and reported that the Penobscots "speak English well, and carry on a large traffic in articles of their own manufacture."[35] Nick Sockbeason earned a little extra money in August when the U.S. Navy sponsored a canoe race on the lagoon. He won two "depreciated" silver dollars by beating out Joe Stoccalette, also a Penobscot.[36]

There is little, if any, record of Penobscot discussion of their experience in Chicago. The state of Maine, Putnam, and the press had nothing but praise for their role in the fair. Other peoples who had unfavorable or difficult experiences made their views known either to officials or to the press. Without negative documentation, it seems that the experience for the Penobscots was largely positive.

As with the Kwakwaka'wakw and the Penobscots, the individuals representing the Haudenosaunee (Iroquois) from New York were drawn from the leading members of various tribal communities. One newspaper reported, "The men who represent the Six Nations are almost all of them men of distinction in their tribes."[37] The Haudenosaunee arrived in late June and early July. They were delayed because the bark they needed to build canoes was not in condition for peeling until early May. The Tuscarora leader Luther Jack (Nay-wah-ta-gont or Two Boots Standing Together) arrived first on June 28 to help set up the village. He was joined by Gai-wah-gwan-ni-yuh or The Whole Truth, also known as Nathaniel Kennedy, a Seneca man. The Reverend John Wentworth Sanborn described him as "a man of considerable property." They completed the work quickly.[38] The Onondaga wampum keeper Thomas Webster and Onondaga firekeeper Daniel LaForte soon followed.[39] LaForte was described as "probably the best Indian linguist in America." Solomon O'Bail, the seventy-eight-year-old Seneca grandson of Cornplanter, arrived later in the summer.[40] Colonel Ely S. Parker also stayed in the Iroquois Village while he was visiting the fair.[41] Parker, a Civil War hero who had gone on to become the first American Indian to serve as the U.S. commissioner of Indian affairs, was near the end of his life.

Sanborn organized the Haudenosaunee exhibition. He was appointed by the New York state fair commissioners, and Putnam arranged for Cornelius Cusick to aid him in organizing the work. Cusick, during his collecting for Putnam, had elicited enthusiasm for participation in the fair in the Haudenosaunee communities he had visited. Sanborn's vision of the exhibit reflects the way it was built on the fairgrounds. "Not only are the regular Indian tents going to be set up in village style at the Fair, but a 'long house,' the usual seat of government, will be provided," the *Buffalo Express* reported in a September 1892 article about Sanborn. By November 1892 the Haudenosaunee had either built or gathered the materials for the longhouse, four houses, and two wigwams. Sanborn also commissioned elm bark and birch bark canoes for the fair.[42] The State of New York donated these to the new Chicago museum at the conclusion of the fair.[43]

Sanborn described the work the Haudenosaunee did during their time at the fair. "The chiefs were constantly questioned about their customs, history, and social life, and by their intelligent answers courteously given, did much to further the laudable purpose in view in the installation of this exhibit. They explained the peculiar uses of the articles on exhibition, and performed certain of the most interesting ceremonies peculiar to the Iroquois."[44] He also proposed to Putnam that Luther Jack could present a paper on "The Present Condition of the New York Iroquois" at the Indian Congress to be held in August.[45] After the fair, Putnam wrote that the Iroquois "were frequently to be seen dressed in their native costumes paddling their canoes about the water ways on the Exposition Grounds or joining in the boat races and evening parades on the lagoons."[46]

The women who came were skilled in basket making and beadwork. Emma Reeves, an Abenaki woman who identified herself as Iroquois for purposes of the fair, was a renowned basket maker. The women sold their handiwork throughout the run of their time at the fair. A newspaper article described the public view of the Iroquois village thus: "The council lodge now is used as a bazar, in which relics of the days when the Six Nations were the warriors of the continent are shown side by side with beautiful basket and bead work and fans and trinkets of scented grasses. The sales are conducted by pleasant-faced young women of the tribe." The article described the women as indistinguishable from non-Indian women, adding "A visitor referred to one of them in her hearing recently as a squaw, and six men felt an impulse to kick the offender, which only disappeared when they discovered that the culprit was another woman."[47] Though visitors may or may not have been aware of it, *squaw* was a derogatory term applied to Native women; the Haudenosaunee at the fair, who viewed themselves as participating in modern society on equal grounds with other Americans, had no desire to be so insulted.

One observer said of the Iroquois, "The Indians sell many curios."[48] Another popular sale item was masks made from corn husks.[49] These were sold with cards of authenticity stating, "The article accompanying this Souvenir is hereby guaranteed to be of New York State Indian Manufacture and made for the World's Fair."[50] This helped insure against forgery or the sale of "Indian" objects that were not Indian made. This was already becoming a problem which Congress would finally begin to address more than four decades later in the Indian Arts and Crafts Act.[51]

The men also participated in events that included numerous other groups of people, including the Kwakwaka'wakw and the Penobscots. When replicas of Columbus's ships sailed into Chicago in early July, the Haudenosaunee along with other Native groups from several continents were among the troops that lined the shore to help create a spectacle for the viewing audience.[52] They also paddled their birch bark canoes in a boat procession put on for the public on September 19.[53]

The Haudenosaunee seemed to earn money only from the tourist trade through their sale of curios. It is possible also that they rented out their canoes; in at least one case, an Apache youth from Carlisle rented a canoe from the Indian encampment. Their room and board was covered for them. By all accounts, they enjoyed their time in Chicago. At the fair's end, O'Bail famously said, "'Had good time all summer; no mad words; good time.'"[54]

The Navajo had a different experience. Putnam had engaged Antonio Apache to collect in Navajo country in May 1892, and Antonio went there that summer. Putnam asked him to encourage two or three Navajo families to attend the fair as living exhibits, as part of his original intent to display peoples from all across the Americas.[55] Putnam's plan stalled when budgetary realities limited the scope of his work. However, the State of Colorado was eager to bring Navajos to Chicago, and Putnam and the state reached an agreement whereby Colorado would support the Navajos. They would live in the ethnological village under Putnam's supervision.[56] Colorado also agreed to hire Antonio to provide direct oversight of the Navajo group.

A Navajo silversmith named Peshloki or Peshlakai and two female blanket weavers, Cheeno and a Mrs. Walker, together with two children, Ned Manning and his sister Lucy, thus came to Chicago to ply their trades and sell their goods. Colorado agreed to pay the adults $25 a month and the children $10 a month each for four months. The state's fair commissioners also agreed to cover travel and living expenses and to pay Antonio Apache $50 a month to oversee the Navajo visitors.[57] This would have been a good opportunity for Peshloki, who was "widely respected" and served as an Indian judge on the Navajo Agency, where he earned just $10 a month.[58]

Conditions were dire in Navajo country in the years leading up to the fair. The Indian agent E. H. Plummer issued a frank report to the commissioner of Indian affairs in August 1893, writing that the Navajos were "discouraged by continued failures of crops, loss of stock, decrease in the yield of wool, and the low price of that staple." He added that the Indian Office had been made aware that "unless these Indians received material assistance they must steal or starve. The assistance has not been rendered and both starvation and stealing are in progress and increasing, and will lead to bloodshed and serious trouble in the near future. . . . Their condition is not only pitiable but extremely dangerous."[59] An Office of Indian Affairs 1893 report indicates that no Navajos received government rations. They all reportedly earned a living by "civilized pursuits," which would have largely meant farming and to a lesser extent selling woven products and jewelry.[60]

Putnam requested permission from the Office of Indian Affairs to bring the Navajo employees to the fair on May 16.[61] On June 17 they departed the Navajo Agency for Chicago, after arrangements had been made for their salaries and "all necessary living expenses."[62] Plummer wrote, "Mrs. Walker is a very fair representative of her tribe and excellent blanket weaver, a woman of good character and very trustworthy and reliable and will keep a general watch over the children. Ned Manning is considered one of the brightest boys of the school and the trip will no doubt be of great advantage to him."[63]

Navajo lodging on the fairgrounds was to be provided in hogans, but that apparently did not include heat when the weather turned cold. Putnam commented, "The idea of placing a stove in their habitation was of course out of the question when we wished to represent their native mode of life." It is ridiculous to conceive of Navajo people not heating their homes—it can be very cold in Navajo country. Putnam's intention was to display Indians in a pre-Columbian lifestyle without any modern amenities.[64] Nonetheless, the women set up their looms and wove blankets of sheep's wool outside the hogan, and the men made silver jewelry.[65] Sheep's wool was a decidedly post-Columbian commodity, and silver jewelry was made for the tourist trade. Antonio Apache purchased groceries for the Navajos throughout the fair to provide board for them.[66]

Like many of the other Native people who came to the fair, they became homesick, but their case seems to have been more extreme. A language barrier probably made them feel more isolated than others. According to the *Chicago Tribune,* "As they do not speak English they have nothing to say." One of the women wrote a letter to her daughter in September urging her to study hard in school. She told her that she herself would have a much better time in Chicago if she spoke English. As it was, speaking only Navajo, she felt isolated and alone.[67]

The Navajos had initially resisted making the trip due to homesickness on a previous trip to Washington, but Antonio Apache convinced them that this trip would be different.[68] Mistreatment of the women by Antonio Apache was alleged, but Putnam defended him, arguing that the problems the Navajo experienced were caused by the Colorado representative overseeing the exhibit, A. F. Willmarth, and not Antonio.[69] Antonio Apache seems to have been a poor choice to oversee the troupe at any rate. Agent Plummer told Putnam that Antonio "has been unfortunate in this part of the country in making people mistrust him, both whites and Indians, everywhere that he has visited."[70] Indians probably recognized him for who he was—an impostor. A visitor to the fair reported to Plummer that the Navajos in Chicago "claimed that Antonio was not keeping them in very good shape; that they hadn't as much to eat as he had promised them. They also wanted beds, a stove etc. but claimed that he refused to furnish them."[71] No doubt problems like this exacerbated the feeling of homesickness.

Near the end of their stay, another group of Navajos arrived in Chicago for a weeklong visit. Eleven men, two boys, and a girl traveled to Chicago under the sponsorship of the Indian Rights Association. The stated purpose of the trip, given to federal officials and donors, was to show leading men from the northern part of the reservation the strength of America and to encourage them to have their children formally educated for the purposes of civilization and assimilation. Putnam put them under the charge of Antonio Apache, and they lived in the ethnological village. They did not work there, but toured the fair and the city.[72] Still, it seems likely that having more Navajo speakers in the camp would have boosted the spirits of those who had been there all summer.

In the months preceding this visit, the Navajos working the fair were moved around the fair's grounds for commercial reasons, which added to their frustrations. The failure of the exhibit to bring in the amount of money that the state commissioners had hoped was the cause of this. Putnam had told them before they agreed to come "that in my opinion the sale of objects of native manufacture, which will be allowed on the Ethnographical Grounds under my direction, will largely or entirely defray the expenses of the exhibit."[73]

This did not occur. Willmarth complained that he had agreed on a visit that was too lengthy to be profitable. By the end of August Putnam had permitted Willmarth to move some of the Navajos from their homes in the ethnological village to the Midway Plaisance, a commercial strip, reporting, "They are rather restless, I understand, and wish to come back to their hogan. They have unquestionably been a little homesick at times as are all the Indians who are here." [74] The ethnological village was located in a somewhat remote spot, and there seems to have been a sense of comradery and comfort among the various Indians there. For many, it was likely a good place to get away from the cacophony of noises and crowds of people constantly surrounding them in other parts of the fairgrounds. The Midway was raucous, and while Indian people were there as well, the move upset the Navajos. The move also failed to bring about the economic infusion that Willmarth hoped it would.

He wrote in September, "I find that I can do nothing further for the Navajos, in the way of paying money to or for them." He added cryptically, "It was a mistake to keep them so long, but it was done in the hope that they might have some faint glimmering of what was decent and right."[75]

They received their first payments from Colorado, and though arrangements were slow, they sent some of the money home. In August Peshloki sent $20 to his wife with a postal money order, and Cheeno sent $5 for her son with Mrs. Walker's help.[76] Shortly after this, Willmarth refused to pay them the rest of their salary. His refusal to pay the full amount contracted to the Navajos led to a lengthy dispute that the Navajos eventually lost.

After their four-month stint was over and they returned home, the Navajos brought the nonpayment to Agent Plummer's attention. Colorado had simply refused to pay them for the final two months of their work. Plummer took the issue up with Putnam, who responded that "Mr. Willmarth, who had charge of the Indians, and Col. French, secretary of the [Colorado] board under whose authority the Indians were engaged, declined to pay them." He suggested that Plummer write to the Colorado board for remuneration. Putnam also commented that since "it was not an Exposition affair," he could not procure the money. "This problem has caused me an endless amount of trouble recently," he added.[77]

The trouble was worse for the Navajos who went unpaid. "It seems very hard that the poor Indians should be deprived of what was promised them, through no fault of their performance of their part of the contract," Plummer wrote in response.[78] Plummer wrote the Colorado board without getting a response. Then he wrote Putnam again in February 1894 "and told him that the Indians were very much in need of the money, that I had been compelled to advance them a great portion of the amount, to assist them to support their families."[79] They had foregone any work at home in order to fulfill their contract in Chicago.

When Putnam did not respond to that letter, Plummer wrote to the commissioner of Indian affairs. "The Indians were taken away with a distinct understanding that they were to receive due compensation. I am sure that they would not have consented to go and remain away under any other conditions. They were and are miserably poor and it is not right that they should be longer kept out of what is justly due."[80]

In March Putnam wrote the commissioner of Indian affairs reiterating that the Colorado fair board was responsible for the Navajo salaries. "They were well taken care of, but did not receive their pay for the last month and a half, as the Colorado Commissioners did not furnish the money," he said, adding, "The recent correspondence shows that there is little hope of getting the money from the Colorado Commissioners." He explained that the matter was now before the fair director. He also defended himself. "You can rest assured that no Indian will ever suffer by any act of mine, and that I shall do all I can to rectify the present matter in which I am unfortunately involved by the failure of the Colorado Commissioners to do as they agreed."[81] The correspondence continued as the situation remained unresolved.

In May 1894 Plummer wrote to the commissioner again, arguing that Putnam should pay the Navajos and collect the money himself from fair officials. "The only inducement for the Indians to go to the Fair was the opportunity to earn a little money. They needed it. Nearly all due them has been advanced to them by their friends or myself and it is not right that we should be compelled to make good what is the right of the Indians."[82]

Putnam wrote to one of the exposition officials at the end of May, hoping to shame him into paying the total bill of $171.66. He pointed out that "non-payment would reflect on everyone connected with the Exposition and be looked upon as another instance of cheating the poor Indian."[83] The next day he reported that he had forwarded a letter from the commissioner of Indian affairs to the president of the World's Columbian Exposition "with an earnest appeal that this matter may be attended to."[84] None of this worked, either.

In the end, the Navajo employees were simply swindled out of a significant portion of their promised salaries. Local officials paid them from other funds in dribbles. During a time of great hard-

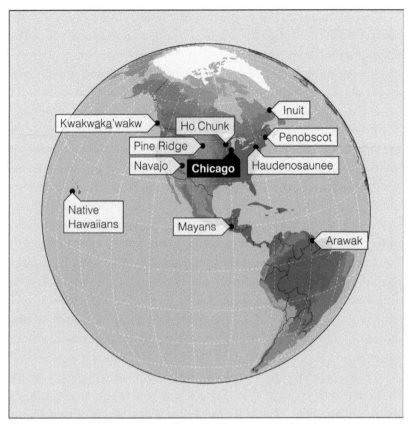

Map 3. Homelands of fair participants. Courtesy Lucien Liz-Lepiorz.

ship in Navajo country, they had counted on this money to support themselves and their families. The amount was minuscule in relation to the entire fair's budget, but the fair had been organized as a for-profit venture.[85] In the end, the stockholders' interests proved to be more important to fair organizers than those of the Navajo employees. And Colorado's failure to anticipate costs justified cheating the Indians they had hoped to profit from as far as their commissioners were concerned.

The ethnological display of living Native peoples extended beyond North America, but just barely. One individual from South America turned out to be the distillation of Putnam's extravagant hopes for hemispheric representation south of North America. British Gui-

25. Arawak house. From Bancroft, *The Book of the Fair*, 2 of 2:635.

ana hired a Christian Arawak man, Adolphus Daniel, as its national
exhibit guide for the fair. One observer referred to him as "the Indian
pilot of the gold rivers" of British Guiana. Daniel told visitors about
his country's flora, fauna, minerals, manufacture, and agricultural
products. He apparently gave a detailed explanation of the Indians'
use of cassava. "With an active brain, an intelligent comprehension
of what a visitor wants to know and a thorough knowledge of his subject, the little riverman, true to his calling, pilots his guests all over
British Guiana, through sugar plantations and gold fields, tangled
jungles and grand forests, giving an object lesson at every step," the
newspaper reporter wrote.[86]

In February, at the expense of the British Guiana government,
Daniel arrived on the fairgrounds where Putnam hired him as an
assistant at $30 per month for a brief time.[87] In March, before the
fair opened, Daniel built an Arawak style house in the outdoor ethnology exhibit.[88] Originally the British Guiana government planned

to bring a village of Arawak people to display in their homes at the fair, but none but Daniel made it to Chicago.[89] Putnam attempted to hire him permanently through the fair's run at $30 a month to work for the ethnology department. Daniel gained the title of assistant, which gave him a pass to the fairgrounds, but apparently his salary was eliminated from the budget.

Daniel must have tired of living on the fairgrounds once he stopped being paid. By July he was writing from an address on the 700 block of 65th Street. It is unclear for how long he was paid by Putnam as an assistant, but now he was on his own. The British Guiana government paid for food and clothing for him and expected him to live in the hut. He had no expense money, however, and wanted to purchase agricultural and mechanical souvenirs before he returned home. He had known in advance that he would not be paid by his government, and he emphasized that this was not a cause for complaint. "Before leaving British Guiana I plainly told Mr. Quelch that if he (Mr. Quelch) only take me beyond the limits of my country I shall esteem it a favour."[90]

Daniel explained that upon his return, he would like to show other Arawak people how others in the world lived. "My lecturing them on the Industriousness + economical habits of other nations in foreign lands (especially the American) will be useless to them unless I show them the Technical parts of my subject and my trying to do so will be worse than useless unless I have, about me, the proper implements to begin with." He hoped to raise the money to do this by lecturing about South American Indians.[91] Putnam was unable to provide him this opportunity. In August he won a swim race seen by 60,000 spectators and earned $5.[92] There is no evidence of other money he may have earned.

As with North American Indians, Daniel hoped to use his fair experience in a modern way. In addition to seeing new parts of the world and meeting people, he hoped to take knowledge back to his Arawak countrymen and women. He hoped this would give them an opportunity to use the tools of empire to carve out better economic conditions for themselves. On the one hand, this would seem to be supportive of Christian and governmental assimilation programs. But on the other hand, the world was rapidly changing, and Indians in British Guiana, like those elsewhere, needed ways to survive in it. Daniel, like many others, hoped to use the fair as a launching pad for a way forward.

Table 1. Earnings at the fair

NAME OR GROUP	TRIBE/GROUP	JOB	PLACE	PAY
74 employees	Pine Ridge Lakota	Entertainers	Buffalo Bill's Wild West	$10–$70/month. Total $1890/month
Antonio Apache	Impostor	Oversee village	Ethnological Village	$45/month or $50/month plus 10% of sales
Francis Cayou	Omaha	Columbian Guard	Grounds	$60/month
Tom Deer	Inuit	Carpenter	Grounds	$1.75–$3.20/day
Hawaiian hula dancers and chanters	Native Hawaiian	Dance, sing, sell tickets	Midway	$5/week each
Hawaiian quartet	Native Hawaiian	Sing	Volcano	$50/month each
George Hunt	Kwakwa̱ka'wakw	Cultural broker	Ethnological Village	$90/month
Kwakwa̱ka'wakw villagers		On display	Ethnological Village	$20/month for 7½ months, plus expenses
Inuit families (9–12 families)	Inuit	On display	Fairgrounds	$50/year/family modified to $50/month
Peter Meshe	Inuit		Buffalo Bill	$1.50/day
Nallook or Joe	Inuit	Dog sled rides	Esquimaux Village	$100 during fair
Pomiuk	Inuit	Entertainer	Esquimaux Village	pennies and nickels

Table 1. Earnings at the fair (*continued*)

NAME OR GROUP	TRIBE/GROUP	JOB	PLACE	PAY
62 employees	Potawatomi, Sioux, Ho-Chunk	Entertainers	T. R. Roddy Village	unknown, but raised $1.50/week
Weavers	Navajo	Weave	Village and Midway	$25/month when paid
Nick Sockbeason	Penobscot	Canoe race winner	Lagoon	$2
Adolphus Daniel	Arawak	Swim race winner	Lagoon	$5

Note: Most, though not all, had some of their expenses paid, primarily for food, lodging, and travel. Sources include Annual Reports of the Commissioner of Indian Affairs; Cash Book FMNH; Derks, *The Value of a Dollar*; Frederick Starr Papers, University of Chicago Special Collections Research Center; FWP Papers HUA; LR 1881–1907, RG 75, NARA-DC; Payroll Ledgers F.C.M. 1894 FMNH; SIA RU000070; Time Book FMNH.

Table 2. Comparative earnings

NAME OR CATEGORY	JOB	PLACE	PAY
Frederic Ward Putnam, 1891–94	Chief, Department M	Anthropology, World's Fair	$300/month first 16.5 months; $416.66/month for final 23 months
Putnam's staff		Department M	$30-$200/month
Franz Boas		Department M, Anthropology, World's Fair	$50/month until fair; $200/month during fair
Boas, 1894	Curator, Ethnology	Field Museum of Natural History	$200/month
James Mooney, 1891–92	Collecting in the field	Smithsonian Institution	$116.67/month
Walter James Hoffman, 1891–92	Collecting in the field	Smithsonian Institution	$116.67/month

Frederick Starr, 1892–93		Assistant professor, Sciences	University of Chicago	$2,000/year ($166.67/ month)
Frederick J. V. Skiff, 1894		Director	Field Museum of Natural History	$500/month
Dr. G. M. West, 1894		Assistant, Ethnology	Field Museum of Natural History	$100/month
E. R. Cooper, 1894		Furrier, Ethnology	Field Museum of Natural History	$100/month
Antonio Apache, 1894	Impostor	Assistant, Ethnology	Field Museum of Natural History	$11.50/week based on $50/month
Laborers, 1894		Ethnology Department	Field Museum of Natural History	$9/week @$1.50/day
Carpenters and Painters, 1894		Ethnology Department	Field Museum of Natural History	$16.80/week @ 35¢/hour
Indian police, 1893		Reservation police force	Various communities	$10–15/ month
Quanah Parker, 1893	Comanche	Indian judge	Kiowa, Comanche and Wichita Agency	$10/month
Herders, 1893	Crow	Ranching	Crow Reservation	$300/year
Emily Peake	Ojibwe	Schoolteacher	White Earth Reservation	$600/year
Daniel M. Browning		Commissioner of Indian Affairs	Washington DC	$4,000/year ($333.33/ month)
George Steell		Agent	Blackfeet Agency, Montana	$1,800/ year ($150/ month)
B. S. Coppock		Superintendent	Chilocco Training School	$2,000/year ($166.67/ month)
Carlos Montezuma	Yavapai	Physician	Carlisle	$1,200/ year ($100/ month)
Byron Bancroft Johnson, 1893		Sports editor	Cincinnati Commercial Gazette	$30/month

Table 2. Comparative earnings (*continued*)

NAME OR CATEGORY	JOB	PLACE	PAY
Carpenters, Connecticut, 1893	Average pay		$2.53/day or $15.18/week
Farm laborers, New York, 1893	Average pay		$1.17/day or $7/week
By advertisement	Photography retoucher	*San Francisco Examiner*	$10/week

Note: Due to the recession, wages dropped precipitously in 1893.

The Education Exhibits

American Indian children also worked at the fair. Despite one proposal, none worked for compensation. Some even paid their own way for the privilege to attend. Indian children were put on display in the federal school building doing schoolwork. The children were not paid; they worked in the government school exhibit for travel, room, and board expenses. The students from Albuquerque Indian School, the first to come to the fair, were almost the exception. As the fair drew near, it became clear that the school building, like other buildings across the grounds, would not be ready to open on time. Due to the limited federal funding to build the school, it would not be furnished with dressers or shelving or wardrobes. The Office of Indian Affairs under Commissioner Morgan suggested that the carpentry students from Albuquerque come early and do the work. Ten students would have been brought in early, and they would have been paid $3 per day for the work, nearly the same amount as the non-Indian carZpenters negotiated as fair pay for their work building the fair.

The new administration of President Grover Cleveland brought in a new commissioner of Indian affairs, and for some time in April all decisions in the department were put on hold. In the end, there was not enough time, or perhaps there was no budget to pay these pupils to come early to do the work, and it was done on-site by exposition work crews. It seems, however, that these young men would have been paid a fair wage to do the work, which the acting commissioner argued, on their behalf, "will be of decided advantage to these young men who are just learning how to support themselves in civi-

26. Boarding school students at the fair. From Bancroft, *The Book of the Fair,*
2 of 2:646.

lized ways."[93] The Indian Office did support the principle of Indian
youth participating in wage labor as an inducement to assimilation,
but could not organize itself to support it in practice in this case.

Children from both federal government and private schools came
to live and work in the U.S. school building. The children from Haskell Indian Industrial Training School in Kansas reportedly hosted
between twenty and twenty-five thousand visitors a day during their
stay in August. Forty-six students from a variety of tribal backgrounds
attended, including school band members. The band played two
half-hour concerts a day, and the school was open for visitors for two
hours in the morning and two hours in the afternoon. A Sioux man
visiting the fair, Black Tomahawk, heard the music and was attracted
to the Indian school, which he had not realized was one of the exhibits. He reported that he was pleased with what he saw. The school, he
observed in broken English, shows the "Indian good as white man,
read book, read paper, blow horns. It's good for Indian." He remained
with the students for an entire day and was invited to spend the night,
but he declined since he had a hotel room in downtown Chicago.[94]
The children had reading and writing lessons and exhibits as well as
manual labor work. The band also entertained visitors.

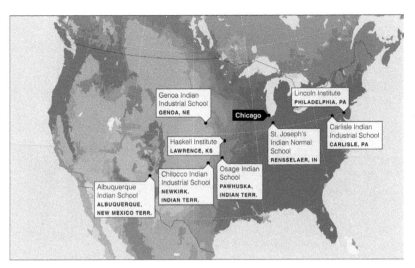

Map 4. Locations of U.S. boarding schools whose students came to the fair. Courtesy Lucien Liz-Lepiorz.

Lincoln Institute, a private Indian boarding school located in Philadelphia, also brought Indian students who performed music at the exposition's recital hall and in the manufacturer's building. Several gave recitals on piano, organ, and cornet. Others sang solos, duets, and quartets. The musicians included children from the Modoc, Mohawk, Pawnee, and Sioux tribes.[95] Rensselaer Indian School in Indiana brought thirty boys and two "working" girls to the fair.[96] Records do not indicate whether the girls were paid for their work. The other schools participating in the government exhibit were Chilocco Indian Agricultural School, Genoa Indian Industrial School, and the Osage Boarding School.

Carlisle, though not sending children to the school, mounted its own exhibit in the Liberal Arts Building. Pratt refused to work with Putnam, since he believed that "ethnologists were the most insidious and active enemies of Carlisle's purposes." He believed that both ethnologists and the Office of Indian Affairs worked to keep Indians from becoming fully "civilized," and therefore they kept them dependent on the federal government.[97]

One Carlisle student worked at the exhibit, probably for room and board. Chauncey Yellow Robe, whom Pratt described as "one of our foremost pupils" and "a fine specimen of gentlemanly young manhood" came to help show off Carlisle. His role was to serve "as a sample" of

Carlisle's work and to provide descriptions of it to visitors.[98] He boarded with an African American woman who, with her sons, oversaw the Hampton school exhibit.[99] In May he gave a speech that was reportedly well received to a Congress of Women at the fair.[100] In August he gave a speech at a Woman's Home Missionary meeting in Des Plaines with a student from Haskell.[101] By September he had "full and complete charge" of the exhibit.[102] "I have many questions to answer," he reported.[103]

For Yellow Robe, the fair itself was a great learning experience. In August he said, "When I first came, I walked hastily through the buildings and saw how big and beautiful they were, but there was so much I could not understand, it made me tired to look, and I did not see much. But now . . . I'm beginning to see and learn and understand."[104] In September he wrote that he enjoyed seeing a "wedding procession in the streets of Cairo. The camels and donkeys made a funny sight as they moved along."[105] Though he was not paid cash for his work, he seemed to have been delighted with the personal education he received through the fair experience. Yellow Robe went on to become an educator, a coach, and a national Indian leader in the early part of the twentieth century.[106]

When Pratt brought his 450 Carlisle students to the fair in October, they paid for part of the trip themselves. Pratt negotiated costs in advance with the railroad company, a Chicago trolley company, a hotel in receivership, and a lightly visited restaurant. The latter provided breakfast and dinner food, and packed lunches for 50 cents a day per person. The children cooked, washed dishes, and waited the tables for their group. They also did the hotel cleaning work. Pratt had difficulty convincing the fair's managers to permit the children to enter the grounds free of charge. Their policy permitted no free passes. However, he argued convincingly to the Council of Administration that the children's activities on the grounds would draw more visitors to the fair. Two of the council's three members agreed that the children would make money for the fair, and so their passes were not considered free but given in exchange for valuable work.[107]

Pratt later recalled the cost as $19.50 per student, including $5 spending money, but it might have been slightly less. Records indicate that at least a significant number of the students withdrew $13 for Chicago from their financial accounts on September 21, probably for rail fare. Many also withdrew cash for spending in Chicago nine days later. While at the fair the students gave daily military drills, drawing wide attention from the fairgoers. Pratt recalled, "The military demonstration attracted many thousands of spectators daily."[108] The girls were invited to a reception at the Women's Building and given a tour there.[109] The boys' band gave a concert at Festival Hall.[110]

The children all wrote journals of their experiences at the fair as homework. Those who kept the journals were permitted to take them home as souvenirs. Pratt reported their experience as exciting. Indeed, it was. In addition to touring and working together on the fairgrounds, students apparently had the freedom to explore on their own, taking Ferris wheel rides, renting canoes, and going out on the lake in a barge with Pratt to watch fireworks.[111] The students who chose to go had to work hard in advance to pay for the experience and work while at the fair to keep costs affordable. The three hundred male students who had participated in the 1892 opening ceremonies had made a favorable impression on the audience and the soldiers whose barracks they slept in. They brought a buzz of excitement back to the Carlisle campus, causing hundreds of students to either want to return for the fair or attend the event for their first trip.

Pratt viewed the fair as an opportunity to show the world that education was the path to civilization for American Indians. He challenged the students to earn $20 to pay for it, which some did working for the school, and most did through Carlisle's annual summer Outing work program on nearby farms. Instead of earning money at the fair, they earned money to attend the fair. Unlike the children in the government school exhibit, the students from Carlisle paid their own way to Chicago. Pratt would argue that the students' money brought profit to the restaurant, the hotel, and the world's fair corporation.[112] The profit to the children, in his view, was the education they received.

The Canadian government also brought Indian children to perform their daily educational tasks on the fairgrounds. The Canadian Department of Indian Affairs wanted "to demonstrate" to fairgoers "the result of the liberal and paternal policy so long pursued by the Canadian Government in its treatment of the Indians."[113] The Canadians were especially proud of their school display. Like the U.S. Office of Indian Affairs, Canadian officials hoped to accomplish their goals by bringing children from a variety of the "Manufacturing schools" to demonstrate their work.[114] The plan was to bring boys and girls in shifts, similar to the U.S. program. They brought children from both Protestant and Roman Catholic schools of Manitoba and the North-West Territories. The program was intended to show Canada's benevolent treatment of Indians.

The children would benefit as well, the Canadian government argued. "By sending children from the different schools in relays it is expected that some pupils from all of these institutions will have the opportunity of showing the results of their training and evidence of their skill at some period of the Exposition."[115] The Canadian government paid for the travel, boarding, and lodging of the students, but did not pay them for their work.[116] These children conducted their regular school activities, such as weaving, sewing, shoemaking, and printing—even printing a newspaper on the grounds—for the amusement of fairgoers.[117] When Frederick Starr visited, he wrote in his diary, "Model of the Industrial schools at Winnipeg + Sault Ste. Marie; food supplies in birch bark baskets; pemmican; several girls sewing +c; a boy printing; a 'Sister' in charge."[118]

Canadian officials reported that "many Americans expressed their surprise at our treatment of the Indian, and the great success attending our efforts in civilizing him. In fact, a great many of them said, judging by our success in teaching them useful arts, that it could no longer truthfully be said that 'the only good Indian is a dead Indian.'"[119]

Some of the Native people who worked at the fair did indeed earn decent wages. The Kwakwaka'wakw are an example. Though they had good opportunities for work back on the Pacific coast, the trip to the fair was economically worthwhile. It also brought prestige to those already in leadership positions. George Hunt was highly paid for his specialized work at $90 a month. In comparison, Boas made $50 a month leading up to the fair.[120] Once the fair began, ethnology department employees under Putnam earned salaries ranging from $30 to $200 a month, with Boas making the most.[121]

The other adults in Hunt's group received $20 a month, in a nice lump sum paid at the end of the fair, plus tips. The Navajo too, at least by contract, received a fair wage, especially in comparison to conditions back home. Unfortunately, when they were cheated out of their earnings, they returned home to dire poverty. Their homesickness during the fair probably only exacerbated the discontent they felt by their treatment. And their ill treatment probably worsened their homesickness as well.

The Haudenosaunee and the Penobscots, who came at the expense of the States of New York and Maine, did not receive wages for their work. Although they sold handmade objects for the tourist trade, in comparison with others who earned monthly salaries, they did not fare as well. Likewise, Adolphus Daniel did poorly. He did not expect to make money, and he came primarily for the experience. Once he arrived in Chicago, however, he realized that without cash he could not bring tools back to British Guiana that would improve agricultural conditions among the Arawak.

The children who came to the fair in the Indian schools were brought by the U.S. and Canadian governments both to broaden their own experiences in the world and to show off the government's work among them to fairgoers. The Carlisle children conducted wage-labor work during the summer of 1892 to help pay their way to the fair, where their work was given in exchange for passes to the fairgrounds.

There was no singular work experience for individual Native people from the various tribal groups, even if the work itself was similar. In terms of salary and work environment, people's experiences varied, sometimes significantly. This was true even among the children who attended the fair.

To get an even broader perspective, it is necessary to turn our attention to the Native people whose work comes under the category of commercial entertainment. Separate agreements permitted entrepreneurs on and off the Midway to bring in displays of Native peoples on a for-profit basis, and their experience in relation to wages for their labor mirrored those described above; some earned good wages, others were badly treated and poorly paid. And to further complicate matters, dozens of Lakota people worked for Buffalo Bill Cody *off* the fairgrounds, since his Wild West show was denied official sanctioning by fair organizers.

7

Working the Commercial Displays

Numerous commercial displays and exhibitions of indigenous peoples were scattered across the fairgrounds, many on the Midway Plaisance, but others elsewhere. These were the places where most Native people spent their time during the fair. In most cases people both lived and worked with others from their home communities or their own tribal groups. They nonetheless regularly interacted with other Native people. The relationships that people developed created social bonds that could lead to sharing information about employment conditions and salary, among other things. Some people were gregarious. For many, however, there was an isolation caused by being constantly on display. As with those in Putnam's village, the Native people working in commercial displays had a variety of experiences.

Putnam initially hoped to exert control over all of the commercial exhibits, but the fair organizers viewed this as too unwieldy a task for him. In the end, he did maintain a modicum of influence regarding the treatment of those being exhibited. But since these were for-profit affairs, the necessary dealings with entrepreneurs bringing them in proved beyond his capabilities. Putnam and others successfully prevented formal Wild West shows from gaining space on the grounds—Buffalo Bill Cody was forced to lease land west of the fair's site—but most of the displays that did gain contracts depended on gaudy showmanship to draw paying crowds.

Among the commercial exhibits, historians have paid most attention to the Native groups displayed on the Midway Plaisance. To fairgoers it was an exotic, exciting place with adventures at every

new attraction. Throughout the time of the fair, exhibits came and ~~commercial~~
went. Some operated from May until November, others for only a few weeks. The most popular attractions, at least in terms of profits earned, were Cairo Streets, Carl Hagenback's Menagerie, the Ferris wheel, and the German and Austrian villages, in that order. Indigenous American exhibits were not among the most profitable. Exhibits of Native peoples included T. R. Roddy's Indian village, an Aztec village, and a Hawaiian model of the Kilauea Volcano together with Hawaiian musicians and dancers. Other indigenous groups associated with the Midway included a Bedouin camp, a South Sea Island village, a Sami village, and a Dahomey village. The Esquimaux village was classified as a Midway exhibit but was located elsewhere on the fairgrounds.[1]

The Native American and Native Hawaiian displays were spread apart from each other. All of these displays were contracted to pay a percentage of earnings to the World's Columbian Exposition Company, the formal name for the fair's business operations.[2] Each of the contracting entrepreneurs intended to make money from his exhibits. Each had agreements for providing transportation to and from the fair for his employees, room and board while at the fair, and salaries or sources of income for some of his charges. Each charged admission to fairgoers to visit his exhibit. And each attempted to balance the costs and the income to his favor.

The United States and other North American displays included a group of several dozen Ho-Chunk (Winnebago), Potawatomi, and Sioux who encamped on the Midway as part of T. R. Roddy's Indian village; several Lakota people who lived in Sitting Bull's cabin; and a dubious group of Aztecs brought from Mexico. The Native Hawaiians who came began organizing for the journey when Hawaii was an independent kingdom. The United States overthrew and imprisoned their queen just before the fair's run, but it would be several years before the United States annexed the island nation. Probably the most successful of these exhibits, and certainly the one that garnered the most attention from the press, was the Inuit colony brought from Labrador. The individuals who worked in these displays received various rates of pay, and all of them faced difficult work conditions. Many also enjoyed their time in Chicago.

Inuit Colony

The first of the groups to arrive was nine to twelve Inuit families from Labrador brought to the fair by an independent entrepreneur. They were exhibited on a for-profit basis on the northwest corner of the fairgrounds in a site that was not affiliated with the ethnological village. The Inuit arrived at the fairgrounds in the winter, in order to acclimate to Chicago's weather before the spring opening of the fair. They were contracted to come to Chicago as part of a longer trip and were to be paid $100 per family for two years, plus supplies on their return home. Their exhibit was popularly known as the "Esquimaux village."

The families were drawn from those who still lived in their traditional homelands and those who had changed their lifestyle to interact with coastal commercial whalers. One reporter, after receiving a personal tour of the village from the promoter, P. M. Daniel, was surprised to find that the former appeared to be both healthier and happier.

> It is very painful to have to confess it, but of the two classes of Esquimaux in the village—those whose conditions have been ameliorated by the refining influences of civilization and those whose conditions have not—the latter are much the finer looking and happier men and women. Those who have come in contact with the whalers and Newfoundland fishermen about Esquimau Bay [now Hamilton Inlet] are sallow and lean from feeding on the manna of civilization and absorbing its tobacco smoke and rum. On the other hand the poor savages from Nachvak and Kikkertaksoak, who have subsisted on blubber and fish without condiments, are disgustingly fat and healthy and morbidly contented.[3]

One reporter wrote, "The truth of the matter is that out of the fifty-eight in all there are only two families who represent the primitive Eskimo. The others are civilized. They keep house and use sewing machines like Americans would if they had to live on as limited means as they do."[4]

The Inuit village was a hit with the public even before the fair opened. Newspapers reported their arrival, first in Boston and then in Chicago,

27. Eskimo snow hut. From "The Eskimo Village," 18. *World's Fair Number,*
The Youth's Companion, 1893.

in October 1892. "They have brought with them their own reindeer,
snow shoes and sleds, and everything essential to a complete furnishing of their village, and will carry on their native domestic life, as they
are in families."[5] In November Susan Manak gave birth to a fourteen-
pound(!) baby, which she named Columbia.[6] She became a press sen-
sation but died within a week. A second girl, named Nancy Helene
Columbia Palmer, was born a few days later. She too became a press
favorite.[7] This girl's mother, Esther, had come to the fair with her parents, Abile, an Inuit who was also a Moravian missionary, and Helene.[8]

Another baby, Christopher Columbus Tuktootsina, was born a
couple of weeks later. Their birth notices were published widely in
the press.[9] The fairgrounds were open in the months prior to the
fair for a fee of 25 cents; up to twenty thousand people a day visited
the grounds throughout the winter. The early arrival of the Inuits
gave the press a ready-made story. Since newspapers reprinted those
stories regularly, Americans coming to the fair once it opened had
already read about the Inuits and were eager to see the village and,
of course, the babies born on the fairgrounds.

One newspaper reported that the winter weather, hard on most
Chicagoans, was pleasant and normal for the Inuit. Its headline read,

"The Esquimaux Basking in the Eager and Nipping Air." The story was accompanied by a cartoon depicting a white couple bundled heavily against the weather with hats, long coats, and a muff—and the Inuits sitting on ice fanning themselves. "Talk about sun baths, why it was rich to see those people lying and lolling around in the snow just fairly taking supreme comfort in the eager and nipping wind," the reporter wrote. "They were just simply in their element."[10] This would change when the weather warmed up.

P, McDaniel was a ruthless overseer of the exhibit. He paid a very low wage and forced unhealthy working conditions on the Inuits under his charge. One report said that he spent 14 cents per person per day for their subsistence.[11] The contractor used every trick he could imagine to bring in business, which led to the alienation of a significant portion of the Inuit performers. Many eventually left the village in a protest that lasted months and involved the court system, federal and fair officials, and entrepreneurial inventiveness.

One individual, Peter Michaud (called Meshe or Mesher in the newspapers), was kicked out of the village in the winter, and he went to work for Buffalo Bill at the salary of $1.50 per day.[12] That is equivalent to a little less than $40 a day in 2017 value.[13] Shortly thereafter another individual, Zacharias, left and took a job with a contracting company earning $2.25 a day. James Sugarloaf and Peter Locey also left the village and went to work for contractors on the fairgrounds.[14] Tom Deer quit working in the village a month before the fair opened. He claimed poor treatment and inadequate food as his reasons. He reportedly became a carpenter on the fairgrounds.[15] According to a New York newspaper report, a district attorney in Chicago "was Inclined to believe that President P. M. Daniel [superintendent of the Inuit village] was liable under the Contract Labor law in each case where an Esquimaux goes to work for wages in competition with American workmen."[16] If Deer did get work as a carpenter, he would have earned $3.20 per day. If he was hired instead as a laborer or helper to the carpenters, the wage would have been determined by him and his employer, most likely between $1.75 and $2.40. This was a time of increasing worker activism in Chicago, and representatives of the various trades had negotiated pay rates for all classes of laborers working at the exposition.[17]

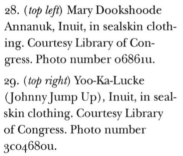

28. (*top left*) Mary Dookshoode Annanuk, Inuit, in sealskin clothing. Courtesy Library of Congress. Photo number 06861u.

29. (*top right*) Yoo-Ka-Lucke (Johnny Jump Up), Inuit, in sealskin clothing. Courtesy Library of Congress. Photo number 3c04680u.

30. (*right*) Inuit woman in sealskin clothing. Courtesy Library of Congress. Photo number 06860u.

Michaud petitioned in court on March 30 for the release of five Inuits imprisoned in the village.[18] He argued that they were being held in virtually slavelike conditions. The *Daily Inter Ocean,* a Chicago newspaper, covered the story and reported with sympathy for the Inuits. The judge ruled that their rights were being denied and that they could return to court without formally petitioning if it happened again.[19] They were also covered by U.S. contract labor laws.[20]

The complaint centered around their being misled about work conditions before they came to Chicago. Thomas Pallacier reported being held by guards in one of the houses in the Eskimo village. According to the newspaper, "John Lozey said that Pallacier was locked up because he would not wear his sealskin dress. 'They did not treat us right,' he said in fairly good English. 'When they coaxed us from Labrador they told us we would be fed well and only have to wear the skin clothes half the day, but when they got us here they made us wear them from 9 o'clock in the morning until 6 o'clock in the evening. No man can stand that here.'"[21] In early April the temperatures doubled to more than 60 degrees.[22]

To make matters worse, according to one contemporary report written by anthropologist Frederick Starr, the sealskin clothes were not the accustomed attire of the Labradoreans. "Dressed in their furs these people looked truly polar, but we are assured that as spring came on they rebelled against wearing these heavy garments, which were unlike anything they ever wore before. It seems they came from a part of Labrador often visited by vessels, and are used to clothing made of white men's cloth."[23]

James Sugarloaf's family was also locked under guard for about six weeks.[24] This caught the attention of the national press. One West Virginia newspaper opined that this clothing "was not intended for a temperature that melts a ton of ice in two seconds." Sometimes that clothing would be appropriate in Chicago. "But this is not the time and in a month or two it will be less so."[25] Daniel attempted to have the Columbian Guard, the fair's police force, enforce the imprisonment, but fearing a lawsuit, they refused. Instead he hired his own security guard.[26]

The court ruled that the Inuits were being illegally deprived of their liberty.[27] Once that occurred, they secretly planned an escape. Three weeks later, after measles and heat-induced illnesses swept through the camp, a mass exodus from the village occurred. During a stormy night in late April, five families numbering more than half of the Inuits left the fairgrounds and moved into a hotel on Sixty-Fourth Street. They were led by their Moravian minister, Reverend Abile, and Peter Michaud, who snuck over the fence "dressed a la Americ-aino" to spirit them out. The *Daily Inter Ocean* reported the story on its front page as if it were a crime thriller. The Inuits talked their way past the guard with the help of the interpreter, who convinced the guard that they were within their rights and "busied himself about the gate in expediting the exodus and bidding each dumpy little figure god-speed." They left their luggage behind but took six dogs with them.[28] Daniel reported that he tried unsuccessfully to have the Columbian Guard prevent them from leaving the grounds.[29]

A Hyde Park judge paid for their hotel and helped them set up their own exhibit on Stony Island Avenue, a street just west of the fairgrounds that held numerous nonsanctioned exhibits and retail stands.[30] The newly incorporated "Esquimaux Exhibition company" was reported in the *Chicago Tribune* on April 26.[31] Peter "Mesher" (Michaud) and Thomas Deer were listed on the legal corporation, and Abile and Zacharias set up and oversaw the rival camp on Stony Island. Both camps, on and off the fairgrounds, claimed "without dispute" to be the original camp brought from Labrador.[32]

The Inuits protested not only their employment conditions but their rate of pay. The remaining families planned to join those who had left, but Daniel quickly renegotiated their contracts. They were originally to receive room and board for their work and were prom-ised five hundred Newfoundland shillings (approximately $100) per family for the duration of their two-year contract, plus supplies when they returned home. In late April Daniel promised each fam-ily an astonishing salary increase: immediate payment of $50, and then $50 per month until the end of their two-year contract, as well as the supplies when they returned home. The families still on the grounds decided to stay with him and wear their sealskin clothing at least part of the time throughout the run of the fair.[33] One of the women, however, acquired a sewing machine. One reporter wrote, "None of the Eskimos are wearing furs. The men are attired in white

31. Peter Pallacier, Inuit. From *Photographs of the World's Fair*, 327.

cotton raiment, cut after the established style of Labrador, while the women appear in calico dresses, thus destroying much of their value as curiosities."[34]

The agreement between Daniel and those who remained did not end the conflict, however. In May the U.S. Superintendent of Immigration ruled that his office viewed their dispute as private, so those who had left the fairgrounds would not be forced by U.S. law to leave the country.[35] Then in June Thomas Pallacier and Peter Pallacier, a popular fiddle player in the group that left the fairgrounds, sued Daniel in federal court. They both sued Daniel for $10,000 for imprisonment for more than a month for their incarceration when they refused to wear the sealskin clothing. Daniel responded that he was within his rights, and then argued that *they* had broken the law by trying to break out of the building he had locked them in, in order to enter the exposition grounds from which he had banned them. He argued that they were attempting to trespass onto the land that he had leased. It was not until late August that he dropped the lawsuit, and the two sides came to a relatively amicable agreement.[36]

Though Daniel agreed to a significant salary increase, he continued to try to make money in every way possible. Even the funeral for Degoulick, a fifteen-year-old boy who "drowned while bathing in the village pond" in August, was open to the public for a fee. Hundreds of tourists paid to watch the observances of the young orphan, who received both a traditional and a Christian service and was buried in a private ceremony in Oakwoods Cemetery after the funeral.[37]

One boy who remained in the village all summer was Pomiuk, nicknamed "Prince Pomiuk" by promoters because he was a crowd-pleaser. Pomiuk, an orphan, was quick with a smile and adept with a dog whip. He was injured on the fairgrounds and died of meningitis in the fall of 1897, but he gained fame before his injury. Visitors would stand nickels or pennies into the ground, and whoever could hit the coin first with his twenty-four-foot long whip would get to keep it. "Pomiuk always hit it first," according to a children's book published about him ten years after the fair.[38] One account says, "When lookers-on grew inattentive, and no more money seemed forthcoming, he would cry out in very understandable English, 'Put up a nickel! Put up a nickel!'"[39] In this way Pomiuk and other boys earned little bits of money using their skill with the whip.

Another teenage boy, Nallook or Joe, drove visitors on dog-sledge rides for a fee. He reportedly took home $100 for his work at the end of the fair. His experience at the fair served him well later in life. He became comfortable traveling and marketing his wares. In 1901 he brought furs directly to New York to sell to furriers, bypassing the middleman at home in Hopedale. He struck up a relationship with a New York City furrier after he brought him a beautiful silver fox fur that he sold for "considerably more than seven hundred dollars."[40]

Another individual who apparently paid close attention to the business side of the exhibit was Esther, later called Esther Eneut-

32. Prince Pomiuk, Inuit. Courtesy Peabody Museum of Archaeology and Ethnology, Harvard University, PM#2004.29.2925 (digital file# 170100092).

seak, who remained in the United States after the fair. She would participate in eight more expositions and build a career in which she took over organization of the Eskimo villages at several of these, as well as at Luna Park on Coney Island. She and those she hired toured not only the United States but Europe and North Africa as well. She and her parents and daughter reportedly earned as much as $150 per week working for Barnum and Bailey's Circus in

33. Inuit people with whips. From Bancroft, *The Book of the Fair*, 2 of 2:631.

1894–95. In 1911 her daughter Columbia wrote and starred in what was probably the first Hollywood film to feature Inuit people. They lived a comfortable middle-class existence in the United States. By contrast, most of the Inuit who worked in Chicago returned home after their two-year contract. Many probably felt the same as Zacharias, who reported, "We are glad to be at liberty once more, and not to be continually looked at as if we were animals. We shall never go again."[41]

One fair observer bemoaned the fact that the first American word the Inuit learned in Chicago was *money*.[42] But without money they would be fully under Daniel's control. They had no curios to sell, and so upon their arrival, to augment their meager funds, they had to ask for money. After the salary renegotiation, the Inuits went shopping and used their money as other fair visitors would. Numerous stands were set up outside the grounds on Stony Island Avenue, selling food and providing recreation and entertainments for a fee. A Chicago newspaper reported on "An Eskimo family in American Clothing" who made an outing on Stony Island one Sunday afternoon in July.

The father bought himself and one of his daughters a soda, the mother spent 10 cents on two oranges, and the father bought himself two cigars. The man lit a cigar, and the family then continued on "to Washington park for an outing just like American folks," according to the newspaper.[43]

In many cases the indigenous people who worked on the fairgrounds used their leisure time to make new acquaintances, to see other exhibitions, and to leave the grounds and experience parts of Chicago. This family simply enjoyed a day in a foreign city, having an experience that broke up the monotony and drudgery of constantly performing for people who often viewed them as primitive otherworldly curiosities. It probably would not have been possible had Abile and Zacharias and Peter Pallacier not used the American legal system to force Daniel to renegotiate the pay of these performers.

Indians on the Midway

T. R. Roddy, an Indian trader from Black River Falls, Wisconsin, home of the Ho-Chunk (Winnebago), brought a mixed group of Ho-Chunk, Potawatomis, and Sioux to the fair to be displayed in a village on the Midway at the end of June. They stayed for four months. They performed music and dances, the men made arrows, and the women beaded deerskin dresses while the fair's visitors watched.[44]

A report from Black River Falls said, "The Winnebago Indians that were taken from here to the world's fair, after getting there and learning the ropes a little, refused longer to 'perform' at the old prices."[45] It is not clear what they were originally being paid, but after their threatened strike they and the Potawatomi and Sioux people working in the village each earned an extra $1.50 a week. This report came out soon after the Inuit case was settled out of court. Whether that, or the knowledge of what other Native people were earning, either on the Midway or working for Buffalo Bill, was the cause of their efforts to get better compensation, it is clear that as the fair went on, performers increasingly knew the relative value of their work.

Some Lakota people were stationed in Sitting Bull's cabin next door. These included the well-known Rain-in-the-Face, Black Bull, and Pretty Face, who was Sitting Bull's niece. One fair visitor, Ida Zerbe, described Rain-in-the-Face as "extremely neat," wearing "a white shirt with crimson tie, blue pants bound with yellow, blue blanket with white stripes, and large black hat over his long black hair." She also wrote, "He is a pathetic sight, only forty-six years of age, with his brave, bold spirit like a prisoner within himself, unable to read, with no personal resources, sitting day by day to be stared at by the curious, restive and homesick for his reservation, where he can break the monotony of life by riding horseback."[46]

Nonetheless, he apparently enjoyed being wheeled around the fairgrounds to see its attractions, and he especially enjoyed the fireworks. He also did other odd jobs on the fairgrounds; in early June, for example, he agreed to greet fair visitors in the North Dakota Building as a distinguished resident of the state. There are no records indicating whether or how much the individuals on display in Sitting Bull's cabin were paid. Pretty Face made embroidered and beaded moccasins, which she sold for $4.50 a pair.[47]

An "Aztec" Indian village was erected on the Midway in September and was open the last two months of the fair. The admission was 10 cents. Weavers, metal workers, and musicians all performed there. Not many people came to see this exhibit, according to reports. One observer said, "There was some doubt, too, in the public mind as to the genuineness of these Midway Aztecs. Their serapes were said to have been made in Germany."[48] Nonetheless, some visitors took it on faith that the Indians they saw were Aztec. A fifteen-year-old boy wrote in his diary that Aztecs were among the foreigners he met. In typical teenage manner, he succinctly noted his observations of the exhibit: "In the Astec [sic] Village I saw Sitting room scene. Place of worship. Store of Souvenirs. Prison. Implements of war. Bed room scene. Music of their instruments. Seen the cliff dwellers at a distance."[49] Not much more is known about this exhibit. There is no record of whether those on display were Indians from Mexico or whether they were paid. These several groups were not among the more popular exhibits on the Midway Plaisance. They made little money for the people who brought them and were not there for the entire duration of the fair. Records do not clearly show how much money they were paid, but Roddy's villagers had salaries, and the others at least earned some money from the curio trade.

34. Rain-in-the-Face, Lakota. Courtesy Library of Congress. Photo number
3c04681u.

Native Hawaiians

Other indigenous peoples with relations to the United States also worked the Midway. Three groups of Native Hawaiians provided music in two venues at the fair. At least fifteen Native Hawaiians came from Honolulu to provide entertainment to fairgoers. The kingdom of Hawaii, in the years before the overthrow of Queen Liliʻuokalani, attempted to organize an exhibit. It was supported by both the Honolulu Chamber of Commerce and the Planters' Labor and Supply Company. The latter had no interest in supporting "an exhibition of curios relating to ancient times [that] would mislead strangers, and give a wrong impression in regard to the present condition of Hawaiian civilization and affairs."[50]

Political events overtook the islands as the queen was placed under house arrest and a provisional haole (white foreigner) government took over. However, Lorrin Thurston, who worked both at the queen's behest and toward her overthrow, organized an exhibit which he referred to as both an artistic success and a business failure.[51] He developed a cyclorama of the Kilauea Volcano on the Island of Hawaii that proved to be a popular Midway exhibit. It stood nearly 60 feet high and measured 140 feet in length, in a sixteen-sided building. As he described it, the paying customer stood in the center on a model of the crater floor. "At one side, there was a representation of a molten lake; on the other side, the floor of the crater appeared, with cracks from which steam was rising; at the bottom of the cracks, molten lava was simulated; and the walls of the main crater surrounded the whole." It was electrically lit. The cyclorama, initially estimated to cost upwards of $25,000 to build and install, in the end cost more than $80,000.[52] A small part of his expenses went to pay Hawaiian entertainers.

A group advertised as the late King David Kalākaua's "favorite quartet," which included the famed Nulhama "William" Aeko, performed outside the exhibit to draw attention and again inside during tours of the cyclorama. The singing group was also advertised as the Volcano Singers.[53] In addition to this quartet, Thurston brought five more musicians to perform. One of them was Duke Kahanamoku, whose son would later become a renowned swimmer. A *Chicago Tri-*

35. William Aeko. Courtesy Library of Congress. Photo number 3c06482u.

bune advertisement proclaimed, "Native singers from Hawaii singing their beautiful songs on the banks of the burning Lakes of Kilauea."[54] The members of the quartet each received $50 a month plus their round-trip fare from Honolulu to Chicago.[55] They worked from 8 a.m. to 11 p.m.[56]

Six Native Hawaiians also worked the Midway as singers and hula dancers under the direction of their managers Harry Foster and

Charles Warren.[57] The dancers included Kini Kapahukulaokamāmalu (later known as Jennie Wilson), Annie Grube, Nakai, and Pauahi Pinao. The chanters were brothers Kanuku and Kamuku.[58] Kini was adamant that she wanted to go. She approached Queen Liliʻuokalani, who provided her with a passport, and she and the others took off for the mainland in late May 1893.[59] They performed in California and up the coast before heading to Chicago.[60] Kini described the experience in an interview nearly seven decades later:

> And I wanted to go. And I said we can't go unless the queen gave us a pass. So it was all right, I went to the queen, Lilioʻkaulani. "Well, Jenny what is this?" . . . We talk in Hawaiian. I said, "you know your majesty, I want to go to the mainland." "Ahh," she laughs, she says, "aren't you afraid?" I said no. "Everyone was afraid to go." I said, "not me, I want to go." "How many of you?" I told her these other girls were going with me, but I don't know whether they will go or not, but if they don't go I'm going. So she wrote the pass right out and gave it to me. I went back and told those girls, "I am going. How about it, do you want to go?" Ahh. I says, "you don't have to go but I am going." They came! They went with me all right."[61]

She told a newspaper reporter, "And I went, even though many thought I was awful to do the hula in a foreign country where they thought it was a dirty dance."[62]

Though the dancing was culturally meaningful, American audiences viewed it merely as titillating. Kini visited church every week when she traveled, and she stood up to men who treated her as a sex object. Her husband's biographer, Bob Krauss, told of one such experience. "Once a man pinched Kini. She swung at him but missed." She told him not to touch her. Napua Stevens Poire later told Krauss that the dances had a genealogical basis. "When you're dancing about your ancestors or the ancestors of the *alii* [chiefs], you can't be playful or promiscuous."[63]

Modern kumu hula (hula master) Kealʻi Reichel has described the relationship between movement and words in the hula. "All hula springs from expressing oneself physically through the poetry of the text. So hula cannot exist without the text, without the chant, with-

36. Jennie Kini Kapahu. Photo taken in 1893 at 389 State Street, Chicago.
Courtesy Hawaii State Archives. Photo number PP 82-1.039-S, in folder
People-Wilson PP 82-1.

out the word. . . . To me that's what hula is. It's the physical manifestation of the chants."[64]

Like the dances and performances of American Indians on the Midway, what consumers purchased with their entry fees differed significantly in their minds than from the perspective of the performers. Kini and her troupe were paid to carry on cultural tradition and to see the world from their own perspectives; audiences generally missed this and paid simply to be entertained.

"'When we got to Chicago,' Aunt Jennie said, 'I did the bally hoo out in front and sang and played the ukulele and everybody stopped. Our concession was right behind the "Streets of Cairo" show.'"[65] After she did the ballyhoo to attract customers, she went to the ticket counter to sell tickets and then went in to the performance. She played the ukulele and danced. The troupe put on five shows a day, beginning at 11 a.m. with the last one at 9 p.m. The ten-minute performances were held in a 300-seat auditorium that, according to Kini, was often full.[66]

Chicago newspapers took notice of the hula dancers in late July and early August. They reportedly began a six-week gig at the Madison Street Opera House on July 30.[67] According to Adria Imada, in addition to their work conducting five shows per day on the Midway, they also staged performances at a nearby burlesque theater as part of *The Creole Show* in July.[68] This coincides with their appearance in Chicago newspapers. These artists reportedly earned $5 a week plus expenses for their six-month contracts, which were extended for some after the fair as they continued their tour. They may also have earned small amounts of money having their photographs taken, although they were not compensated for any official pictures made under the authority of fair administrators.[69] By late November the *Hawaiian Star* reported that Foster had taken four singers and hula girls to New York for their next engagement.[70]

The Hawaiians enjoyed the fair and made new friends. Kini specifically mentioned the Samoans who lived right next door on the Midway and the Egyptian belly dancers—one of whom gave her a bracelet that had to be soldered onto her arm, and that she never removed. She also had a beaded gift from one of the American Indian women. "We like to make friends with girls like that from different countries," she said near the end of her life.[71]

37. Pauahi Pinao and Jennie Kini Kapahu Wilson dressed for performance. Photo taken at 389 State Street, Chicago. Courtesy Hawaii State Archives. Photo number PP 82-1-032-s, in folder People-Wilson PP 82-1.

Others on the Fairgrounds

Other Indians came to the fair and worked, but little about them is known. For example, Guatemala made a popular exhibit of coffee that included young Maya women from Antigua serving the coffee in their indigenous clothing and young Maya men or older boys playing the marimbas. The men, Antohn Molina, Pedro Chavez, Samuel Chavez, and Lucio Castellanos formed a quartet.[72] One guidebook said, "A coffee garden is located in the rear with native orchestra furnishing sweet music."[73] The men also played to a full house in the second international concert at the fair's Festival Hall in late August. The *Chicago Tribune* referred to their music as "both unique and interesting." The *Daily Inter Ocean* called it "melodious."[74]

As with other performers at the fair, the Mayans participated in events such as the concert, even though their main duties were elsewhere. The Guatemalan commissioner had gained permission to sell coffee for 10 cents a cup without having to pay a percentage to the World's Fair Commission, and he needed every advantage over other coffee sellers.[75] The hopes for exhibits such as this were to draw attention to the product that Guatemala hoped would become a staple import for the United States. The Mayans helped attract customers in competition with other Central American countries also selling coffee on the grounds. The *Chicago Tribune* touted the Guatemalan exhibit, which included "the superb collection of relics of the Guatemalan Indians, nine or ten centuries old," as one of the fair's best.[76] There is no evidence that the Mayan workers were paid for their efforts.

Other indigenous people proved popular at the fair. The Sami Village, whose residents were referred to as "Laplanders," numbered twenty-four individuals of several generations, "nearly all of one family," whose surname was Bull. Neil Bull was a wealthy man. He was said to own two thousand reindeer in Norway, valued at $50 apiece.[77] They stayed at the Dearborn Hotel before moving onto the fairgrounds in late May. Like the Inuit, they had trouble with the hot weather—five of the seven dogs they brought with them died. Their reindeer seem to have survived, however. They erected both winter and summer homes. According to a photo book of the fair, "Five Delacarlian [an area in Sweden] girls made hair ornaments, and used no little skill

38. Sam Blowsnake and other American Indian members of the Roddy encampment on the Midway Plaisance. From Todd, *"Snap Shots" or World's Fair from a Camera through Recent Photos*, 117.

in selling to visitors."[78] The terms of their contract with the company that brought them is not in the record, however, so it is not clear how much money they may have earned for their work.

Indian people participated in a number of entertainments for which they did not receive pay. On the one hand, there is evidence that many enjoyed dressing in their traditional clothing and participating in parades, and on the other hand, there is evidence that they did not always have the choice whether or not to participate. For example, when the Spanish reproduction of Columbus's caravels sailed down Lake Michigan and arrived at the fairgrounds, Indians were at the forefront of the official welcoming ceremony. According to a Chicago newspaper, "The Indians, as they held first place in this country when the first caravels sighted its shores, led the column in march." Dozens of Indians marched in the parade, led by a contingent of Lakota from Buffalo Bill's Wild West, followed by Indians under Putnam's authority, including those from Vancouver Island, Penobscots, Haudenosaunee, and Navajos.[79]

It is likely that a very small number of American Indians got work on the fairgrounds, like Tom Deer, under the same circumstances as any other workers. Francis Cayou (Omaha), who would become a leader within the Chicago Indian community by the early 1920s, said he first came to the city to work as a Columbian Guard at the exposition. He served as one of some twenty-five hundred guards who were hired because the fair's organizers believed the Chicago police force would not be able to protect the fairgrounds. The guards, primarily college students and military men, protected some three million objects at the fair, and they also helped the various offices control the intake of visitors and conduct business.[80] If Cayou were hired as a guard, as he claimed, he probably earned $60 a month.[81] It is possible that he was hired as a short-term "paid special" guard, which paid $2.50 per day. Some guards also received lodging on the grounds.[82]

A Carlisle Indian Industrial School alumna, Emily Peake, also came to the fair to work. After graduation she had returned home to the White Earth Reservation in Minnesota where she was hired first as an interpreter and then as private secretary to Sybil Carter. She did lace work with Carter as well. Records do not indicate how much money she earned working for Carter, but in December 1893 she took a job as an assistant teacher at a Leech Lake, Minnesota, Indian school where she earned $600 a year.[83] That professional salary was in line with the higher paid salaries for Indians who worked at the fair.

Outside the Fairgrounds: Buffalo Bill

The Inuit were not the only indigenous people to work outside the fairgrounds. Wild West shows were a wildly popular form of entertainment at the end of the nineteenth century, and Buffalo Bill's was the most popular of them all. Bill Cody employed hundreds of cowboys, Indians, frontiersmen, and women at a time and traveled extensively across the United States and Europe beginning in 1883.[84] The Chicago fair seemed a golden opportunity to draw an enormous audience for nearly six months.

Cody's partner Nate Salsbury unsuccessfully tried to secure a spot within the fairgrounds for the show and the large encampment that

39. Buffalo Bill's Wild West show camp. Courtesy Buffalo Bill Center of the West, Cody WY; Vincent Mercaldo Collection, photo 71.1368.

accompanied it. Instead, he leased land across the street, west of the main grounds and south of the Midway, between Sixty-Second and Sixty-Third Streets. More than seventy Indians employed by Cody camped there and participated in the cast.[85] According to historian Sam Maddra, Cody exclusively employed Lakota people from the Pine Ridge Reservation in South Dakota.[86] Vine Deloria Jr. tells us that the programs for Buffalo Bill's shows often listed the Indian participants as hailing from a variety of tribes, but that the characters were played by Lakota people—and their tribal affiliations changed to give the audience a better understanding of the variety of tribes on the plains. Many of the participants were leading members of Lakota society who, had they not been part of the traveling show, would likely have had serious conflict with the Indian agent assigned to their oversight back home.[87]

Buffalo Bill opened his show on April 3, nearly a full month before the fair itself opened. According to one of his biographers, Nellie Yost, the show attracted some twenty-five thousand people a day, with many of them returnees who came again and again.[88] The program

40. Cowboys and Indians of Buffalo Bill's Wild West and Congress of Rough Riders of the World. *World's Fair Puck,* 5 June 1893, 54–55.

was so popular that one South Dakota newspaper wryly observed, "'Buffalo Bill' is scalping more white people in Chicago than he ever scalped Indians on the plains."[89] Part of the attraction of the show was the campground, through which visitors were encouraged to wander before the program. The Lakota lived in tipis at the camp, and except when they were indoors with closed flaps, they were on public display.[90]

According to Maddra, working for Cody "was a prized job for a number of reasons."[91] The contract paid in cash, which provided an important supplement to the meager annuity payments made to individual tribal members. There were few jobs on the reservation, and they paid far less than Cody paid.[92] This gave individuals an opportunity to support their families in ways that were not possible for Indians in rural South Dakota in the 1890s. Performers were able to send part of their earnings home to help their families survive. Tribal life was heavily circumscribed following the army's massacre of Lakota at Wounded Knee just a few years previously. The work was also valued because it involved skills such as horsemanship that had been a key part of Lakota life since the horse came to the plains. As a bonus, the job provided the opportunity to travel. As one reporter covering the aftermath of the Wounded Knee massacre said, Cody's Wild West show "is a better place" for Indians "than an Indian agency on half rations with nothing to do."[93] Historian Louis Warren has observed, "The show was the reservation's most lucrative employer."[94]

Sitting Bull, who performed in the show in 1885, was a prize addition that gave legitimacy and authenticity to Cody's Wild West. He earned $50 a week plus expenses for four months and profited from the photographs taken of him.[95] At the end of his run, Cody gifted him with "a trick riding horse that he admired." By the time of the fair, Indians were integrated into the cast. The Indian horsemen who performed for Cody did so as part of a larger contingent of master horsemen from across the United States and Europe and even beyond. "Instead of degrading the Indians and classifying them as primitive savages," according to Deloria, "Cody elevated them to a status of equality with contingents from other nations."[96] To some extent, documentary evidence supports Deloria's view. However, white cowboys were paid a better wage than the Lakota performers. According to Warren, this "was in keeping with the show's overall racial hierarchy and ideology."[97]

Cody's treatment of Indians would contrast significantly with the role of Indians at the fair across the street. Cody had largely earned the respect of the Indians who worked for him, in contrast to the entrepreneurs who brought many of the Indians in for the fair. The largest single contingent of Indians who came to work for the fair— some seventy-four men, women, and children from the Pine Ridge Reservation in South Dakota—worked for Cody in Buffalo Bill's Wild West and Congress of Rough Riders of the World. One reason that Indian people liked to work for Cody was that they were well paid. They received travel expenses, clothing, lodging, and medical care in addition to their salary. They earned from $10 to $70 per month apiece, for an amount totaling $1,890 per month among them.[98] Individuals spent some of the money they earned. For example, one observer wrote:

This Agreement, Entered into this _15_ day

of April, 1893, by WILLIAM F. CODY, President, and NATE SALSBURY, Vice-President, of Buffalo Bill's Wild West Company, parties of the first part, and an Indian _Plenty_ _Horses_ of Pine Ridge Agency, South Dakota, party of the second part.

Witnesseth, That the parties of the first part have, and by these presents do, engage the party of the second part to accompany the Exhibition ("Wild West") of the parties of the first part on its tour in America and Europe, within the time specified by the Interior Department, the object of such tour being to give public exhibitions of American frontier life; and the party of the second part agrees to do whatever in reason and justice may be required of h___im___ while in the service of the parties of the first part, and which may be necessary and incident to such exhibition not inconsistent with the laws of morality and the ordinary rules of propriety; and the parties of the first part agree to pay to the party of the second part, in lawful money of the United States, a monthly salary of _Twenty Five/100 ($25.⁰⁰/₁₀₀)_ dollars, from the date of the departure of the party of the second part from the said Agency and during h___is___ absence therefrom and until h___is___ return thereto.

The parties of the first part further agree to supply the said party of the second part with proper food and raiment, and to discharge all h___is___ traveling and needful incidental expenses from the date of leaving said Agency until h___is___ return thereto, and to protect the said party of the second part from all immoral influences and surroundings, and to provide all needful medical attendance and medicine, and do all such other acts and things as may be requisite and proper for the health, comfort and welfare of the said party of the second part, and to return h___im___ to said Agency within the time specified by the Interior Department from the date hereof without charge or cost to the said party of the second part, or to the United States.

In Witness Whereof, The above parties have executed these presents at Pine Ridge Agency, South Dakota, the day and year first above written.

WITNESSES AS TO SIGNATURE BY MARK:

Geo F. Comer,

Fred D. Heil

Cody and Salsbury
W. William day Snyder
Plenty Horses his mark +

I **Certify,** on honor, that I explained to the above-named Indian the nature of the agreement hereto attached, and am satisfied that h___e___ fully understood the same at the time of signing it.

Louis Menard
Interpreter.

PINE RIDGE AGENCY, April _15_ 1893.

Approved; _____

Captain 11th Infantry, Acting U. S. Indian Agent.

41. Buffalo Bill's contract with Plenty Horses for work at the fair. From LR 1893:28007 RG 75, NARA-DC. Courtesy National Archives and Records Administration.

Nine Sioux Indians from Buffalo Bill's Elysian Fields filed into a gent's furnishing store on Sixty-Third st., and whiled away some of the happiest moments of their lives trying on hats and coats, and contemplating their increased charms before a mirror.

The broad-rimmed gray hats like Mr. Cody's especially captivated their fancy, and one by one they tried the effect of placing them on their heads at different angles. Some put them on one side, some on the other, some on the back of the head or down over their eyebrows, denting and crushing them here and there, and when they had sufficiently spoiled them bought half a dozen from the delighted proprietor at six dollars apiece."[99]

Six dollars was anywhere from a few days to a week's salary for these men. Other favored purchases for those in Buffalo Bill's camp included peanuts, popcorn, souvenir hats, and candy. Merry-go-round rides were also very popular.[100]

But much of the money was also sent home to support families, which would have been a culturally appropriate use of it. At one point in 1891 an astonished Herbert Welsh, director of the Indian Rights Association, wrote to the Office of Indian Affairs to learn if it was really true that Buffalo Bill's Indians had sent some $18,000 in earnings back home to Pine Ridge.[101] It is likely an accurate amount if it represented money accrued over time for those who worked for Cody over a period of years. It is likely, according to experts, that this was the one time in early Pine Ridge history when there was a significant flow of cash into the reservation.[102]

Another important feature of employment with Buffalo Bill was the opportunity to maintain aspects of Lakota culture that were prohibited back at Pine Ridge. Some of the activities were simply fun. For example, one of the show's features was racing by "Indian boys on bareback horses."[103] In addition to riding horses and camping while wearing traditional regalia, the Lakota performed traditional songs and dances. "Down to the present day," Warren tells us, "Lakota dancers credit Wild West show performers with taking dangerous journeys to protect vital traditions of music and dance that had been driven underground on the reservation."[104]

42. Lakota performers in Buffalo Bill's camp at the World's Columbian Exposition. Courtesy Buffalo Bill Center of the West, Cody WY; Vincent Mercaldo Collection, P.71.1563.P.71.1368.

Cody took every opportunity to parade the Indians who worked for him before the public, in order to attract attention to his Wild West show outside the fairgrounds. One newspaper correspondent wrote of Cody, "Buffalo Bill never lets an opportunity to extend hospitality to all notables that visit the Fair go by. He strives to ingratiate himself with all foreign powers."[105] Another reported that "Buffalo Bill's Indians took a look over the fairgrounds" on May 13. "They created considerable excitement themselves, dressed up in their savage toggery."[106] This was just the type of publicity that Cody aimed for. Yet this also gave the Lakota performers opportunities to engage with the fair and other people. Rocky Bear, Rain-in-the-Face, and Flat Iron all attended the fair's opening ceremonies in their regalia and paint, for example. When Rocky Bear asked to say hello to President Grover Cleveland, whom he had previously met in Washington, he was able to do so.[107]

Cody also permitted special guests free range within his encampment. When the well-known reporter Amy Leslie visited his camp in May, she met with a broad variety of the cast, including Lakota people from both the Wild West show and Sitting Bull's cabin. Rain-in-the-

Face was especially hospitable to her, as was a medicine man who, in her words, "Wants to bless me, shake hands, and recite an inspiring incantation over my trembling head."[108]

Cody gave the sculptor Alexander Proctor a free access pass, and Proctor used this to photograph and make sculptures of Indians and others in Cody's camp. Proctor tells the story of one occasion which led to a near serious conflict with one Lakota man. Proctor made a six-inch bust of Kills Him Twice from a photo but wanted the man to sit for him so that he could perfect the image for a statue he was commissioned to build on the grounds. Kills Him Twice was shocked to see the sculpture and quickly grew angry, bringing a war club and several compatriots with him to confront Proctor. Through an interpreter Kills Him Twice said that this was "bad medicine." He feared that by using the sculpture, either malevolent spirits or his enemies could attack him surreptitiously. Proctor observed, "I had removed a part of his soul + now, if I carried it away, evil spirits would harm him, where he was not there to defend himself. It was a terribly serious matter."

In the end, Proctor said that Kills Him Twice was ambivalent. He resolved the conflict by paying Kills Him Twice $2, "but my willy [sic] savage would pose no more + he avoided me after that."[109] Proctor concluded, "I had to use Jack Red Cloud, a Sioux, for my mounted Indian, instead of the fierce, majestic Kills Him Twice."[110] Kills Him Twice was paid for the sitting, but it is not clear whether Red Cloud was.

This touristic and display aspect of the work was not in the contract. It allowed outsiders access to the Lakota that they would not otherwise have, and this led to intercultural interaction that was sometimes positive and other times conflicted. On occasion, it also allowed the Lakota to enter the fairgrounds without paying a fee.

In the late nineteenth century, Americans were enamored with visions and images of the West. For many people, whether newly arrived immigrants or not, these images helped define their conception of national identity. Popular interest in American Indians among those living in the East was high, at the same time as the popular notion of Indians as a disappearing people permeated the minds of policy makers, scholars, and the general public.[111] In relation to Indians, this created what anthropologist Renato Rosaldo has termed "imperialist nostalgia"—a longing for that which the colonizing society has recently destroyed.[112] This was evident in the popularity of the Indian displays at the fair, at the ethnology exhibit, in the state exhibits, and on the Midway. It was especially evident outside the fairgrounds at Buffalo Bill's popular Wild West show.

The labor experiences of the Indian people who came to Chicago in 1893 and worked on the Midway and across the fairgrounds varied from bleak to positive. Like those in the ethnological village, their work conditions, their salaries, and the provision of their room and board all varied. Indigenous people from a variety of backgrounds gravitated to each other, sharing experiences at the fair and stories of their lives back home. They also seem to have shared stories of the treatment and remuneration; how else to explain the successful strike of the Potawatomi, Ho-Chunk, and Sioux in T. R. Roddy's Indian village? How else to explain the drastic change in Inuit salaries that brought them more in line with those of other groups' earnings? Those who had longer experience with the wage labor market, such as the Kwakwaka'wakw, the Native Hawaiians, and the Lakota working for Buffalo Bill, set the standard. Some of the others quickly caught on, learning the market value of their labor and using modern labor tactics to gain new contracts. Yet others did not or could not take advantage of such opportunities. Still, even those most highly paid earned less than their white counterparts in most cases, as evidenced with the cowboys and Lakotas in Buffalo Bill's employ.

A whole different category of people failed to gain the opportunities they had hoped for. Numerous tribal people from across the United States, Canada, and Latin America hoped to come to Chicago in 1893, either to display themselves as they wished to be seen by the world, to earn some money, or to simply visit the fair. For a variety of reasons, these people's hopes and plans were never consummated.

8

Those Left Out

A bewildering variety of Native individuals participated in the making and enactment of the fair. Some, like the schoolchildren from Carlisle, paid their own way. One such group consisted of Mohawk lacrosse players. They had asked to be invited to participate, but according to David Blanchard, "Natives deemed 'acculturated,' such as the Kahnawake Mohawk, were not invited to the fair to exhibit lacrosse, pantomime dance, or to sell their crafts." So they "traveled to Chicago using their own resources."[1] On October 9 they staged a competition with a rival lacrosse team that was probably made up of Potawatomi and Ho-Chunk players. Some were living on the fairgrounds in Roddy's village, and others may have been visiting for the Chicago Day celebrations.

The game was held in the stock pavilion, with Simon Pokagon serving as honorary umpire. Tali Keno captained the Mohawk team, which handily won the game. The Potawatomi and Ho-Chunk team included Blowsnake, Red Cloud, and Red Bird. Among those who came to celebrate Chicago Day was the Ho-Chunk leader Black Hawk, who would "smoke the pipe of peace" with Pokagon in order to recognize that conflicts between their two tribes were in the past.[2]

Many others never made it to Chicago, however. Putnam's original intent was to bring Native peoples from throughout the hemisphere together in a vast ethnographic village. In February 1892 his secretary wrote, "The American Ethnographical Exhibition, as planned by Professor Putnam, is intended to present a living picture of the actual home life of typical native peoples in different parts of America from the Arctic regions to the Island of Tierra del Fuego, including many tribes of the U.S. Indians which will be represented."[3]

As late as August 1892 Putnam still hoped to bring, from Central and South America alone, a Yucatan Maya family, a Miskito Indian family, natives of Guatemala, a Venezuelan Indian family, a group of Caribs ("the lowest of the native races of people that met Columbus"), Aymaras and Quechuas from Bolivia and Peru, Patagonians, and Tierra del Fuegans.[4]

Word of these plans spread across Indian country in the United States and Canada and indeed throughout the hemisphere. As a result, individuals in Indian tribes, bands, communities, and nations planned to attend the fair. Some hoped to come and show themselves off to the world. Others hoped to earn some money. And some simply hoped to travel.

In addition, Putnam had planned to allow tribes to develop their own exhibits on a par with other displays. In his instructions to assistants sent into the field, he wrote:

> Several tribes are preparing exhibits illustrative of their customs and manufactures, which will be sent to Chicago as exhibits by the tribes. Whenever there is a desire on the part of the leading men of the tribe to thus make a special tribal exhibit, it should be encouraged and aided in every possible way, that the people of the tribe may realize that they are to have equal rights with other exhibitors.[5]

Those equal rights proved nonexistent. For a variety of reasons, many Native people who planned to come to Chicago failed to make the trip. When the reality of the fair's budget sank in, Putnam significantly scaled back his plans.

The dilemma of Indians who wanted to participate in the fair was this: the Department of Ethnology, according to Putnam, could "have nothing to do with the civilized Indians of the United States, without breaking faith with the United States Government, unless there may be some of pure blood among them who may be willing to return to the aboriginal ways and come to the Exposition as part of the Ethnographical Exhibition."[6] The U.S. government exhibit with its limited budget focused solely on schoolchildren. The only remaining paths were the avenues of curiosities on the Midway Plaisance or sponsorship by state, territorial, or foreign governments.

Probably because of Putnam's early hopes to have Indians from across the hemisphere attend, numerous people in tribal communities believed they would have an opportunity to do so. After all, Putnam's assistants in the field had been instructed to identify people who would be willing to come to Chicago. They could not do so without broaching the topic to prospective candidates.

In addition, numerous entrepreneurs hoped to profit by bringing Indians to the fair. Their hopes often extended beyond their capabilities of bringing their plans to fruition. Time and again newspapers and even contemporary scholarly journals reported confidently the imminent arrival of Indians from various tribes, in many cases based on plans rather than reality. Guidebooks for the fair carried misleading information based on the advance marketing materials that the authors received. This has created a confusing historical record. A list of proposed exhibits included various doomed displays that would have brought people from Comanche, Kiowa, and Wichita from Indian Territory; Utes, Sioux, Cheyenne, and Apache; Sioux, Northern Cheyenne, and Arapaho; Lakota from Pine Ridge; Kiowa, Comanche, Apache, Cheyennes, and Arapaho; "Flathead," Blackfeet, Pend d'Oreilles, Nez Perce, and Kootenai; Minnesota Chippewa; Ontario Indians; Kickapoo from Mexico and Indian Territory; "Mexican nations"; Navajo, Utes, and Apache; Pima and Papago from Arizona and Mexico; "Canadian Indians"; Bolivian Indians; and "Digger" Indians from California.[7] Several of these groups were actually reported to be in attendance in contemporary guidebooks, although they never did make it to the fair.

Putnam seemed to genuinely believe that he was giving Indians opportunities to participate in the fair on their own terms. In the summer of 1892 he said, "It has been my object throughout to give the Indian a chance at the Exposition if he wishes to avail himself of it; and I am satisfied that a large number of Indians in various parts of North America are grateful to me for this opportunity."[8] But he turned away those he thought to be too civilized or advanced to portray the ancient lifeways of the Americas. As a result, numerous tribal groups hoping to establish their own displays were never given the opportunity. Many were led to believe that they would be welcomed at the great celebration in Chicago. They planned accordingly, only to be unexpectedly denied their chance. Individual Indians too were thwarted in their efforts to attend the fair in some official capacity or other. These people's stories help shed light on the new world to which American Indians were adapting and the obstacles they faced in becoming recognized as a vibrant part of modern American society.

Conflicts with Putnam

Putnam hoped to have a large variety of Indian tribes represented in the ethnographic village display practically until the fair began. First he hoped to bring them together with funding from the fair, then with support from states or foreign governments, and finally through the work of either Indians themselves or non-Indian entrepreneurs. He had urged his collectors in the field to identify and recruit Indian families and individuals to live on the fairgrounds, and several did so. This would cause high hopes followed by disappointment for those who were ultimately unable to join the festivities in Chicago. Some of the field agents were college students, but others had long experience in Indian country and already had made acquaintance with a variety of people who they believed would benefit from attending the fair, either for educational or economic reasons.

Alice Fletcher was one such person. She was a reformer and ethnographer who would later become the first woman to hold an endowed chair at Harvard University. She had helped write the 1887 General Allotment Act. She worked closely with the Nez Perce tribe in Idaho, serving as their federal allotting agent when their reservation was broken up in the years just prior to the fair.[9] In November 1892 Fletcher wrote to Putnam urging him to work out a way for a Nez Perce acquaintance of hers, one of the tribe's leaders, to attend the fair to sell a book about his tribe. "James Reuben (a full blood Nez Perce) is writing out the myths of the Nez Perce, and wants to have the volume published + to sell it at Chicago in the Exposition. What steps should be taken or can I take for him? I think James R. will make a readable book."[10] Reuben does not seem to have made the trip to Chicago.

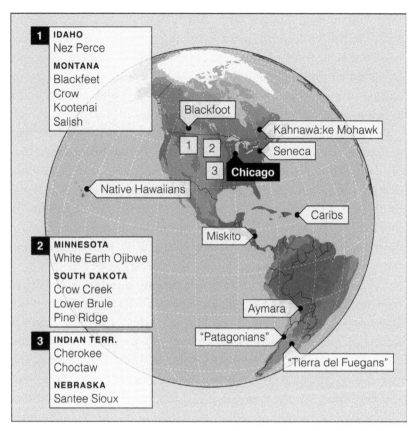

Map 5. Communities who could not attend the exposition. Courtesy Lucien Liz-Lepiorz.

Fletcher also told Putnam that a Winnebago man from Nebraska, whom she did not name, would bring a bark house to the fair for the cost of transportation. She said he could also set up a mat house that could be purchased inexpensively. She especially urged Putnam to bring the bark house to the fair because "it is typical of so large a number of Indians."[11] This does not appear to have occurred either.

Other efforts failed as well. In March 1893 Putnam sent an application for space to the Minnesota Board of Fair Managers for a living display with twenty-five Ojibwe (Chippewa) Indians. "I am very much pleased to learn that the State will represent this tribe," Putnam wrote of the proposed exhibit. He said that he had already corresponded with William Bonga of the White Earth Reservation regarding such a display. Just two months prior to the fair's opening, he mentioned that New York and Colorado were sponsoring similar displays, and he added confidently that Wisconsin was planning to bring a group of Menominee, Ho-Chunks, and Ojibwe, while Louisiana was going to bring a Choctaw village.[12]

By now the expense and responsibility of bringing any new displays were to be farmed out to states. Bonga had apparently organized people from White Earth to attend, together with help from Theodore Beaulieu and Capt. Charles Beaulieu. In the end, however, the White Earth Indian agent was too busy to help with the arrangements on short notice. Without his help, the state could not get permission for the Ojibwe people who intended to go to leave the reservation and travel to Chicago.[13] Other problems surfaced as well.

At Putnam's suggestion, Minnesota proposed to bring a group of Dakota Sioux with the Ojibwe. However, the Minnesota board was discouraged when it learned that Putnam wanted only two lodges of Dakota people and two lodges of Ojibwe. The president of the board wrote, "My remembrance of the discussion in the Board regarding this matter is that from twenty to thirty Indians, including bucks, squaws and papooses, was the number suggested when only the exhibit of Chippewas was thought of." Since it was scaled back, he recommended abandoning the exhibit.[14]

In a last ditch effort to organize the Ojibwe exhibit, the board sent a representative, George Lamphere, to White Earth. He was scheduled to meet with Theodore Beaulieu, but skipped out on the meeting. Beaulieu reported his disappointment to the board's secretary, Charles McCormick Reeve. He heard that Lamphere had met with "certain parties" on the reservation that he considered unsavory. If the state followed Lamphere's lead, "the general place of the Minnesota Indian Exhibit will have assumed hippodromic developments rather than the archaic feature of . . . the true intention of the original movement"—a place in the ethnological village. Beaulieu described the people that Lamphere intended to employ as "'show Indians,' and 'Dime Museum' freaks, that is they are Indians who made the 'patent medicine fake' and 'Dime Museum' freak a professional pastime, and of which element there is always an unenviable surplus."[15]

Lamphere had a different take on the situation. According to him, no one aside from the Indian agent was interested in Theodore Beaulieu taking a leadership role in organizing the trip to Chicago. He also reported that it would be difficult to find Indian men without their "hair shorn" at White Earth, and wondered whether they would be allowed to wear wigs, or if men would have to be recruited from the Leech Lake or Red Lake Chippewa Reservations. Nonetheless, he believed he had found "good specimens" of Indian men and women who would attend, and who had agreed to accept a pay rate of $15 a month for each man and $10 a month for women. No other expenses would be included. At that rate the state could afford to employ ten families for the duration of the fair, and pay them $25 a month per family. Lamphere suggested hiring William Warren, the twenty-two-year-old son of Tyler Warren. Tyler was respected but already employed as a surveyor, and he could not take the summer off from work. William Warren agreed to lead the group for $15 per month, the same as the other Ojibwe men and much less than George Hunt received for a similar position leading the Kwakwaka'wakw.[16]

The display seems to have already been ill-fated by this time, however. But the conflict between Beaulieu, whose support did not extend beyond the Indian agency, and those already making a living as "show Indians" does provide an insight into Indian life in the late nineteenth century. Some of the diversity of experiences and goals within individual communities are reflected here. Some tribal members hoped to come to Chicago to continue to make a living in showmanship, which they were already doing in Minnesota. Beaulieu seems to have wanted to come to Chicago to support Putnam's educational goals for the exhibit. Both efforts depended on portraying Indians as peoples of an imaginary past. The show people used this past to earn money; Beaulieu hoped to use it to educate the broader public. In the end, neither group was successful. Minnesota decided to restrict its tribal display to "Indian curiosities."[17]

As Putnam recognized the limitations of his own fiscal resources, he even encouraged his assistants in the field to urge tribes to send their own representatives and create their own exhibits. In July 1892 he reported, "In some cases they have aroused the enthusiasm of the Chiefs of the tribes to make special exhibits illustrating their old time customs and industries, with the understanding that the collections shall be sold at the close of the Exposition for their benefit or returned to the respective tribes. In other cases individual Indians will bring together characteristic collections and send them as private exhibitors."[18] Putnam would have viewed this as a pre-Columbian exhibit, while tribal leaders would have viewed this as a way to both participate in the fair and make and sell collectors' items and souvenirs to fairgoers.

Putnam also arranged for space for a Canadian government exhibit on the village grounds. (The Kwakwaka'wakw exhibit was sponsored through Putnam's budget.) An official Canadian government document in December 1892 reported that Putnam had set aside space on the lagoon "sufficient to accommodate three lodges of Canadian Indians from the North-West belonging to tribes not represented in the United States." The Northwest Territory Indian commissioner, Hayter Reed, was assigned "to provide these families of Indians with their equipments representing their wild condition."[19] In response to this, the Blackfoot of Alberta, Canada, held a council meeting in April 1893 and told their agent that they "understood that a family was to be sent to represent the North West Indians at the World's Fair." They asked him to request that Reed "select a family from the Blackfeet."[20] In the end the Canadian government failed to sponsor this exhibit.

Other nations as well declined to financially support bringing Native peoples to Chicago. By February 1893 Putnam was resigned to the fact that "it looks very doubtful about the Central and South American tribes." He added morosely, "I wish the Central and South American Governments would send up some of their natives to complete our Ethnographical Exhibition. I am glad the Arrawaks are coming but I wish I could have many other types."[21] By then he was embroiled in a nearly all-consuming effort to have his space built out in time to organize his exhibits and open them to the public. Latin American governments appeared to be willing that their indigenous inhabitants be displayed at the fair, but not at government expense. In the end, just one Arawak Indian and half a dozen Mayans worked at the fair.

In September 1892 Putnam told the director general of the fair, "It is worthy of mention that the Indians as a rule are very ready and anxious to join in this exhibition, and many letters have been received from the chiefs and leading men of different tribes expressing interest and offers of cooperation."[22] Unfortunately, most faced barriers too steep to overcome in their efforts to get to Chicago.

Indian-Organized Exhibits

Various Indian groups hoped to come to Chicago and exhibit themselves on their own terms. They objected to the Wild West show portrayals of them and desired to present themselves as part of modern America. Their perspective stood in contrast to the images ultimately created at the fair by the ethnology exhibits, those on the Midway, and Buffalo Bill's show just outside the fairgrounds. Some opposed the fair's representations of Native peoples consciously, and others focused on ways to participate.

The Indians who proposed to exhibit themselves were primarily concerned with how Indians would be portrayed to the public. They wanted to work the fair, but not for a salary. They wanted to show the world who they were. Their focus was on how Indians were adapting to the modern world at the end of the nineteenth century: not how they had appeared when Columbus first arrived four hundred years earlier, but how they had changed since then.[23]

In June 1891 tribal leaders from two Lakota Sioux reservations in South Dakota—Lower Brule and Crow Creek—sent two identical petitions requesting participation in the fair. One was addressed to the president of the United States and the cabinet, though it was apparently never forwarded to either, and the other to the commissioners of the fair itself. The petition lamented the current state of Indians in the United States and proposed that participation in the fair could help Indians to feel part of the nation that had thus far subordinated them.

The petitioners also believed that an Indian exhibit should be organized and run by Indians: "With a Native American or Indian Exhibit, in the hands of capable men of our own blood such as are willing and anxious to undertake it, a most interesting and instructive and surely successful feature will be added." In words that Simon Pokagon would later echo, they said, "Do not, we pray you, leave us all, the worst and best alike, to regret and continually and forever regret that your race discovered America and us. Give us, rather, some reasons to be glad, with you, that it was so discovered." Albert Hopkins, a non-Indian who organized the petition drive, suggested that physician Frank Powell, a mixed-blood Indian also known as White Beaver, who lived in La Crosse, Wisconsin, would be an ideal person to oversee and organize the exhibit.[24] The suggestion went nowhere.

Emma Sickels, whom Putnam was forced to hire and fire twice, also lobbied for inclusion of Indians in the fair on their own terms.[25] She tried to organize Indian tribal groups to create their own exhibits for the fair. She worked with Henry Standing Bear, who coauthored the 1891 protest of any proposed Wild West type exhibits. Then in the summer of 1892 Sickels reported that numerous tribes desired to attend the fair, including Creeks, Peorias, and the chiefs of the Cherokee. The Cherokee were willing to pay their own way. Sickels reportedly gained approval for participation from some fourteen tribal delegations when they visited Washington DC in 1892.[26] In the spring of 1892 Principal Chief Wilson N. Jones wrote from Indian Territory, "saying the Choctaw nation has decided to make an educational Indian exhibit" for the fair.[27]

At some point, perhaps spurred by Sickels's recruitment efforts, the Five Civilized Tribes of Indian Territory proposed to work together to bring an exhibit to the fair. Commissioner of Indian Affairs Thomas Morgan told George Davis, the director general of the fair, that the Indian office would not be involved in such a display. "It seems to me," he wrote, "that this is a matter for the authorities at Chicago to work up in connection with the authorities of the five civilized tribes in Indian Territory."[28] Davis told Morgan that he agreed. He added that the fair officials would not aid the Indians in the planning for such an exhibit, but would "rely upon their taking action in the matter themselves, as the residents of any other state or territory would do."[29]

The Cherokee leader Joshua Ross then petitioned the State Department to be appointed as a commissioner representing the five nations of Indian Territory to the fair under the congressional authority to recognize commissioners from U.S. territories. He was turned down in August 1892 due to legal complications, when the State Department referred the question to the Justice Department. Indian Territory was unlike other U.S. territories. The State Department argued that it had no jurisdiction in the matter because Indian Territory did not have a governor, and fair commissioner appointments were required to come from governors of states and territories.[30] The attorney general wrote that the proposal was legally invalid. "As a political organization the [Indian] Territory has no existence," and therefore it was not authorized to be represented by commissioners at the fair.[31]

Taking a different tack, the Cherokee established a world's fair organization at their tribal capital in Tahlequah, Indian Territory, and requested a building for Indians at the fair that they "would like to pay for with their own money," the *Chicago Tribune* reported in February 1893. The story added that Sickels had visited Indian Territory and that "all the leading men and women of the different nations were preparing to visit Chicago during the Fair."[32] None of this occurred. Despite the various efforts of the tribes in Indian Territory, the obstacles to establishing an exhibit were too many. Their state of legal purgatory must have been especially galling. What may seem like a technicality, that Indian Territory had no governor, was actually a harsh reminder of the limits of tribal sovereignty. Indian Territory operated under tribal leadership, but the Justice Department failed to recognize it as either domestic or foreign. This left tribal governance in legal limbo.

The Miskito Indians of the Mosquito Coast were also thwarted in their efforts to attend the fair and establish their own exhibit. They were hindered in part because of a misunderstanding of their legal status. Although their land was technically part of Nicaragua, they had retained self-governance over their own affairs in the 1860 Treaty of Managua. "Nicaragua will not invite us. We wish to do business direct with the World's Fair Co.," said their government agent, Miskito surgeon general Roland Kuehn. He anticipated that this might be an intractable issue. He added that if all else failed, "I will ask for space as a private exhibitor, and bear the expense myself, if not too much."[33]

Putnam told the fair's head of the Latin American division, William Curtis, "We want the exhibit, and we must manage it somehow." He thought he could arrange funding for Kuehn to bring one or two families and to feed them while at the fair, so long as they dressed in old style clothing and lived in traditional lodgings. He also held out hope that Kuehn could fund the exhibit.[34] Just before the fair opened, Putnam learned that an entrepreneur hoped to make money by bringing Indians from Nicaragua. Putnam did not know who this man was, but stated that the two groups could not both come.[35] In the end, neither did.

The Crow Indian tribe of southeastern Montana also hoped to participate in the fair. They worked through a contact in Chicago, P. B. Weare, to try to secure a place at the fair. In June 1893 he wrote, "Their own idea would be to send a sufficient number of their men and families to represent what would make a fair representation of their people, say five lodges or families. They want to get up new lodges and native dresses, which will take considerable time to do it." Weare described the Crow as "among the very best of the North American Indians, both as to intelligence and physique" and "anxious to be represented in a creditable manner to themselves and their friends." Despite the fact that the Crow had "many good farmers amongst them and are all owners of good horses," which made their lifestyle too modern for his purposes, Putnam supported the idea. He called Weare's suggestion "entirely in accordance with the plans which I am developing." He indicated that he still did not know which tribes he would sponsor, but in the end, the Crow tribe was not one of them. The plan was doomed, probably because their proposal was not pre-Columbian in nature, and so separate funding would be necessary. Since this was not a commercial exhibit, it would require funding from Congress or the Office of Indian Affairs, both of which were managing their finances frugally.[36]

Honoré Joseph Jaxon, a white impostor who claimed to be Canadian Métis, attempted in various ways to work with Indian people to bring them to the fair throughout 1891 and 1892.[37] His efforts brought him into an ugly conflict with Sickels, and he was never able to bring his plans to fruition. Together with Henry Standing Bear and Manuel S. Molano, he claimed to represent "the Nations of the Indian Territory; of the Dakotah Indian Nation; of the Six Nation Indians of New York; and of the Latin-Indian Nations of the North and South."[38]

Jaxon initially proposed organizing an Indian village of two thousand people. This was a direct response to Buffalo Bill Cody and Nate Salsbury, the latter of whom had told him that "the Indians must not be accorded the dignity of free action, but must be kept under, as disturbers in posse, by white overseers." Instead, Jaxon argued, "The Indians of all classes and ranks are determined that on the occasion of this dress parade gathering of the nations, they will not appear in any other character, or with any lesser dignity than that which properly pertains to them as the scions of the Aboriginal race which welcomed Columbus." Putnam agreed enthusiastically.[39]

Henry Standing Bear wrote to Commissioner Morgan seeking support to bring Lakota people from Pine Ridge to the fair under Jaxon's plan. "My people are not willing to put themselves under the hands of Indian exhibitors," he said in reference to Buffalo Bill's and other entrepreneurial exhibits. He urged the commissioner to pay the expenses of tribal elders out of the tribe's funds in the U.S. Treasury. He believed this would provide an opportunity to educate the fair's visitors about the dignity of his people and to educate his people on the rapidly changing nature of U.S. society.[40]

Sickels, in a desperate effort to wrest control of the living Indian exhibits from Putnam, attacked his plans for the fair, attacked the Indian commissioner, and attacked Jaxon as well, calling him "an escaped lunatic." Jaxon had indeed suffered a mental breakdown due to the events surrounding Riel's Rebellion, a Métis attempt at separate nationhood in western Canada. He had been imprisoned in an insane asylum and had run away from it.[41] As the fair approached, Jaxon scaled back his plans and promoted an effort to set up a campsite outside of the fairgrounds for visiting Indians. Putnam offered him free entry tickets to the fair for Indians who encamped there.[42] In the end, Jaxon failed to organize even this.

Another group that hoped to participate was a musical band of Santee Sioux tribal members. "The Santee Band," a self-organized brass band, unsuccessfully lobbied Commissioner Morgan "that you detail our Band for the columbia world fair for which we ever pray."[43] Only a few of the band's sixteen members spoke English. They had organized themselves and hired a Bohemian music teacher whom they brought into the Santee Agency in Nebraska from fifteen miles away to help with their training when they were able to afford it.

An attorney introduced Henry M. Jones of the brass band to Nebraska senator Charles Manderson, indicating that both Indians and whites liked Jones. "They desire employment at the World's Fair.

I think their employment would prove satisfactory to the management, and would be a great encouragement to the Indians."[44] Local newspapers had hailed the band as "Pure American" and detailed its members' efforts to become proficient and to play locally. The men held "ordinary" jobs, but had a love of music. "Some are school teachers, some are farmers, others carpenters and still other trades are represented," according to one newspaper.[45] Like many others, they wanted an opportunity to come to Chicago and show off to the world. They hoped to be paid to do so.

Commissioner Morgan indicated that he too had hoped to have an Indian band at the opening ceremonies. But fair officials refused to pay the expenses for it, perhaps in part due to the participation of Carlisle Indian School. "I do not see how it will be practicable to make any arrangements for having the Santee band, as such, employed at Chicago during the Fair," Morgan told the Santee Indian agent. He added, "I do not see how, as an Indian band, arrangements can be made for having them employed during the progress of the Fair; especially as bands from Carlisle, Haskell and perhaps other schools will attend the Fair in connection with the respective school delegations."[46]

Such bands were popular in Indian country in this era. Brass bands had been introduced to Indian children in boarding schools in the late nineteenth century. Their purpose, in the words of John Troutman, was "inculcating the male students with the regimented disciplinary movements associated with military brass bands."[47]

The Seneca National Band and Orchestra also hoped to participate in the fair, asking only for expense money. Their leader, C. C. Lay, identified the group as a military band of forty to fifty members, all from the six nations of the Haudenosaunee. In response to his query in February 1892, Morgan told him essentially the same thing he had told the Santee Band. He informed Lay that the Indian schools would bring bands and that any other Indian bands would only provide duplicating exhibitions. Since the fair's policy discouraged that, he said, "I do not see how we can give you any assistance in the way of getting your band to Chicago."[48] Cornelius Cusick had also dismissed the idea of this band attending in a letter to Putnam when he was collecting for the fair in 1891. He pointed out that the Seneca were "progressive," and "they have a fine brass band, but of course it will not be needed."[49] It did not fit into Putnam's definition of Indians of the past. These bands and their members were too much a part of modern society for his purposes.

Individual Indians also hoped to come to Chicago to participate in the fair. Some proved to be too advanced in Putnam's definition of civilization, and so they hoped to come on their own. Such was the case with one Mohawk woman, who met one of Putnam's collectors, S. K. Fenollosa, a Harvard student. Fenellosa wrote to Putnam at length about his inability to find Iroquois Indians who were not modern. "On the Reservations which I have visited, the Indians have been so civilized, and have given up their old customs to such an extent, that it has been impossible for me to get up a good collection of objects," Fenollosa said.[50] The Haudenosaunee had for centuries developed relations with Euro-Americans; to think they were untouched by western society was absurd.

The Haudenosaunee had learned at least by the eighteenth century the value of some of their children gaining an English education in order to deal effectively with the invaders of their homeland, and they sent children to English schools. There is also good evidence that the Founding Fathers adopted Iroquois political structures in the establishment of their new government.[51] The Iroquois and the Euro-Americans had a long history of interaction predating the establishment of the United States. Little surprise, then, that Fenollosa could not find an untouched Native society in upstate New York.

Nonetheless, he did find skilled beadworkers over the border in Canada. He thought their work, and especially the work of one woman who worked as the local telegraph operator at Kahnawà:ke, merited showing at the fair. He told Putnam, "All the Indian women [there] are engaged from morning till night in the manufacture of beadwork. . . . The telegraph operator does about the best work + is a thoroughly reliable woman." Fenollosa told Putnam that for $25 she would spend a month making objects for the display. But more than that, she hoped to come to Chicago and sell her wares herself. "She desires me to ask you, to whom she could write to find out how to obtain space within the Fair Grounds, for a booth. She wants to have beadwork for sale on her own account."[52]

Unfortunately this Mohawk woman was ahead of her time. In the 1890s it was acceptable for non-Indian entrepreneurs or government officials to bring Indian artisans to such events to sell their wares—paying the expenses of the businessmen or exhibit organizers—but not for Indians themselves to set up and make the profits for themselves. Like the Mohawk lacrosse players and the brass bands, she was deemed too civilized to participate in the fair.

Putnam may also have been influenced by his assistant, Thomas Holgate of Ontario, whom he sent to measure people and collect at the Mohawk Bay of Quinte Tyendinaga community. Holgate wrote to Putnam, "These people have been so long under the influences of civilization (nearly 200 years in all) that they have almost entirely forgotten the primitive habits and what they know of them is simply from traditions and these are now very vague." Their status as a federally recognized Indian community also worked against them in terms of being considered truly aboriginal. "On account of the recognition paid them by the government, the Indians pride themselves in their nationality and it is all but impossible to ascertain to what extent they are mixed with the whites. I have been informed that there is not a pure Indian on the reserve and so far as I have seen I believe it to be true. There are a large number however who retain the characteristic Indian features."[53] Holgate was simply following instructions he received from both Putnam and Boas to be on the trail of what was considered precontact Indian life. As both the Mohawk woman Fenollosa reported on and the Mohawk lacrosse players had learned, the relationships they had established with their white neighbors in their long development as independent communities within Canadian and U.S. society disadvantaged them when they wished to participate in the festivities in Chicago. In numerous cases, then, tribal groups and independent Indian groups such as the musical bands, as well as individuals, were shut out of their opportunity to come to Chicago.

Entrepreneurial Exhibits

Numerous non-Indians, either on their own or through patrons, also tried and failed to oversee or be part of the Indian exhibits, either for prestige or profit. They ranged from people who knew Indian people or communities well to opportunists hoping to make a quick buck. Putnam tried to work with some of them in their efforts, as he had with some of the Indian-organized efforts. Others were turned down by Putnam or the fair's oversight board.

Frank Miles, a rancher from Demersville, Montana, had Putnam's enthusiastic support. He proposed to work with two mixed-blood individuals from the Flathead Reservation in western Montana, Charles Allard and Michel Pablo, to bring their bison to the fair along with several families of Indians who would oversee the exhibit. Flathead was home to the Salish, Kootenai, and Pend d'Oreilles tribes. The last Salish holdouts, who had lived in the homes in their Bitterroot Valley south of Missoula, had been forcibly removed to the reservation in 1891. This occurred just two years after Montana gained statehood. The Salish had established a viable herd of bison, commonly called buffalo, by bringing specimens from the few surviving remnants of the great herds of the plains. One man had traveled over the mountains to Canada to bring back buffalo, and others had been brought from nearby Fort Shaw.[54]

Miles and Allard must have met by January 1892 to discuss the proposed exhibit. In early February Miles wrote to Allard that he had met with fair officials to broach the subject of the bison exhibit.[55] Miles then wrote to Commissioner Morgan seeking permission to bring Allard and Pablo's bison along with ten to twelve lodges of Indians "belonging to the Flathead or Kootenai tribes."[56] Morgan responded that he did not object but that fewer Indians would be needed, since the focus of the exhibit was to be bison. He added that if Putnam wished to have Flathead Indians in his exhibit, the Office of Indian Affairs would help facilitate it.[57]

In March Miles wrote to Putnam asking "whether or not I can have the use of these Indians." He pointed out that since the bison were near extinction, there were very few people who could handle them. "The owner of these buffalo, being a half-breed, will not consent to my employing inexperienced white men to handle them." He also argued that he needed to bring the Indians as families, since the men could not be away from their wives and children for that long without problems arising.[58]

As in other cases, family was often such an important feature of tribal life that individuals could not conceive of being separated from it for more than half a year. Indeed, anthropologist Christina Gish Hill has argued that extended kinship relations should be considered the very basis of tribal nationhood.[59] This led to conflict with fair organizers such as Putnam who worked to keep the number of employees of any particular tribe to a minimum. It also helps explain why a proposed exhibition such as this one would need to include such a large number of people.

Peter Ronan, the agent at the Flathead Agency in Montana, supported the idea of Allard and Pablo leading the exhibit. He wrote to Morgan in March 1892:

> In my opinion, if this matter will be carried out and receive your attention, it will successfully show to the world that men of Indian blood are not only capable of raising a herd of buffaloes, but are as capable of handling them on the grounds of the World's Fair as on their native plains. It will also show that they are as capable of their own business management as if under the management of the writer of the attached letter, or any other management.[60]

Morgan responded that Putnam had the ultimate authority to decide.[61] Putnam approved. He reported that he advised Miles that the Indians should wear their native clothing and live in their native habitations. "The fact of their herding the buffalo would not interfere with their being seen and studied as native Americans."[62] Morgan then told Ronan, "Prof. Putnam and I both agree with you that, if it is practicable, it is better that the entire exhibit should be planned and carried out by persons of Indian blood." He warned of the difficulties of carrying out such a complex proposition from a business perspective. Allard and Pablo would need to "think it out in all its details and be perfectly sure of what they are going to do, and what it will cost, and whether they have sufficient capital to undertake such an enterprise without risk of bankruptcy." They would need to be astute in considering costs, such as leasing concession space, employing people in various roles, and transporting everyone from Montana and back. Morgan also informed Ronan that, per Putnam's instructions, the Indians should be prepared to wear their "native costumes" and live in "their native habitations; so that those who attend the exhibition of the animals may see as nearly as possible a transcript of life in the Indian country as it used to exist in the days of buffalo hunting."[63]

These two directives—that the Indians must work as modern businessmen and that they must portray themselves as part of a bygone era—neatly define the dilemma that Indians faced in the late nineteenth century. They were considered to be part of a rapidly fading past in American history, and at the same time they needed the skills to effectively participate in present-day society. They had to address both aspects of outsiders' perceptions of them in order to succeed. Many became skilled at the chameleon-like adaptation necessary to do so. But in other cases, the two contradictory demands proved overwhelming.

By May 1892 Putnam was worried that Miles's plans would lead to the fair's endorsement of "a wild west show before we know it." He also warned Miles that the exhibit should be "in no way degrading to the Indian or does not savor of the wild west show character."[64] Miles by this time had changed plans slightly to include one hundred Indians from a broader variety of backgrounds and to create more of an extravaganza.[65]

An article in the Kalispell, Montana, newspaper *Interlake* seems to bear out Putnam's concern. It reported that Flathead, Kootenai, Pend'd'Oreilles, Blackfeet, and Nez Perce would participate, "surrounded by deer, buffalo and prairie dogs." The article continued, "The war dance and Messiah craze will not be forgotten and will be an important feature. They will not be half breeds or squaw men but genuine thoroughbred red skins of the woods that have participated in the war dance when it meant blood and lots of it." In addition, deer would be sent live to the fairgrounds where the tribal members would slaughter them and then tan the hides and use them to make items for sale.[66]

Putnam told Miles in no uncertain terms that neither war dances, "which would tend to impress the public with the idea of wild savagery in connection with the Indians," nor killing and processing deer would be permitted.[67] He had been given control of the Indian exhibits, and he exerted it here. Apparently killing deer for food and skins was too visceral a representation of pre-Columbian Indian life. The Indian Office also maintained control in its own way, restricting who could and could not travel on and off reservations.

In October 1892 Assistant Commissioner Robert Belt approved Miles's plan to bring Flathead, Blackfeet, Pend d'Oreilles, Kootenai, and Nez Perce people as part of his exhibit. The only requirement was that the Indian agents would review the names of individuals Miles would bring to determine whether they were "proper persons to be allowed to go to Chicago."[68]

The next April, just weeks before the fair opened, Putnam reported that Miles's exhibit was a go, and that "in return" for "my endorsement" of it, "I am promised of the loan to this department, from day to day, of families of the following tribes in the out-of-door section: Flathead, Blackfeet, Pend de Oreille, Nez Perce, and Kootenai." Miles now called his exhibition the "Miles Montana Buffalo and Indian Company."[69] As with the anticipated Minnesota Ojibwe exhibit, Putnam expected to augment his own ethnological village with Indian people sponsored by others. And like the Minnesota case, Miles's plans fell apart in the end.

Even after the fair opened, Allard, who was described as having "100 buffaloes on the Flathead reservation, the only live herd of such magnitude in the world," was "thinking seriously of bringing them to Chicago to be exhibited during the world's fair."[70] In May 1893 the *New York Times* provided clues as to why Miles was unable to pull his plan together. It intimated that Buffalo Bill opposed Miles on the basis of competition. It reported, "Nothing . . . has been heard of the Montana gentleman since it was learned that he and Major Burke had locked horns, the latter threatening a damage suit," adding, "Col. Cody and Mr. Burke assert that, 'deed and double deed,' they know nothing about it." The article concluded that Putnam "entertains strong suspicions, especially since the Wild West combination offers to lend him Indians, out of which gift, it is safe to say, they will take the incidental advertising as a return of the favor."[71] This article seems likely to be referring to Miles's proposal, and perhaps he was bought out by Cody and Burke in order to keep him from bringing a sanctioned popular exhibit that would rival their Wild West show.

Numerous poorly planned proposals also brought Indian people hopes of visiting Chicago in the summer of 1893. A Chicago newspaper reported in July 1893 that three families, fifteen people in all, would be brought to the fair by E. H. Ellison, "an old scout and interpreter among the Sioux for thirty years. . . . The old scout says that he will have no trouble in getting a party; the difficulty will be to make his choice from the swarm that will turn out when it becomes known that there is a tour in prospect."[72] This was just one of a number of efforts reported on in correspondence or the press. Numerous non-Indian groups, both U.S. and foreign, also hoped or planned to participate in the fair with Indian or indigenous exhibits or concessions, but were unable to do so for various reasons.[73]

Native people in South and Central America also hoped to come to Chicago. A variety of people devoted considerable effort throughout 1891 and 1892 to bring Latin American Indians to the fair. A number of individual entrepreneurs, government officials, and U.S. collectors proposed bringing Native families and individuals with the enthusiastic support of Putnam and William Curtis, the man in charge of the Latin American Department, but most never arrived.

The list of proposals is stunning in its breadth. Putnam was most enamored with the planned exhibits from Argentina, including Patagonians and Tierra del Fuegans. One of his men in the field instructed an entrepreneurial collector to retain families from both places. "The idea is to represent in all its filth and savagery what you find on the barren island of Tierra del Fuego or the pampas of Patagonia."[74] This reflected Putnam's view of the Indian people of the furthest south. Others planned to bring Caribs from the Dominican Republic, Natives from the Lake Maracaibo region of Venezuela, Costa Rican Indians, Jibaras from the Brazilian-Colombian frontier, more than half a dozen Colombian tribes, and Amazonian Indians from Peru.[75] In February 1892 Putnam assured Commissioner Morgan that Brazil, Peru, and Guatemala would be including indigenous people as part of their exhibits.[76] Only Guatemala did—their coffee servers and marimba players were Mayan.

Most of these failed arrangements clearly fit into already existing economic patterns that had developed, in which entrepreneurs profited from bringing Indians to display, and Indians earned little or nothing. But in at least one case the Indians who agreed to come to Chicago insisted on being paid in cash for their work, similar to the systems that had developed within the United States. Their experience was also the most startling. A contingent of Aymara Indians from Bolivia (sometimes referred to as Peruvian Indians in the press) almost succeeded in attending the fair. They made it as far as New York and Philadelphia in their desperate attempt to get to Chicago. The Bolivian Aymara story is confusing and incomplete, yet instructive.

William E. Safford, an officer in the U.S. Navy, was the fair's designated collector in Bolivia. Putnam had given him a charge similar to his other collectors in Latin America, which included collecting ethnographic objects, measuring people, and arranging to bring individuals to the fair for display. Safford informed Putnam that it would be difficult to bring Indians from Bolivia who still practiced the old ways, since they seemed loath to leave home. If they did go, they would need to bring all of their household goods and "a supply of their own food should accompany them. The Fuegians taken to Paris died from overeating and from being given food too rich for them." As with other cases in Latin America, Safford ultimately was unable to bring Native individuals to Chicago. He believed the major problem to be that the Indians who lived in La Paz would be most likely to want to come, but that they no longer knew their ancient crafts. On the other hand, he said, "It will be difficult to induce" those women who still wove and those men who made pottery in the old way and lived in their remote villages "to leave their country."[77] But word of the opportunity spread among both entrepreneurs and Aymara people in Bolivia.

When the government-sponsored plans to bring Native Bolivians to the fair fell through, August Stumpf developed "two possible arrangements with private individuals" to do so, according to Nancy Egan.[78] In April 1892 Stumpf recommended hiring a "catholic Indian preacher" in whom the Indians "have the fullest confidence." They could be brought for 30 cents a day in Bolivian money so long as a supply of food brought from home accompanied them.[79] Stumpf wrote again in September 1892 that he had found someone who would bring Bolivian Indians to Chicago.[80]

A local mine operator in La Paz eventually succeeded in bringing seventeen Aymara men by steamship to New York. They arrived there on April 1, just a month before the opening of the exposition.

These men planned to make their way from New York to Chicago to take part in the fair. Egan surmises that they were mine workers.[81]

Egan has aptly observed, "In many regions with significant indigenous economies and population, any depiction of these communities as completely unfamiliar with Western markets, capitalism, or Western 'civilization' would have to rewrite the lived reality of export economies at the turn of the century."[82] Indeed, as part of the periphery that fed the expanding core—not just in the United States but in remote tribal communities throughout the Americas— that held resources of value to the colonio-national empire, Native individuals had forged new economic and social identities and practices that conformed to their new realities. In Bolivia's mining communities these economic practices dated back centuries. By 1893 Aymarans knew well the value of their labor or at least the pay level it would command. They worked under conditions where the rates of pay for various skill levels had long been regularized.[83] They would likely not know the exchange rates of Bolivianos and U.S. dollars, however.

Once the Aymara arrived in New York, no fair officials would agree to pay their fare to Chicago. They ended up being contracted to a circus in Philadelphia, but when that failed to be lucrative to their contractor, they were let go—and walked back to New York. They made the trek during heavy rains, during the week that the fair in Chicago opened. Along the way a man named Santos fell ill and was hospitalized in Bellevue, where he died alone. His companions were not permitted to visit him, and his body was held as unclaimed in the morgue.[84] At this point Emma Sickels intervened. She arranged a funeral and had him buried in the hospital cemetery, in a ceremony that brought Potawatomi people from the Midwest.[85] Sickels said she blamed the fair's officials "for the sufferings endured by Santos and his companions since they landed in this country." She claimed credit for bringing the "Peruvians" to the states. She said she was authorized to do so.[86] If she was responsible for authorizing their trip to New York, she deserves a lion's share of the blame for their trials. In her attempts to control the Indian exhibits and her consequent conflict with Putnam, she proved to have even less political clout than he did.

In this case it seems she attempted to force her will on Putnam, but the bottom line was that neither he nor other fair officials had any interest in providing funding for the Aymarans.

Not all Native groups who had an opportunity to attend the fair actually decided to do so. Members of the Hawaiian National Band were offered the opportunity to work at the fair, but refused. Their work was tied in with the politics related to the overthrow of Queen Lili'uokalani, but their refusal hinged on the employment conditions specified in their contract. They considered the contract offer they received seriously and attempted to modify the contract. When its sponsor refused to do so, they voted not to go to Chicago.

Music was long an important feature of Hawaiian culture. The Hawaiian National Band was a brass band sponsored first by King David Kalākaua and later by Queen Lili'uokalani. They spent as much as $50,000 a year on the band.[87] After the queen's overthrow in January 1893, the band members were asked to sign an oath of allegiance to the provisional government led by Sanford Dole. They refused and told the bandleader, Henri Berger, that they were *pau*, or finished with the band. A cornet player, R. W. Aylett, told Berger "that he was ashamed to be a Hawaiian citizen and he would rather swear allegiance to Portugal or some other country" than to the pro-visional government run by U.S. businessmen.[88] At the time more than forty thousand Hawaiians and "half-castes" and fewer than two thousand Americans lived in the islands.[89]

A new band was formed, but over the next several months the old band was reconstituted. In September Lorrin Thurston, whose Cyclorama company operated the volcano exhibit at the fair, tried to contract with the original band to bring them to Chicago near the end of the fair. He hoped also to bring them to San Francisco for the midwinter fair after the Columbian Exposition ended. He was apparently desperate to stanch the financial losses he was suffering in Chicago.[90] On September 10 the band members met at Aylett's home to discuss the contract with Thurston's attorney.

They were offered transportation, room and board, and 25 percent of receipts. They were also told they could earn extra money with outside engagements, although they would be expected to play ten hours a day for Thurston. Aylett had proposed the band members be paid $50 a month plus expenses, but had been turned down. Band members were concerned that the 25 percent would not amount to much per member, and wondered whether it would be paid only after Thurston's expenses. Most band members had families at home that they needed to support, so uncertainty of income was a real issue for them. They were also concerned by living and travel accommodations. Would they be housed in seedy hotels? Drummer Hack Kuamoo wondered whether "we might be packed in freight trains on the way to Chicago." Thurston's attorney refused to modify the contract to answer their concerns, so the band voted 24 to 3 not to go.[91]

In the end, support for their families back home was a key consideration for the musicians. Unlike the Inuits, or the Sami, or the Penobscots, they would not travel to the fair with their families. And unlike the Lakota working for Buffalo Bill or the Navajo weavers or the other Hawaiian musicians Lorrin Thurston had hired for his volcano cyclorama exhibit, they were not guaranteed a salary that could be used to support family at home. Their story provides insight into the various advantages and disadvantages in participation for this group of men. Their choice shows the complexity of competing factors in determining whether to work in Chicago. But these young men read the contract offered to them closely, and their ultimate choice was a business decision.

Despite Putnam's hopes and promises, the fair kept out seemingly even more Native people than it brought in. Putnam's budget allowed him to do far less than he had initially intended. Some of the entrepreneurs who planned to bring Indians to the fair were poorly organized. Others, like Honoré Jaxon, probably underestimated the amount of work and coordination necessary to bring together a far-reaching exhibit. But Indians faced a deeper problem at the end of the nineteenth century. They were viewed as anachronistic by a society that had forced them to its edges and worked to keep them there.

Those Indian people who hoped, but failed, to participate in the celebration at Chicago pushed back against societal perceptions of them. Although they were unsuccessful in coming to Chicago, they were mounting a challenge to the definition of Indians as incapable of managing their own affairs. They opposed the idea that they did not want to participate in the modern world on their own terms. For some, working at the fair would be a way to make a living. For others, the work would provide an opportunity to show the public who Indians were from a Native perspective rather than from a governmental or scientific one. The people working to get to Chicago, like many of their compatriots who successfully came to the city, believed that they were part of a modern society that did not accept them as such.

Afterword/Afterward

American Indians and Their New World

Historian James Gilbert, writing about the 1904 Louisiana Purchase Exposition in St. Louis, observed, "Sometimes the meaning of an event is best understood by those looking in from the margins, those excluded for one reason or another, who could not attend but recognize the importance of being present." He is referring to the way that organizers of that fair blunted participation of African Americans.[1] But in 1893 in Chicago, although Indians were not always excluded, they were on the margins. They were brought in to portray one thing, but their experiences were something entirely different. The meaning for them to a significant degree was participation in the larger American industrializing economy—the very thing the fair intended to portray about Chicago and the United States. Unfortunately, they were consigned to a role that did not reflect their reality. They protested that role, some in words, others by their actions.

To the fair's organizers and the vast majority of visitors to the fair, the Indian displays, both the displays of individuals and of tribal artifacts and objects of material culture, showed a past that illustrated how far industrial society had risen from its prehistoric past. But to many of the Indian participants, both those at the fair and those back home who prepared objects for sale to the ethnologists and collectors who built their displays, their participation in the extravaganza of the exposition represented a relatively new place in a changing world.

The early 1890s were harsh, difficult times in Indian country. In the western great plains in the United States and Canada, the vast herds of bison, a major foundation of the economic, political, religious, and social lives of tribal people for millennia, had only recently been demolished.[2] Settler communities displaced Native peoples on much of their lands, "opening" the West to national development and growth in both nations.

Across the United States and Canada, American Indians and First Nations people were confined to reservations and reserves on much diminished portions of their homelands, and their economies were largely destroyed. As a consequence, tribal communities lost political power and control of their political institutions and many of their social institutions under the heavy hand of federal paternalism. As the United States sank into depression, even the meager payments owed to tribes for the sale of their lands and resources were at times withheld. Tribal members were forced to attempt to grow crops on lands not suited for agriculture. In 1893, for example, potato crops failed across southern Canada from Nova Scotia and New Brunswick to Manitoba and the North-West Territories, which includes present-day Saskatchewan and Alberta as well.[3] Individuals often were restricted from leaving reservations to look for resources to support their families. Even in the face of all this, Indian people found ways to adapt. Indeed, as part of the periphery that fed the expanding core—not just in the United States and Canada but in remote tribal communities throughout the Americas that held resources of value to the colonio-national empires—Native individuals had started the process of forging new economic and social identities and practices that conformed to their new realities.

American Indians had begun consciously entering the cash economy by the time the fair opened. In many cases, the federal annuity and ration system was failing to provide the support they needed to feed their families and live a healthy life. Cash could be used to directly purchase needed food, clothing, and materials at market value. A letter from Henry Standing Bear to the commissioner of Indian affairs, written the day before the fair opened, clearly shows this. Standing Bear was secretary of the Pine Ridge Reservation, which sent seventy-four tribal members to earn money working for Buffalo Bill during the exposition.

Standing Bear's letter was written for those who stayed home and probably those who left the reservation for work as well. Pine Ridge

Lakota people in one district, representing differing reservation factions, asked the Office of Indian Affairs to have their annuities and rations converted to cash and not sent in goods. "One party, the most advanced and progressive people want cash payment for the rations and annuity goods, and all other rights and the other party largely composed of the so called hostile people want only annuity goods to be commuted into cash payment," he wrote. "These people are sincerely in earnest about this matter and they are anxious to send a delegation of four men to present reasons for their desire, and to show the evils and folly of issuing these rations, annuity goods to this people."[4] Annuity goods were often of inferior quality and subject to theft or devaluation by corrupt or negligent officials. All reservation members needed cash, which they knew to be of more value than the meager goods they received.

These Lakota individuals did not desire to be cheated of fair value by middlemen and traders or to receive low-quality goods not of their own choosing. The goods were intended to serve civilizing purposes, but they failed to provide for the people. The Lakota hoped to use cash to purchase the goods they most needed to support their families. This letter reflects the situation across Indian country. American Indians were in dire economic conditions and wanted the authority to spend their own money in their own way. The federal government did not grant them this wish, and so many began looking for jobs elsewhere in order to earn cash themselves. Some fortunate ones got jobs at the fair. Federal paternalism, however, showed no signs of loosening its grip on Indian country.

Indians, legally wards of the federal government, were considered incompetent to manage their own affairs. In fact, barely more than a decade later in the case of *Lone Wolf v. Hitchcock*, the Supreme Court would declare that incompetency defined the relationship between individual Indians and the United States.[5] This attitude relegated Indians to a place outside of modern America. It continued a long-standing backward-looking policy of management of Indian affairs that conformed with and helped shape popular perceptions of Indians.

The role of the various non-Native groups contesting each other to represent the place of Indians in late nineteenth-century America followed the same pattern, freezing Indians out of both the right to self-definition of Indianness and out of history. Lee Baker has observed, "Under the aegis of science, anthropologists of the era cemented a very narrow image of an authentic Indian by staging, fabricating, authenticating, and editing what was and was not Indian." He goes on to say that "this scientific intervention . . . precluded any variation, culture change, or diversity within traditional American Indian practices and worldviews."[6] Simply put, authentic Indian culture was viewed as static, not dynamic.

Similar observations can be made about the Indian school exhibits, Buffalo Bill's program, and the Indians exhibited by entrepreneurs on the Midway. They all narrowly defined Indians for the public. By doing so they limited Indians' possibilities to break out of their prescribed place on the margins of American and Canadian society. The non-Indians were so successful that their contestations also shaped the historiographic debates over the role of Indians at the fair. In essence, these debates led most future scholars to ignore the role of Indians in using the fair as an opportunity to enter the wage labor market and find new ways to support their families. Instead, their role as romantic or savage reminders of the past or as scientific specimens was reified. Indians were thus denied the possibility of exerting their own agency in terms of self-definition. This did not stop them from trying.

Indigenous people's labor at and for the fair was wide-ranging. Their work was part of the newly evolving economies reshaping Indian country and Indian relations to U.S. society in the late nineteenth century. As the Office of Indian Affairs stymied economic development in tribal communities, individual tribal members found new ways to make a living by participating in the cash economy. Scholars have recently begun to explore these experiences, but the field at large is only beginning to recognize the agency of Indians and the development of a changing economy.

The Indian people who worked at the fair recognized that they were on society's margins. They were trying to shift that position and move into a space where they could at the very least support themselves and their families. Some hoped to reeducate the American populace about current Indian realities. Many simply wanted to participate in the modern cash economy. They were trying to turn the tables. In a sense, whether consciously or not, they were trying to make the periphery over into the core. But the core, of course, resisted, strengthening its hold on both the representation and the employment and labor profits of the periphery and keeping it in its place, maintaining the imperial stranglehold it had on the weakened Indians.

It is important to recognize that the Indians who worked for the fair did so as wage laborers or volunteers. Those who had hoped to work for themselves by mounting their own exhibits were excluded. These groups included the Indian Territory tribes, those working with Honoré Jaxon and Henry Standing Bear, and the brass bands as well as various individuals. For a short time some of the Inuits succeeded in working for themselves by leaving the fairgrounds and establishing their own village outside the gates where they could manage the funds. This was reactionary to the condition they found themselves in, however. It was not what they set out to do when they left Labrador.

The work of Native peoples for the fair in Chicago set the stage for later American Indian participation in the fairs and expositions that were so popular with the public. Just two years later, in 1895, several Native groups were represented at the Cotton States Exposition in Atlanta, though not nearly on the scale that had occurred in Chicago. The place of Indians in southern society was somewhat problematic, since race was thought of in binary terms, black and white.[7] Andrew Denson has argued that in these years, the only place that white southerners could envision American Indians in their world was in the past.[8] This was reflected in the Indian exhibits in Atlanta in 1895.

Buffalo Bill brought his Wild West extravaganza to Atlanta for a two-week run. Other Indian displays included an exhibit and marketing of lace made by women from the White Earth Ojibwe Reservation in Minnesota, a Midway Indian village inhabited by Rosebud Lakota, an Eskimo village, and a group of Zapotecs from Tehuantepec in Mexico.[9] Except for a Chickasaw-run asphalt company from Indian Territory that marketed its work, these exhibits all firmly placed American Indians and Native peoples in the past. Even the White Earth exhibit, Theda Perdue argues, was looking backward, since the lace was handmade at home and not made by machines in a factory. So though there was a small opportunity here for Native peoples to earn some money, for the most part they did so as representatives of a bygone era. In their own minds they may have been participating in a modern American endeavor, but in the minds of fair officials and visitors they clearly were not.

At the 1904 Louisiana Purchase Fair in St. Louis, the anthropology village and Indian school were built on a much grander scale even than at Chicago. Hundreds of Native individuals from more than twenty tribes set up camp in the Indian village alone.[10] Their transportation was paid by the fair, and they were to live in traditional homes, wear traditional clothing, and carry on traditional activities. As in Chicago, these were not to be tainted by use of modern accouterments. This proved impossible to maintain; as Nancy Parezo and Don Fowler have pointed out, Native "participants wanted souvenirs just as much as visitors."[11] The village was to be a scientific object lesson in racial classification and comparison, and it included a series of anthropological villages with other indigenous people who were not Indians.[12]

People from various tribal groups were paid to gather material and build traditional homes. They were also invited to sell artisan objects of material culture and trinkets, which some did. Even Geronimo sold bows and arrows that he made at the fair. He claimed that when he went home after the fair, "I had plenty of money—more than I had ever owned before." He and others also earned money for allowing fair visitors to photograph them. Some tribal people were paid to put on performances. One Navajo woman set up a cooking school and was paid to teach fairgoers how to make frybread. Frederick Cummins brought Dakota and Lakota people to the fair as part of his Wild West show. He was a popular employer because, like Buffalo Bill, he paid a good wage to his cast, who desperately needed to earn money.[13]

The Chicago fair opened the doors for Native people to participate in and earn money from such expositions in the United States. The ways that Native people earned money in St. Louis seems to have been more reflective of the ways that this would occur in later fairs. Although Indian people had earned money through such sales in Chicago, the salaries that were paid to some of Putnam's charges seem to have been less available in later years. Artisans in St. Louis were encouraged to make and sell goods at the fair, and they often had items shipped to the fairgrounds at no cost to themselves.

In another example, at the 1915 Panama-California Exposition, Indians were limited in their roles, but nonetheless were able to market their crafts. They were exhibited by the Fred Harvey Company, which had exclusive rights to display them. María and Ramoncita Martínez did well with pottery sales, "but they were tired, lonesome, and homesick." Nonetheless, as Matthew Bokovoy has written, "Show Indians decided how they would portray their culture and heritage to audiences, so long as they appeared to 'play Indian.'"[14] Although the goods they produced were considered reflective of the past, they were actively participating in a cash economy that had become an increasingly important part of their lives.

Indians in Chicago had worked hard to be part of the modern economic system, but they had to face many barriers to achieve success. Though they succeeded in important ways, the same pattern would continue into the future. Indians could only participate in a modern cash economy by portraying their past. Still, they consistently pushed back against this.

The answer to the question implied in the title of this book, to what extent did American Indians participating in the Columbian Exposition receive fair compensation, is of course mixed. Some were well paid, some were ripped off, and most received enough money and food to live on during the fair but not enough to take home a profit. On the fairgrounds, those few Native people who held official jobs, such as Francis Cayou, Tom Deer, and the impostor Antonio Apache received fair compensation for their work and services. For the others who came to be put on display, the experiences varied widely. The Indians whom Buffalo Bill hired were treated better than most; they were part of a well-oiled commercial machine that Cody had developed long before 1893.

Other Native people came under contracts of varying terms. The Native Hawaiian quartet members each earned $50 per month, while the hula dancers and chanters each made $5 per week and supplemented their income with work outside the fair. The dancers, at least according to the recollections of Kini Kapahukulaokamāmalu (Aunt Jennie Wilson) nearly seventy years after the fair ended, came for the adventure as much as for anything. The Penobscots and the Iroquois who came without pay (but sold their crafts for cash) nonetheless seemed to appreciate their time at the fair. They did not take the job for the money. The Kwakwaka'wakw came under the direction of

George Hunt, who was handsomely paid $90 a month and used this work to further both his career and his place in his home community.

Not everyone was satisfied, however. The Navajo who came under the sponsorship of the State of Colorado would have received a decent wage had they not been cheated out of a significant portion of their pay when the state refused to abide by its agreement with them. The Ho Chunk, Potawatomi, and Sioux who came to the Midway with T. R. Roddy apparently came under a contract that reflected their pay in the Wisconsin Dells, but they renegotiated their weekly salaries after they arrived. They no doubt quickly learned that others were paid better than they were.

Chicago was a hotbed of the labor movement in these years; craft unions negotiated pay scales for those who built the fair. Whether or not the larger labor movement played a role in these Native negotiations, the Native people used similar tactics to protest pay and working conditions. The Inuit went to court on more than one occasion and walked off the job to gain better treatment and pay. Amazingly, they succeeded in getting a twelvefold salary increase. The Hawaiian band tried to negotiate a favorable contract in Honolulu and refused to come when they were unable to do so. Clearly, goals and experiences varied to such an extent that there is no simple answer to the question of how equitably they were remunerated.

In comparison with the money spent to develop the ethnology division, the wages received by American Indians for their various contributions must be considered paltry. That does not make it any less meaningful for the individuals or communities that received it, however. Despite the barriers and setbacks, individual Indian experiences were valuable for several reasons. For those already participating in the wage economy, it gave them an opportunity to make a living for a few more months, and in some cases led to further opportunities in the coming months and years. Those just entering the cash economy began to understand its workings, and they began to learn some of the tricks of the trade in terms of negotiating treatment and salaries from some of their peers. They were in the curious position of many Indian people of their era, being both exploited . . . and active agents at the same time.

Appendix

*American Indians and Other Indigenous People
Affiliated with the United States at the Fair*

Collectors (fair attendees also listed under tribe name)

Antonio Apache (impostor)	Collector for Putnam; hired to work with Navajos; worked for Putnam
Terrill Bradby (Pamunkey)	Collected for Mason / Smithsonian
Cornelius C. Cusick (Tuscarora)	Collected in Northeast for Putnam; visited fair
George Hunt (Fort Rupert Kwakwaka'wakw)	Collected for Boas; oversaw Northwest Coast exhibit
Francis LaFlesche (Omaha)	Display with Alice Fletcher on Omaha Sacred Pipes
Joseph Laurent (Abenaki)	Collected for Canadian officials
Odille Morison (Tsimshian)	Collected at Skeena River

Native people at the fair

Affiliation unknown

Jack Blackhawk

Abenaki. *See* Emma Reeves in Iroquois Village

Arawak

Adolphus Daniel	Agricultural Building lecturer, won $5 in swim race

"Aztec"	Individuals not identified

Cherokee

Carrie Blue Jacket	Peace Congress delegate; singer
Rena Blue Jacket	Peace Congress delegate; singer
Ross Blue Jacket	Peace Congress delegate; singer

Chippewa. *See* Ojibwe

Cree	Several Canadian families from Northwest Territories

Creek

Ben Marshall	Stock ranchman, attended fair with sister

Crow

Curley	Met with Rain-in-the-Face in Sitting Bull's cabin (Note: There was also a Curly identified as Sioux)

Haudenosaunee. *See* Iroquois

Ho-Chunk	Arrived June 30; part of group of 61
Blackhawk	Came to watch lacrosse game at Pokagon's invitation
"Young Blackhawk"	Roddy's Indian Village
Sam Blowsnake/Carley	Roddy's Indian Village
Angel Decora	Probably attended fair, stayed in same boarding house as Chauncey Yellow Robe
Frisk Cloud	Roddy's Indian Village
Green Cloud	Roddy's Indian Village
Henry Mike	Roddy's Indian Village
Jerry Red Horn	Roddy's Indian Village
John Smoke	Roddy's Indian Village
Wah-Ka-Cee-Gah	Yellow Thunder? Roddy's Indian Village. Arrow maker
War Eagle	Roddy's Indian Village

Inuit Colony (9 to 12 Families. Age is from *Evelena* passenger list, October 14, 1892)	From Labrador: Forbush: 12 families. Spellings vary greatly from source to source
Reverend Mr. Abile or Apila (38)	Head of family; Esther's father
Helene Abila (36)	Abile's wife, Esther's mother
Esther Abila (later Eneutseak) (15 or 19)	Mother of Nancy; became a businesswoman organizing Eskimo villages
Nancy Helene Columbia Palmer, 3-week-old baby at start of fair	Father unknown (Esther unmarried at time); lived most of life in United States; wrote and acted in films
George Deer (30)	Maggie's husband
Maggie Deer (28)	George's wife
Peter Deer (6 months)	George and Maggie's baby, born in Labrador, died April 18, 1893
Sarah Deer (5)	
Tom or Tommie Deer (25)	Carpenter
Degoudlak or Degoulick Also referred to as Aella Ta-M-Loch or Aelia Taloch (14)	Drowned at fairgrounds; stepson of Tucklevina and Konnegottchock
Miss Easter	May be same as someone with Anglicized name or Francophone name; not on passenger list
Miss Geghatemi	May be same as someone with Anglicized name or Francophone name; not on passenger list
Kam-i-Kameha	A leader; may be same as someone with Anglicized name or Francophone name; not on passenger list
Kaugi Geghatchook, or Kangegatchook (38)	From Kikkertaksoak
Tuklivena, wife of Kangegatchook (45)	Stepparents of Degoulick
Kamialuit Kangegatchook (f) (16)	
Sikipa Kangegatchook (f) (7)	
Kupah or Kooper (40), Pomiuk's stepfather	From Cape Chidley region
Kututicook or Kootookatook or Kuttukittok (38), wife of Kupa	Daughter Evelina born in Chicago

Mollie or Mali Kooper (7)	Little girl, adopted a kitten
Tigujak Kooper (2)	
Evelina Cooper orig. Kotuktooka	One of three babies born at the fair in November 1892
John Lozey or John Lucy or Locy (50)	Same as John Log? Head of family
Katatina Locy (48)	
Hetvick Jula Locy (22)	
Abraha Locy (20)	
Simon Locy (18)	
Jonasik Locy (16) Same as Nallook or Joe?	Drove dog sledge and earned $100
Joseph Locy (42)	
Charlotte Locy (32)	
Tomasi Locy (14)	
Sarah (Sally) Manauk or Manok (30)	
Simon Manauk or Manok (35)	
Maria Manok (14)	
Jakobus Makus Manok (18)	
Sarah Manok (Jr.) (16)	
Peterus Manok (8)	
Abraha Manok (2)	
Columbia Susan Manak	First baby born at fair; died within a week
Peter Meshe or Mesher (22)	Listed as Peter Michaud on passenger list; worked for Buffalo Bill
Peter Pallacier (45)	Fiddle player; sued Daniels in U.S. 9th Circuit Court; head of family
Mary Magdaline Pallacier (17)	
James Palacier	Head of family; same as Jonas?
Mr. Tuktootsina (Jonas Pallister) (56)	
Mary Magdaline Pallacier (18)	
Lucy Pallacier (5)	

Sam Pallacier (20)

John Pallacier (18)

Tom or Thomas Pallacier (same as   Involved in lawsuit
Thomas Jones?) (25)

Esther Pallacier (23)

Susan Pallacier (5)

"Prince" Pomiuk or Pamiuk (15)   Aka Kikkertasoak; became famous at 16

Punniniok, 3-month-old girl

Joe Sugarloaf   Four sons came with him; may be one of
                 the Suglas

James or Jimmie Sugla or
Sugarloaf (50)

Salomie Sugla (f) (43)

Maggie Sugla (18)

Augustinich Sugla (16)

Liza Sugla (6)

Tom Sugla (1½)

Mrs. Tuktootsina (Susie   Later became Mrs. Jonas Pallister
Pallaciker?) (32)

Abraha Tooktootsina (17)

Christopher Columbus Tuktootsina Born at fairgrounds in November 1892

Uksuk (male)   May be same as someone with Anglicized
                name or Francophone name; not on
                passenger list

Yoo-Ka-Lucke   Uncle of Prince Pomiuk; may be same
                as someone with Anglicized name or
                Francophone name; not on passenger list

Mary Dookshoode Annanuck   Wife of Yoo-Ka-Lucke; may be same as
                            someone with Anglicized or Francophone
                            name; not on passenger list

Zacharias (35)   A leader; head of family

Naimi Zacharias (35)

Justina Zacharias (13)

Tapia Zacharias (f) (4)

Iroquois. *See also* **Mohawk lacrosse team**

Dr. P. Johnson	Of Pekin NY, visited August 1893

Iroquois Village (15)

Mrs. Kittie Coates (Oneida)	Basket maker and singer
Deerfoot, Chief Lewis Bennett (Seneca) (65 or 75)	
William Dockstator (Oneida)	With wife and daughter
Emeline Garlow (Tuscarora)	
Chief Luther W. Jack (Tuscarora) (30 or 34)	Came early to help set up village in June; aka Nay-wah-ta-gont or Two Boots Standing Together
Louisa Jack, Luther's wife	Needlework, beadwork, ornamentation; aka Mrs. Louisa Two Boots
John Jacket (Seneca) (85)	Grandson of Red Jacket
Nathaniel Kennedy (Seneca)	Came early to help set up village in June; aka Gai-wah-gwan-ni-yuh or The Whole Truth
Chief Daniel LaFort or Otataho (Onondaga) (70), Firekeeper	"Best Indian linguist in America"
Solomon O'Bail (Seneca) (78)	Aka Owa-No-Oh or "Wise Old Man"
Col. Ely S. Parker (Seneca)	
Miss Emeline Patterson (Mohawk)	
Mrs. Emma Reeves, (Oneida, self-identifies as "Abnaki")	Basket maker and singer
Myron Silverheels (Allegany Seneca)	
Ananias Silverheels (16)	Myron's son
Thomas Webster (Onondaga)	Wampum keeper
Chief Williams (Tuscarora)	

Kwakwaka'wakw

Chicago Jim	
Dōqwăyis, in newspapers: Taquasay, Toquaysa, Toquasa	Chief Wanuk's wife, Fort Rupert

John Drabble	From Nuwitti
Rachel Drabble	John's wife; aka LaLahlewildzemkæ
Hais haxēsaqemē	Man from Koskimo
David Hunt	George's eldest son
George Hunt	$90/month
William Hunt	George's brother, Fort Rupert
King Tom	Tlatlasikwala tribe from Nuwitti
Kroskirass	Son of Chief Wanuk and Dōqwăyis
Malete or Matele	Possibly the fifth woman
MÉ'līd	Hunt's father-in-law, Fort Rupert
Quany	Woman from Koskimo
QlūLelas or Q!wélelas	Tom's brother
Chief Johny Wanuk	Fort Rupert
Whane	Woman from Koskimo

Maya	Coffee exhibit
Lucio Castellanos	Marimba Quartet, Guatemala Building
Pedro Chavez	Marimba Quartet, Guatemala Building
Samuel Chavez	Marimba Quartet, Guatemala Building
Antohn Molina	Marimba Quartet, Guatemala Building
Female coffee servers	

Mohawk lacrosse team	
Big Thunder	
Louis Deer	
John Kanenho	
John Tali Keno	
Tali Keno	Captain
Red Leaf	
Samuel Thompson	
F. Karl Waken	

Native Hawaiians

Nulhama "William" Aeko	One of the second[?] quartet, played ukulele at Volcano
J. M. Bright	Quartet member sailed 7–19
John Edwards	Quartet member sailed 7–19
Keoui Elemeni	One of the second[?] quartet
Dibble K. Eli	Musician brought by Hobron
Annie Grube	Hula dancer
W. B. Jones	Quartet member sailed 7–19
Duke Kahanamoku	Musician brought by Hobron
A. O. K. East Kahualualii	One of the second[?] quartet or two quartets?
Princess Ka'iulani	Did she visit?
Kamuku	Chanter
Joseph K. Kanepuu	Musician brought by Hobron
Kanuku	Chanter at Midway
Kini Kapahukulaokamamalu	Hula dancer
Keoui Maipinepine	One of the second[?] quartet
John Moses	Musician brought by Hobron
Nakai	Hula dancer
William Olepau	Musician brought by Hobron
Pauahi Pinao	Hula dancer

Navajo

Cheeno	Female weaver $25/month
Lucy	Ned Manning's sister $10/month, aka Chiquita
Ned Manning	School boy $10/month
Navajo Jake	Silversmith [Come to Chicago?]
Pesh-lo-ki	Male silversmith $25/month + expenses
Mrs. Walker	Female blanket weaver $25/month
Fourteen who came with Welsh	

Ojibwe

Emily E. Peake	White Earth; came as private secretary to Sybil Carter

Omaha

Francis Cayou	Hired as guard

Oneida. *See also* Iroquois Village

Benjamin Wheelock	Visitor on way home from Carlisle

Onondaga. *See* Iroquois Village

Pamunkey

Terrill Bradby	Visited fair representing tribe; made objects for Smithsonian

Pawnee

A-Te-Ka	Visited grounds before fair opened; wrote to Carlisle School about it
Robert Mathews	Visited fair August 1893, refused work with Buffalo Bill
Samuel Townsend	Visited fair August 1893

Penobscot — From Oldtown, Maine

Charles Daylight	Charles D. Mitchell?
Jessie or Josie Franeway	Josephine Newell?
Newell Lyon	
John Poras or Porus	
Ada Sockbeason	13-year-old daughter of Nick and Katie
Katie Sockbeason	
Nick Sockbeason or Nic Sackbeson	Canoe race
Susan Sockloxis, wife of Joe	
Joe Stoccolette or Joseph Sockbeason	Canoe race

Potawatomi	Arrived June 30 in group of sixty-one
Chief Jack	From Black River Falls, father of Wah-So-Mah-Nee-Gah [Ho Chunk or Potawatomi?]
Simon Pokagon	Visitor
Simon Pokagon's son	Participated in pageant on Chicago Day
Thad Taylor	Participated in pageant on Chicago Day
John Young	Rang bell Chicago Day; Roddy's Indian Village
John Young's wife	Roddy's Indian Village
"Young William"	John Young's son, Roddy's Indian Village
Wah-So-Mah-Nee-Gah	6-year-old boy, Roddy's Indian Village

Seneca. *See* **Iroquois Village**	

Sioux. *See also* **Buffalo Bill**	Many arrived June 30 in Roddy's group of sixty-one
Black Bull	Sitting Bull's cabin
Black Tomahawk	From Northern Cheyenne on Missouri River SD [Cheyenne River?]
Chasing Fly	Sitting Bull's cabin
Cotton Wood	Sitting Bull's cabin
Curly	Note: There was also a Curley identified as Crow
Charles Eastman	Wrote paper on "Sioux Mythology" for International Folk-Lore Congress, July 18
Flat Iron	Attended opening ceremonies
Grey Eagle	Sitting Bull's cabin
Mary Hairy-Chin	Midway Village
Kills Him Twice	
Lone Dog	Midway village
Prairie Chicken	Sitting Bull's cabin
Pretty Face (Sitting Bull's niece)	Sitting Bull's cabin; interpreter and artisan

Pretty Face's husband	Sitting Bull's cabin. Note: May be one of the men listed in this section.
Rain-in-the-Face	On display in Sitting Bull's cabin
"Red Cloud"	Young Native man claiming to be "the famous Sioux of Western notoriety" in Midway Village
War Bonnet	Sitting Bull's cabin

Tuscarora. *See also* Iroquois Village

| Cornelius Cusick | Visited fair with wife |

| **Winnebago.** *See* Ho-Chunk | Arrived June 30; part of group of sixty-one |

Students from Canada

| Gray Nuns NW Territories (10 students) | |

Students from the United States

Carlisle Indian Industrial School	**305 boys for 1892 opening ceremonies**
Attended in 1893 unless otherwise noted	450 students 1893: 325 boys, 125 girls; boys paid $13 to attend; girls generally are not in the record
Band ca. 30	
Dennison Wheelock (Oneida) bandmaster	
Quincy Adams (Assiniboine)	$13; Fort Peck; became a farmer in Poplar
Joseph American Horse (Sioux)	$13; son of American Horse
Sarah Archiquette (Oneida)	Work she made was displayed in Carlisle exhibit with photograph of her, but she did not attend
Ralph Armstrong (Nez Perce)	$13
Anthony Austin (Piegan)	1892; son of Bear Coat
Star Bad Boy (Chippewa)	1892; from White Earth
Victor S. Bear (Gros Ventre)	$13 Son of Spotted Bear

Charles Bictowsewah (Apache)	$13
Allan Black Chief (Seneca)	$13; son of Charlie Black Chief
Rosa Bourassa (Chippewa)	From Michigan, visited on her own in June 1893; graduated 1890. Work she made displayed in Carlisle exhibit
Julius Brown (Chippewa)	Visited fair on his own in July 1893, performed with Lincoln School musicians
Thomas Buchanan (Nebraska Winnebago)	$13 Shot in Spanish-American war; pensioner 1910
Nellie Carey (Apache)	Slippers she made were displayed in Carlisle exhibit with photograph of her, but she did not attend. Daughter of Cochise
Louis Caswell (Chippewa)	1892; From White Earth Agency, later moved to Red Lake
Clement Ceanilizay (Apache)	$13
Ota or Otto Chief Eagle (Sioux)	1892
Peter Chief Eagle (Sioux)	$13; Pine Ridge; became a doctor's interpreter for three years; later special police
Cloud Bird (Assiniboin)	$13; Fort Peck; became a rancher; originally from Frazer; son of Long Crane
Jacob Cobmosa	1892
Solomon Collins (Chippewa)	1892; from Mount Pleasant
Sylvania Cooper (Crow)	Clothing she made was displayed in Carlisle exhibit with photograph of her, but she did not attend
Peter Cornelius (Oneida)	Probably went to Chicago 1892
Scott Crane (Ottawa)	$13; arrived at Carlisle from Custer MI November 6 1891
William Crane (Ottawa)	$13; arrived at Carlisle from Custer MI November 6 1891
Susie Davenport (Chippewa)	Work she made was displayed in Carlisle exhibit with photograph of her, but she did not attend
Charles Dickens (San Carlos Apache)	$13; became policeman at San Carlos

Peter Dillon (Sioux)	$13; LaCreek SD; became an interpreter and farmer
Benjamin Doxtater (Oneida)	$13; Wisconsin; became a farmer in DePere
Charles English (Nebraska Winnebago)	$13; became a farmer
Eustace Esapoyhet (Comanche)	Went in 1892, then went directly to work as a tailor at Albuquerque Indian School
Humphrey Escharzay or Eshazzay (Apache)	$13
Mark Evarts (Pawnee)	1892; arrived from Indian Territory and went immediately to Chicago with group
George Fisher (Chippewa)	$13; son of Levi Fisher
Bedford Forrest (Assiniboine)	$13; Fort Peck; became a police officer, farmer, and unemployed; son of Afraid of a Bear
Nellie Fremont (Omaha)	Dress she made was displayed in Carlisle exhibit with photograph of her, but she did not attend
Chapo Geronimo (Apache)	$13; son of Geronimo
Thomas Guardipee (Piegan)	$13; became a stockraiser
Ben Harrison/Mon-kah-sah (Osage)	$13
Gilmore L. Hawk/Daheen (Apache)	$13; Kiowa, Comanche, and Wichita Agency
Timothy Henry (Tuscarora)	1892; graduated 1896
Presley Houk	$13
Peter Howe (Assiniboine)	$13; died of TB at Carlisle 1896; son of Checker
Frank Hudson (Pueblo)	$13; Son of Yo I ta su eh
Isaac John (Oneida)	$13
Eva Johnson (Wyandotte)	Visited fair for a week in August 1893, then returned to Indian Territory; graduated 1889
Ida Johnson (Wyandotte)	Visited fair for a week in August 1893, then returned to Indian Territory

Peter Jordan (Oneida)	$13; Wisconsin
Morgan Kahkanethla (San Carlos Apache)	$13; became a teamster
Ka-wa-a-che (Queres Pueblo)	$13
Bertrand Kennerly (Piegan)	$13
Perry Kennerly (Piegan)	$13; later worked in Helena law office; jailed for bootlegging
William Leighton (Crow)	1892; toured Chicago and *Herald* office; graduated 1896
Lewis Levering (Omaha)	May not have made the trip; paid fee, reimbursed, left school October 8, 1893
Laura Long (Wyandotte)	Work she made was displayed in Carlisle exhibit with photograph of her, but she did not attend
Alexander Manabove/Zisk Kalasaka (Sioux)	$13; Pine Ridge; became a rancher
Gail Marko (m) (Apache)	$13
Edward Marsden (Metlakatla)	Probably went to Chicago 1892
George A. Martin (Chippewa)	$13
Charles Mason (Chippewa)	$13; White Earth
Thomas Metoxen (Oneida)	1892; musical performer, went straight home from Chicago
Daniel Morrison (Chippewa)	$13; from La Pointe; became an Indian Service farmer
John G. Morrison (Ojibwe, White Earth)	1892
Hiram Moses/Te-a-yeh-oh (Seneca)	$13; from Tonawanda; became a farmer and state highway worker
Wesson Murdock (Assiniboine)	$13; Fort Peck; became a rancher
Vincent Natalsih/Nah-tail-eh (San Carlos Apache)	$13; became a civil engineer, lived in New York City
Ollie Nicholas (Assiniboine)	$13; son of Swings His Thigh Low
Siceni Nori (Laguna)	$13; also attended 1892
Knox Nosthin (Apache)	$13
Henry Old Eagle (Sioux)	$13; son of Old Eagle

Enos Pego (Ottawa and/or Chippewa)	$13; from Mt. Pleasant; became a farmer
James W. Perry (Assiniboine)	$13; Fort Peck; worked in Indian Service until accident
Ernest Peters (Chippewa)	$13
William Petoskey (Chippewa)	1892; toured Chicago and *Herald* office; from Petoskey MI
Purcell Powlas (Oneida)	$13; son of John Powlas
Delia Randall (Bannock)	Dress she made was displayed in Carlisle exhibit with photograph of her, but she did not attend
Andrew Red Duck (Nez Perce)	$13; became a farmer in Idaho
Elmore Red Eyes (Sioux)	$13; from Pine Ridge; Later worked for agency in Kyle SD; later changed name to Elmore Bennett
Buck Red Kettle (Sioux)	$13
John Sanborn (Gros Ventre)	$13; Fort Belknap; Later in state mental hospital in Warm Springs MT
Caleb Sickles (Oneida)	$13; son of Martin Sickles
Elizabeth Sickles (Oneida)	Work she made was displayed in Carlisle exhibit with photograph of her, but she did not attend
Taylor Smith (Oneida)	$13; Wisconsin; became a farmer
Hugh Sowc-a	1892
Johnson Spencer (Nez Perce)	$13; became a freighter and farmer in Idaho
Thomas Stewart (Crow)	$13; later worked as allotting agent 3 years, then became a farmer
Lee Tall Chief (Seneca)	Probably went to Chicago 1892
Paul Teenabikizen (Apache)	$13
Frank Tewery	1892
Charles Thompson (Assiniboine?)	$13; later owned land near Poplar MT?
Jennie Thunder Bull (Sioux)	Work she made was displayed in Carlisle exhibit with photograph of her, but she did not attend
Shield Thunder Bull (Sioux)	$13; Pine Ridge; became a forest ranger

Daniel Varnes	$13
Isaac Webster (Oneida)	$13; Wisconsin; attended Hampton, worked for Indian Service as teacher and farmer
Daniel Osage West/O-pah-sen-tsa-wi (Osage)	$13
Fred Wilson (Chippewa)	Probably went to Chicago 1892
Samuel Wilson (Caddo)	$13; Left Carlisle October 19, 1893
Reuben Wolfe (Omaha)	1892, musical performer, went straight home after Chicago; became a warehouse clerk at Genoa, joined Genoa band, attended with Genoa in 1893
Charles Yarlot (Crow)	$13; became a carpenter on ditch gang
Chauncey Yellow Robe (Sioux)	Docent in Carlisle exhibit; attended 1892 opening; son of Yellow Robe
John Yellow Robe (Sioux)	$13; son of Yellow Robe

Genoa Indian Industrial School

| Joseph B. Harris (Gros Ventre) | Band member |
| Reuben Wolfe (Omaha) | Band member; see Carlisle listing above |

Haskell Institute (23 tribes represented)

Girls

Elizabeth Alexis

Nannie Block

August Cedar

Jerdie Faber

Belle Gives-Water

Julia Hornback (Sioux)

Ella Koshiway

Eliza Macoonse

Josie Pokagon

Geneva Roberts

Rosa Romero

Nannie Sheaku

Katie Viex

Catherine Walker

Gertie Washington

Boys

Robert D. Argosa

John Block

Henry Bozielle

Gus Bruninger

Frank Eagle

Henry Inkanish

Moses King

John Mandoka

Ernest Oshkosh (Menominee)

William Pollock (Pawnee)   Artist

George Primeaux

Frank Rice

George Shawnee

David Slussman

Andrew Tousey

Haskell band members

Joe Abner

Moses Allen

George Choteau

Henry Cornelius

Nic Herr

George Hicks

Thomas King

Harvey Propeck

John Prophet

Peter Rouillard

Louis Shanborn

Isaac Sidone

George Walker

Charley Wesaw

James Williams

Moses Williams

Lincoln Institute

David Back (Mohawk)	Performed music
Annie Beablien	Performed music
Jane Eyre (Pawnee)	Performed music
Harold Gay Bear (Sioux)	Performed music
Lucy Gordon (Sioux)	Performed music
Nettie Hansell (Modoc)	Performed music
Ida McCabe	Performed music
Dinah Philbrick (Sioux)	Performed music
Philip Robideaux (Sioux)	Performed music

Buffalo Bill Show (all Lakota from Pine Ridge), listed by contract number

1. Ellis Standing Bear	$25/month
2. Hawk Ring	$25
3. Yellow Elk	$25
4. Jealous	$25
5. Lone Bear	$35
6. Hard to Hit	$25
7. Plenty Horses	$25
8. Not Afraid	$25
9. Hard Heart	$25

10. Thunder Horse $25

11. Kills Looking $25

12. Lone Bull $25

13. Pipe on Head $25

14. Easy to Hit $25

15. Comes for Him $25

16. Shows His Tracks $25

17. Little Crow $25

18. Charges Alone $25

19. American Horse Jr. $25

20. Charger $25

21. Dreaming Bear $25

22. Red Star $25

23. Black Man $25

24. Last Horse, Saddle Blanket, and Red Feet $50

25. High Crow $25

26. Two Elks $25

27. Charge at the Enemy $25

28. Little Cloud $25

29. Wounded Horse $25

30. Bad Hair $25

31. White Bull $25

32. Leon White Bird $25

33. Kills Across $25

34. Hand $25

35. Clown $25

36. Wooden Leg $25

37. Bear Pipe $25

38. Chief Man $25

39. Bear Feathers $25

40. Eagle Bear $25

41. Parts His Hair	$25
42. His Roan Horse	$25
43. Warrior	$25
44. White Wolf	$25
45. Black Eagle	$25
46. His Horse Wounded	$25
47. Two Eagle	$25
48. Red Elk	$25
49. Medicine Horse	$25
50. Flatting Iron	$25
51. Painting Horse	$25
52. Red Nest	$25
53. Shot in the Eye	$25
54. Good Voice Elk	$25
55. Little Wolf	$35
56. George Standing Bear	$35
57. Black Bear	$25
58. White Cow Chief	$25
59. High Bear	$35
60. No Neck	$75
61. Rocky Bear	$75
62. Jack Red Cloud	$75
63. Red Plume	$10
64. Charges Enemy	$10
65. Looks Back	$10
66. Night Woman	$10
67. Dog Woman	$10
68. Roan Woman (wife of Plenty Horse)	$10
69. Mrs. No Neck & son Johnnie Burke No Neck	$15
70. John Shangreau	$60

Mentioned in newspaper articles but without contracts

Lone Wolf

Painted Horse

Made money at home or loaned materials from home before the fair. *See also* Collectors

Blackfoot (Canada)

Mrs. Old Sun	Lodge
Crowfoot's daughter	Porcupine dress

Maliseet	May have loaned or sold objects
Gabriel Alquin	His mother's grinding stone
Agathe Athanase of Riviere du Loup Quebec	Victorian style basket
Isidore Augustine	Game (purchased)
Frank Francis of Upper Andover NB	Coat, arrowheads, stone implement
Chief Frank Narris	Coat, 150 years old
Frank Nockgut	Coat, stone pipe
Thomas Thomas of Indian Village NB	100-year-old jewelry box

Maya (Copan)	These individuals may be Mayan or mixed-blood, not specifically identified as such in records
Alejandro Dias	Trabajodor at Copan ruins 1892
Eulogio Esquibel	Trabajodor at Copan ruins 1892
Bruno Insmán	Trabajodor at Copan ruins 1892
Feuso Linares	Trabajodor at Copan ruins 1892
Benancia Mendez	Trabajodor at Copan ruins 1892
Francisca Montenegra	Tortilla maker at Copan 1892
Visente Ramirez	Trabajodor at Copan ruins 1892
Juana	Cook at Copan ruins 1891

| Felipa | Tortilla maker at Copan 1891 |
| Josefina | Tortilla maker at Copan 1892 |

Micmac (Nova Scotia)

Mrs. Bealeu	Child's moccasins
Katie Francis	Basket
Susie Francis	Basket cushion
Mrs. John Hammond	Pair men's socks
John Jeremy	Fly hooks
Maggie Jeremy	Basket
Alec Michael	Moose call and decorated perfume bottle
Mrs. Alec Michael	Basket
Elizabeth Michael	Basket
Harnet [Hamet?] Paul	Basket
Mrs. Penny	Mittens

Piegan (Montana)

| Sharp | Painted steer robe |

Sioux

| Standing Bear (Henry Mato Najin) | From Rosebud; interpreter for Emma Sickels |

Sources: This list was developed using a broad variety of sources. Paige Raibmon, in writing about the non-Indian organizers and the Kwakwaka'wakw participants in the fair, wrote the following, which reflects the process relating to all of the Indian and indigenous participants except some of the schoolchildren, the Inuits who were listed in the *Evelena* passenger list, and the performers who came with Buffalo Bill, for whom he was required to file contracts with the Office of Indian Affairs: "Of the troupe's various promoters and detractors, including Boas, Putnam, Hall, and the Indian Affairs officials, none individualized the 'live exhibits' by keeping a list of their names. Consequently, the identities of the troupe's members can only be gathered piecemeal from scattered sources" (Raibmon, "Theatres of Contact," 176).

Names were gleaned from the following collections and sources: Ancestry.com; Grant Arndt (personal correspondence); Bates, "The Children of the Plaisance"; *Boston Journal*; Browman and Williams, *Anthropology at Harvard*; Canadian Government Expositions WCE Department of Agriculture Letterbooks, RG 72, LAC; Carlisle Indian School Digital Resource Center; Central American Expedition Records, PMA; *Chicago Tribune*; Dickinson College Carlisle Indian School Digital Resource Center; Frederic Ward Putnam Papers, HUA; *Harper's*; Hauptman, *Between Two Fires*; *Hawaiian Star*; *Indian*

Helper; *Inter Ocean* (Chicago); James Wojtowicz Collections, 1880–1929, MS 327, Buffalo Bill Center of the West; Letters Received, entry 91, RG 75 NARA-DC; *Midway Types*; *New Orleans Democrat Times*; New York State Documents; Peabody Museum at Harvard University; Pratt, *Battlefield and Classroom*; Raibmon, *Authentic Indians*; Records of the Carlisle Indian Industrial School RG 75, NARA-DC; *Rock Island Daily Argus*; Rohner, *The Ethnography of Franz Boas*; *Scientific American*; *Springfield Republican*; Stephens, "Eskimo Joe"; *St. Nicholas*; Tranquada and King, *The 'Ukulele*; Troutman, "'Indian Blues'"; Ulrich, *The Age of Homespun*; *Vindicator*; William F. Cody Collection, MS 006, Buffalo Bill Center of the West; *Youth Companion*; Zerbe, *Pins*; Zwick, *Inuit Entertainers*.

Notes

Abbreviations

ACP	Appointments, Commissions and Personal Branch Document File
APS	American Philosophical Society
ARCIA	*Annual Report of the Commissioner of Indian Affairs*
BAE	Bureau of American Ethnology
BMA	Bishop Museum Archives
BWFM	Board of World's Fair Managers (Minnesota)
CAE	Central American Expedition
CAM	Council of Administration Minutes
CHMRC	Chicago History Museum Records Center
CMD-LS	Correspondence Miscellaneous Division, Letters Sent
CPL-HWLCSC	Chicago Public Library, Harold Washington Library Center Special Collections
DIA	Department of Indian Affairs (Canada)
FBPP-APS	Franz Boas Professional Papers, American Philosophical Society
FMNH	Field Museum of Natural History
FWP	Frederic Ward Putnam
HSA	Hawaii State Archives
HUA	Harvard University Archives
LAC	Library and Archives Canada
LR	Letters Received
MHSL	Minnesota Historical Society Library
MRL-BBCW	McCracken Research Library, Buffalo Bill Center of the West
NAA-SI	National Anthropological Archives, Smithsonian Institution

NARA-CPM	National Archives and Records Administration, College Park, Maryland
NARA-GLB	National Archives and Records Administration, Great Lakes Branch (Chicago)
NARA-DC	National Archives and Records Administration, Washington DC
PMA	Peabody Museum of Archaeology and Ethnology Archives, Harvard University
RG	Record Group
SIA	Smithsonian Institution Archives
TNL	The Newberry Library
UCLSCRC	University of Chicago Library Special Collections Research Center
WCE	World's Columbian Exposition
WCEEC	World's Columbian Exposition Ephemera Collection

Introduction

1. Since anthropologist Patrick Wolfe's work caused academics to consider the role of settler societies in advancing the colonial enterprise, anthropologists, historians, and Indigenous studies scholars have increasingly analyzed colonial states from the multiple perspectives of the settler, the colonial, and the indigenous impacts in shaping modern societies. See *Settler Colonialism* and "Settler Colonialism."
2. Baker, *Anthropology and the Racial Politics of Culture*, 98.
3. Rand, *Kiowa Humanity*, 7.
4. Meyer and Royer, *Selling the Indian*, xii.
5. Warren, *Buffalo Bill's America*, 194.
6. Viola, *Diplomats in Buckskins*; Thrush, *Indigenous London*.
7. Hunt, *Writing History*, 70.
8. Johnson, "Performing Ethnicity," 224.
9. See appendix, "American Indians and Other Indigenous People Affiliated with the United States at the Fair." Some 16,000 people worked at the fair "at any one time," and approximately 25,000 total people worked either in constructing or running the fair. Silkenat, "Workers in the White City," 268–69.
10. The OIA was also variously known as the Indian Service, the Indian Bureau, and the Indian Department before it was officially named the Bureau of Indian Affairs in the 1940s.
11. Harmon, *Rich Indians*; Bauer, *We Were All Like Migrant Workers Here*; Rand, *Kiowa Humanity*; Warren, "Wage Work in the Sacred Circle"; Raibmon, *Authentic Indians*. See also Hosmer and O'Neill, eds., *Native Pathways*; Hosmer, *American Indians in the Marketplace*.

12. Raibmon, *Authentic Indians*, 34–73; Zwick, *Indian Entertainers*, 12–25.

13. Rydell, *All the World's a Fair*, 2.

14. Bancroft, *Book of the Fair*, 5:957, cited 27,529,400 as the official attendance. This number includes each individual entrance; some people attended more than one day and thus were counted more than once.

15. Gilbert, *Whose Fair?* 1; Rydell, *All the World's a Fair*, 2–3.

16. Johnson, *A History of the World's Columbian Exposition*, 1:10.

17. Sandburg, "Chicago," in *Chicago Poems*, 4.

18. Algren, *Chicago*.

19. *Dedicatory and Opening Ceremonies*, 55, 259.

20. Smith, *The Plan of Chicago*, 19.

21. Shepp and Shepp, *Shepp's World's Fair Photographed*, 8.

22. Hoffenberg, *An Empire on Display*, xiv–xv, 14.

23. Rydell, *All the World's a Fair*, 2–5.

24. Trujillo, "The Commodification of Hispano Culture," 31. Also briefly discussed in Martinez, "Travels and Image Making in the Land of Enchantment," 6–7.

25. Phillips, *Trading Identities*, 4.

26. Rand, *Kiowa Humanity*, 126–50.

27. Rand, *Kiowa Humanity*, 134–38.

28. Rasenberger, *High Steel*, 132–73; Von Baeyer, "Walking Tall," 69–70.

29. Bauer, *We Were All Like Migrant Workers Here*, 8.

30. Warren, "Wage Work in the Sacred Circle," 156. See Warren, *God's Red Son*, for an eye-opening new interpretation of the Ghost Dance religion.

31. Baker, *Anthropology and the Racial Politics of Culture*, 17.

32. Mooney to Gatschet, 14 July 1891, folder Mooney, James 1891, box 109, Bureau of American Ethnology (BAE) Letters Received (LR) 1888–1906, National Anthropological Archives, Smithsonian Institution (NAA-SI).

33. White, *Railroaded*, xxi, xxiv.

34. Moses, "Indians on the Midway," 218.

1. Fair Representation?

1. Smith, *The Plan of Chicago*, 19.

2. Chicago Day, 9 October, drew the largest crowd at 716,881, more than double the attendance of any other day at the fair. Cameron, *History of the World's Columbian Exposition*, 343.

3. See, for example, Fogelson, "The Red Man in the White City"; Jacknis, "Northwest Coast Indian Culture"; Rydell, *All the World's a Fair*, 38–71; Moses, "Indians on the Midway"; LaPier and Beck, *City Indian*, chap. 2.

4. Campbell, *Campbell's Illustrated History*, 1:291.

5. Hulst, *Indian Sketches*, 93–95; Winslow, *Indians of the Chicago Region*, 12–13; Pokagon, "The Red Man's Greeting."

6. For a more complete description of this, see LaPier and Beck, *City Indian*, 25–29.

7. Rountree, *Pocahontas's People*, 209–10; Hauptman, *Between Two Fires*, 75; "Pamunkey Indians and the World's Fair," letter to editor from Terrill Bradley [*sic*], 3 August [1893], newspaper not identified, box 2, HUG 1717.15, Papers of Frederic Ward Putnam, Harvard University Archives (hereafter FWP Papers HUA).

8. "Pamunkey Indians and the World's Fair"; "Powhatan and Pocahontas," *Indian Chieftain*, Vinita Indian Territory, 20 July 1893, 2; "The Pamunkey Indians," *Alexandria Gazette*, 7 July 1893, 2; "To Prevent Extinction, Pamunkies of Virginia Will Invite Other Indians to Their Reserve," *Arizona Republican*, 14 July 1893, 1; "Chief Bradley [*sic*] Coming West, Special Mission to the Fair of a Leading Pamunkey Indian," *Chicago Tribune*, 17 July 1893, 2; *Progress* (Shreveport LA), 29 July 1893, 3, reprinted in *San Saba County News*, 4 August 1893, 3, and partially reprinted in *Iowa Postal Card*, 4 August 1893, 6.

9. Rountree, *Pocahontas's People*, 215.

10. Rountree, *Pocahontas's People*, 210–12.

11. McNenly, *Native Performers in Wild West Shows*, 82.

12. Standing Bear to Morgan, 15 January 1891, folder s(2) E. Sickels, box 33, HUG 1717.2.12, FWP Papers HUA.

13. A-Te-Ka, "A-Te-Ka's Revery, Buffalo Bill's Wild West Show at the World's Fair, a Disgrace to the Nation," *Indian Helper* 8, no. 24 (3 March 1893): 1, 4.

14. Honoré J. Jaxon, secretary of the Metis National Council, Mato Nazin Cinca (Henry Standing Bear), representative of the Dakotah Chiefs at Pine Ridge, and Manuel S. Molano, South American secretary on the Ind. Rec. Com. to Putnam, 15 February 1892, folder J, box 32, HUG 1717.2.12, FWP Papers HUA.

15. "Miss Sickle's [*sic*] Statement Discredited," *Decatur Daily Republican*, 4 November 1892, 1. Sickels also wrote to the Indian Rights Association demanding action. Their response was to excoriate Wild West shows as inimical to "civilization and citizenship" and discuss the policy actions they had already taken. Sickels to Welsh, 24 September 1893, reel 10; Welsh to Sickels, 15 September 1893, Letterpress 9:991–92, reel 72, both in *Indian Rights Association Papers*.

16. Director General Davis to Edwin Willits, 18 August 1891, LR 1891:30682; Morgan to Davis, 6 June 1892, vol. 7, p. 2:73, Correspondence Miscellaneous Division (CMD), Letters Sent (LS) 1870–1908,; both in RG 75, NARA-DC.

17. Daniel Dorchester, Superintendent of Indian Schools, Redfield SD to Commissioner of Indian Affairs, 6 July 1891, enclosing petition from Santee Sioux Indians, LR 1891:24311; S. Draper, attorney, to Senator Charles Manderson, 22 February 1892, LR 1892:12255; newspaper article, "The Santee Indian Band, a Musician's Estimate of the Only Pure American Banh [*sic*] in the World," n.d. (ca. 1888?), reporting on a letter to the Lancaster PA *New Era*; "The Santee Band," *Sioux City Journal*, 6 October 1888. Both in LR 1892:12255; all in RG 75, NARA-DC.

18. Osage Council authorization of $1,800 to support children from the Osage Boarding School to attend the world's fair, 4 October 1893, LR 1893:36996, RG 75, NARA-DC.

19. Mrs. Emma Reeves to Sir, 24 August 1891, LR 1891:31228, RG 75, NARA-DC.

20. "Report on the New York Indian Exhibit," by Reverend John W. Sanborn, director, *Documents of the Senate of the State of New York*, 500.

21. Bokovoy, *The San Diego World's Fairs*, 117.

22. "Before Colon Came, Primitive Life among the North American Indians," *Chicago Inter Ocean*, 9 July 1893, 20. The Penobscots sent a representative to the Maine legislature, with a mid-twentieth-century hiatus, until 2015 when the tribe discontinued the practice. Kevin Miller, "Tribal Representatives Withdraw from Maine Legislature as Rift with State Grows," *Portland Press Herald*, 26 May 2015.

23. The Kwakwaka'wakw were referred to in the press and documents in a variety of ways, Kwakiutl, Quackahls, and North West Coast Indians among them. I am following current literature in using Kwakwaka'wakw. For a discussion of this, see Raibmon, "Theatres of Contact," 157n1.

24. "Simple as Children, Indians from British Columbia Arrive at Jackson Park," *Chicago Times*, 16 April 1893, box 1, HUG 1717.15, FWP Papers HUA.

25. "Strange Races of Primitive Men, Professor Putnam's Exhibit of Ethnology That Includes Red People Living in a State of Nature," *New York Herald*, 30 April 1893, box 1, HUG 1717.15, FWP Papers HUA; "Famous Indians Arrive," *Chicago Inter Ocean*, 29 June 1893, 7.

26. Philip C. Garrett to Morgan, 26 May 1891, LR 1891:19167, RG 75, NARA-DC.

27. Pratt to Franklin K. Lane, secretary of the interior, 21 May 1913, in Larner, *Papers of Carlos Montezuma*, reel 3. Also quoted in LaPier and Beck, *City Indian*, 22.

28. "To Honor New York: Sons and Daughters of Empire State Have a Banquet," *Chicago Tribune*, 1 February 1893, 6.

29. *Photographs of the World's Fair*, 347.

30. Putnam to Antonio, an Apache, 13 May 1892, folder A, box 31, HUG 1717.2.12, FWP Papers HUA.

31. Putnam to Commissioner of Indian Affairs D. M. Browning, 16 May 1893, folder World's Columbian Exposition, Indians, etc., box 34, HUG 1717.2.13, FWP Papers HUA.

32. "Will Go to the World's Fair," *Philadelphia Press*, 6 April 1893, box 1, HUG 1717.15, FWP Papers HUA.

33. Putnam referred to *prehistoric*, a term coined in 1851 in studies of Scotland, as "that most useful word." Putnam, "A Problem in American Anthropology," 227.

34. Holmes, "The World's Fair Congress of Anthropology."

35. Otis T. Mason, "Report on the Department of Ethnology in the U.S. National Museum, 1891," folder Dept. of Ethnology Annual Report 1890–91, box 3, Department of Ethnology Annual Reports 1881 to 1894–1895, SIA RU000158, Smithsonian Institution Archives (SIA).

36. Mason, "Report on the Department of Ethnology in the U.S. National Museum, 1892," folder 1891–92, box 3, Department of Ethnology Annual Reports 1881 to 1894–1895, SIA RU000158, SIA. For a list of the eighty Smithsonian display sets, some with more than one individual featured, and including tribe along with descriptions of clothing and objects in the displays, see C. Bergmann, "List of Figures and Costumes," MS 7217, NAA-SI.

37. Jacknis, "Northwest Coast Indian Culture," 95–96.

38. See #56 Sioux Indian on Horse, #61 Sioux Woman on Horse, #58 Navajo Weaver, #72 Navajo Spinner, #76 Navajo Belt Weaver, all in C. Bergmann, "List of Figures and Costumes," MS 7217, NAA-SI

39. However, the two exhibits were not as close together as Morgan had initially hoped. Moses, "Indians on the Midway," 213–14.

40. Morgan to Supt. Indian School, 11 February 1893, vol. 8, part 1, 387, CMD-LS, 1870–1908, RG 75, NARA-DC.

41. Morgan to Secretary of the Interior, 10 February 1892, folder February 10, 1892, Letters Received, RG 48, NARA–College Park MD (CPM).

42. Moses, "Indians on the Midway," 210–12; Mary E. Chase diary entry, 27 May 1893, Newberry Library; "Personal Reminiscences: 'Vacation Days,'" folder 8, box 2, World's Columbian Exposition Ephemera Collection (WCEEC), Chicago Public Library, Harold Washington Library Center Special Collections (CPL-HWLCSC).

43. *Dedicatory and Opening Ceremonies*, 246.

44. Minutes of 12 September 1893, Council of Administration Minutes (CAM), vol. 50, World's Columbian Exposition (WCE) records, Chicago History Museum Research Center (CHMRC).

45. Baker, *Anthropology and the Racial Politics of Culture*, 101–2; Mary E. Chase diary entry, 30 May 1893, Newberry Library. Frederick Douglass, however, reportedly said, "I have visited at two different times

the exhibit here of the Carlisle School and am greatly pleased with it." *Indian Helper* 8, no. 44 (21 July 1893): 2; "Indian Girls' Work," *Chicago Tribune*, 26 April 1893, in Item 1: Business–Buffalo Bill's Wild West–Scrapbooks (Chicago, Illinois), 1893, box 26 Oversize (hereafter Buffalo Bill Scrapbook), William F. Cody Collection MS 006, McCracken Research Library, Buffalo Bill Center of the West (MRL-BBCW) (available online in pdf format).

46. Dorsey, "Man and His Works."

47. "Interior Department Exhibit," *World's Columbian Exposition Illustrated* 2, no. 12 (February 1893): 273.

48. Warren, *Buffalo Bill's America*; Carter, *Buffalo Bill Cody*; Deloria, "The Indians"; Moses, "Indians on the Midway"; Maddra, "American Indians in Buffalo Bill's Wild West"; McNenly, *Native Performers in Wild West Shows*; Russell, *The Lives and Legends of Buffalo Bill*; Sell and Weybright; *Buffalo Bill and the Wild West*; and Yost, *Buffalo Bill* are just some examples.

49. Moses, "Indians on the Midway," 206–7; "Personal Reminiscences: 'Vacation Days,'" folder 8, box 2, WCEEC, CPL-HWLCSC.

50. LaPier and Beck, *City Indian*, 1–2.

51. Rydell, *All the World's a Fair*, 97.

52. See, for example, *World's Fair Puck*, 10 July 1893, no. 10, back page; Courtship, 4 September 1893, no. 18, back page; cartoon of "Zulu" and little girl, 16 October, no. 24, 278; "Puck's Au Revoir," 30 October 1893, no. 26, 306–7.

53. The Winnebago people were divided by U.S. policy in the nineteenth century when many tribal members were removed to Nebraska from their home in Wisconsin. In the late twentieth century, the Wisconsin tribe renamed itself Ho-Chunk. Those who worked the Midway were from Wisconsin. It is not clear from the records whether the Sioux people in this exhibit were Dakota, Lakota, or both.

54. Cameron, *The World's Fair*, 647.

55. Hawthorne, *Humors of the Fair*, 57–58.

56. Bancroft, *Book of the Fair*, 5:881.

57. *Photographs of the World's Fair*, 347.

58. Minutes of 24 June 1893, CAM, vol. 48, WCE records CHMRC.

59. Calculated from numbers provided in "Monthly Report," 31 October 1893, Newberry Library.

60. Minutes of 4 August 1893, CAM, vol. 49, WCE records CHMRC.

61. See, for example, numerous issues of *World's Fair Puck*; Hawthorne, *Humors of the Fair*, 138–99; *Midway Types*. The Kingdom of Dahomey is now the Republic of Benin.

62. Captain Jack Crawford, "Captain Jack at the Fair," *Chicago Tribune*, 10 September 1893, 34.

63. *World's Fair Puck* illustration, 21 August 1893, 186–87.

2. Evolution of the American Indian Displays

1. Parezo and Fowler, *Anthropology Goes to the Fair*, 5–7.
2. Tozzer, *Biographical Memoir of Frederic Ward Putnam*, 125.
3. Baker identifies Brinton as the first university anthropology professor after his appointment at University of Pennsylvania in 1886. Baker, *Anthropology and the Racial Politics of Culture*, 129. At the time of the fair the Peabody Museum, where Putnam was appointed as professor, was still quasi-independent; he officially became a "full member of the faculty of Harvard College" in 1897 when the Peabody merged with Harvard. Browman and Williams, *Anthropology at Harvard*, 188.
4. Freed, *Anthropology Unmasked*, 121.
5. Hinsley and Wilcox, *Coming of Age in Chicago*.
6. Fogelson, "The Red Man in the White City," 75.
7. Morgan to Secretary of the Interior, 10 February 1892, vol. 7, 1:32–34, CMD-LS, RG 75, NARA-DC.
8. January 1892 F. W. Putnam Report to the Director General, folder World's Columbian Exposition Monthly Reports to Director General January–June 1892, box 35; Transcript of meeting between Commissioner T. J. Morgan, Putnam, and Alice Fletcher, 30 January 1892, folder World's Columbian Exposition, Indians etc., box 34; both in HUG 1717.2.13, FWP Papers HUA.
9. Putnam letters, 30 January 1892 and 15 February 1892, folder 1891–1900 P, box 11, HUG 1717.2.1, FWP Papers HUA. Emphasis in original.
10. Browman and Williams, *Anthropology at Harvard*, 234; Gilbert, *Perfect Cities*, 87.
11. Putnam to Charles P. Bowditch, 4 March 1892, folder 1891–1900 B, box 8, HUG 1717.2.1, FWP Papers HUA.
12. The British military officer Augustus Pitt Rivers deserves recognition for leading this development. He has been credited as "the first to apply" "the idea of context in excavation." Bowden, *Pitt Rivers*, 154.
13. An unidentified observer wrote of him in 1892, "Ever since F.W. Putnam left Salem (where he was director of Peabody Museum there from 1864 to 1876) when called to Peabody Museum at Cambridge he had struggled against the strong feeling at Harvard College which would not believe there was any *American* archeology." Handwritten note on frontis of World's Columbian Exposition Report of the Auditor to the Board of Directors, 30 November 1892, folder World's Columbian Exposition–Misc. Papers–Administrative and Financial Records (2), box 36, HUG 1717.2.14, FWP Papers HUA.
14. Putnam to Eliot, 17 June 1892, folder 1891–1900 E, box 9, HUG 1717.2.1, FWP Papers HUA. In June 1892 Harvard College granted

Putnam a temporary leave of absence until 1 January 1894 "to enable him to perform the duties which he has undertaken in connection with the Columbian Exhibition at Chicago." "At a Meeting of the President and Fellows of Harvard College in Boston, June 20th 1892," folder 1891–1900 H-I, box 10, HUG 1717.2.1 FWP Papers HUA.

15. 29 December 1893, CAM vol. 46, WCE records, CHMRC.

16. Gruber, "Ethnographic Salvage," 1290, 1295, 1296.

17. See newspaper clippings, including section of article from *Chicago Morning News*, 17 January 1891, which Putnam kept in a scrapbook in box 1, HUG 1717.15, FWP Papers HUA.

18. Minutes of Executive Committee of the World's Columbian Exposition, 11 February 1891, folder 2, box 7, WCE Records CHMRC; Draft of Putnam, "Inception and Organization of the Department," folder World's Columbian Exposition–Misc. Papers–Reports (5), box 36, HUG 1717.2.14, FWP Papers HUA.

19. Browman and Williams, *Anthropology at Harvard*, 232–33; Dexter, "Putnam's Problems," 316, 318–20; Draft of "Inception and Organization of the Department," folder World's Columbian Exposition–Misc. Papers–Reports (5), box 36, HUG 1717.2.14, FWP Papers HUA.

20. Hinsley, "The Museum Origins of Harvard Anthropology," 121, 140.

21. Browman and Williams, *Anthropology at Harvard*, 237.

22. Hinsley, "Anthropology as Education," 74.

23. Summary of Expenses of Department M, folder World's Columbian Exposition–Misc. Papers–Reports (5), World's Columbian Correspondence Miscellaneous Papers, box 36, HUG 1717.2.14, FWP Papers HUA.

24. "The World's Fair," *Boston Post*, 15 June 1891, page number not identified, folder 4.41, World's Columbian Exposition folder #2, Newspaper Clippings (Xeroxes), Frederic Ward Putnam Papers, 1855–1935, Peabody Museum Archives, Harvard University (FWP Papers PMA).

25. Browman and Williams, *Anthropology at Harvard*, 174–75.

26. Minutes, 16 November 1892, in Chicago World's Columbian Exposition 1893 Executive Committee Minutes, 17 August 1892 to 15 November 1893, vol. 35 (hereafter Executive Committee Minutes, vol. 35), WCE records CHMRC.

27. Putnam to Ernest Volk, 28 July 1891, folder V, box 33, HUG 1717.2.12, FWP Papers HUA.

28. Dexter, "Putnam's Problems," 320.

29. "The World's Fair," *Boston Post*, 15 June 1891, page number not identified, folder 4.41, World's Columbian Exposition folder #2, Newspaper Clippings (Xeroxes), FWP Papers PMA.

30. Boas, "The Anthropology of the North American Indian," 37–38.

31. Putnam to Daniel M. Browning, 16 May 1893, folder World's Columbian Exposition, Indians etc., box 34, HUG 1717.2.13, FWP Papers HUA.

32. Boas described the tools in an unpublished manuscript. They included, among other things, a two-meter-long measuring rod with plumb (substituted to a level in 1892); a jointed steel calipers; a small (22 cm) calipers for face measurements; and a 40 cm long millimeter scale with a notch for balancing on the calipers. Folder 8.11 Boas, "The Physical Anthropology of the North American Indian," p. 259, box 8, Office of Director (F. W. Putnam), Series VII, Records of World's Columbian Exposition Records, 1890–95, Frederic Ward Putnam Peabody Museum Director Records, PMA.

33. "Shot from Ambush, Boston Doctor a Victim of Indian Ignorance," newspaper not identified, n.d., byline Kansas City, 23 October [probably 1892], box 1, HUG 1717.15, FWP Papers HUA.

34. Tisdale to Putnam, 5 August 1892, folder T, box 33, HUG 1717.2.12, FWP Papers HUA.

35. For an example of the complex interplay of "storytellers" and "storytakers," as Rosalyn LaPier refers to them, see her book *Invisible Reality*.

36. Boas to Robert Bell, 22 June 1891, folder Boas, Franz 1890–1893, Robert Bell Papers, American Philosophical Society (APS).

37. Antonio, an Apache, to Putnam, 17 June 1892, folder A, box 31, HUG 1717.2.12, FWP Papers HUA.

38. Baker, "Mitochondrial DNA," iv. Boas collected more than 2,800 hair samples from more than seventy tribal groups.

39. Cameron, *History of the World's Columbian Exposition*, 84.

40. Putnam to Lee, 18 June 1891, folder World's Columbian Exposition 1891–93 Ethnological Assets Indexed. See also Putnam to William Curtis regarding Latin American collectors, 23 January 1892, folder World's Columbian Exposition, Indians, etc. Both in box 34, HUG 1717.2.13, FWP Papers HUA.

41. Putnam to Dorsey, 23 July 1891, folder World's Columbian Exposition 1891–93 Ethnological Assets Indexed, box 34, HUG 1717.2.13, FWP Papers HUA.

42. Bancroft, *Book of the Fair*, 4:636.

43. Putnam to Dorsey, 23 July 1891, folder World's Columbian Exposition 1891–93 Ethnological Assets Indexed, box 34, HUG 1717.2.13, FWP Papers HUA.

44. Excerpt from Tisdel letter, n.d., folder World's Columbian Exposition, Indians etc., box 34, HUG 1717.2.13, FWP Papers HUA.

45. Dorsey to Stephen Simms, 31 January 1900, quoted in Browman and Williams, *Anthropology at Harvard*, 202.

46. Browman and Williams, *Anthropology at Harvard*, 92, 123; Hinsley, "Frederic Ward Putnam," 144.

47. "On Methods of Archeological Research in America," a synopsis of a talk by Putnam, reprinted from Johns Hopkins University Circulars 5:49, May 1886. In folder Publications–Reprints + Clippings, box 28, HUG 1717.2.6, FWP Papers HUA. The full quotation is revealing: "He then described the methods which should be followed in explorations, in order that everything found, from a chip of stone to an elaborate piece of carving; from a mass of clay to a perfect vase or a terra-cotta figure; from a splinter of bone to an implement made of that material; from a shell to a carving on a piece of shell; from nuggets of copper and other native metals to beautifully worked ornaments; together with implements and ornaments of various materials, broken or whole, remains of charred fibres, matting and cloth; and seeds, nuts, corn-cobs and bones of animals, and one and all shall show their associations and tell their story as a whole.

"With these should be preserved all human remains, from fragments of bones to perfect skeletons. Skulls are unquestionably the most important, but other parts of the skeletons should be studied as well. All these objects should be studied comparatively; their association should never be overlooked, and individually and collectively, they should be compared with similar groups of objects from near and remote places. Deductions of importance can be drawn only from material obtained by such methods."

48. Dorsey's collection that the Field Museum accessioned into its records consists of a lengthy list of objects. He describes some of the objects collected from specific graves, but not in the depth of context that Putnam called for. Others followed Putnam's instructions more completely. For example, T. L. Bolton, a Clark University volunteer who collected from the Bannock in Idaho, described the use of the objects he collected in detail. A.1/1–193, Ancon Peru, Collector G. A. Dorsey, Accession 48; "Bannock Indians of Idaho," Collector T. L. Bolton, Accession 29, both in Accession Records, Anthropology Department, FMNH; George Dorsey Ancon Peru 1893 Case 11 papers, FMNH Archives.

49. Mead to Saville, Owens and Price, 12 February 1892, folder 1–2 Correspondence 1891–92, box 1 Central American Expedition Records (CAE) Records Unaccessioned, PMA.

50. Holgate to Putnam, 1 September 1891, folder World's Columbian Exposition 1891–1893 Ethnological Assets Indexed, box 34, HUG 1717.2.13, FWP Papers HUA.

51. Baker, *Anthropology and the Racial Politics of Culture*, 17.

52. Dexter, "Putnam's Problems," 320–21.

53. September 1892 F. W. Putnam Report to the Director General, folder World's Columbian Exposition Monthly Reports to Director General July–Dec 1892, box 35, HUG 1717.2.13, FWP Papers HUA.

54. Putnam to Gentlemen of the Committee on Liberal Arts, 21 September 1891, folder World's Columbian Exposition, Indians, etc., box 34, HUG 1717.2.13, FWP Papers HUA.

55. Putnam to Edward F. Wilson, 11 September 1891, folder World's Columbian Exposition 1891–93 Ethnological Assets Indexed, box 34, HUG 1717.2.13, FWP Papers HUA.

56. [Putnam] to Antonio, an Apache, 13 May 1892, folder A, box 31, HUG 1717.2.12, FWP Papers HUA.

57. S. K. Fenollosa [Special Consultant in Field] to Putnam, 7 September 1892, folder World Columbian Exposition 1891–93, box 35, HUG 1717.2.13, FWP Papers HUA.

58. *Report to the Governor of the Board of General Managers*, 27.

59. Tisdale to Putnam, 5 August 1892, folder T, box 33, HUG 1717.2.12, FWP Papers HUA.

60. Antonio, an Apache, to Putnam, 17 June 1892, folder A, box 31, HUG 1717.2.12, FWP Papers HUA.

61. Jacknis, "Northwest Coast Indian Culture," 99.

62. Charles de Cazes, the Canadian Indian agent who oversaw the education exhibit, used the term *wild Indians* in a letter to Hayter Reed, Indian commissioner to Manitoba and the North-West Territories, 27 May 1893, in Indian Affairs, Black Series files, file 85,529, microfilm reel C-10153, RG 10, Library and Archives of Canada (hereafter file 85,529, RG 10, LAC).

63. November 1892 monthly report, 8 December 1892, folder World's Columbian Exposition Monthly Reports to Director General July–December 1892, box 35, HUG 1717.2.13; Putnam to Clarence B. Moore, 29 May 1893, folder M, box 32, HUG 1717.2.12, both in FWP Papers HUA; minutes, 26 May 1893, CAM vol. 48, 19 May 1893–11 July 1893, WCE records CHMRC. The *New York Times* ascribed the late opening of the anthropological exhibit to Putnam's personality. "He is an active and an erudite little man," the newspaper reported, "but he seems to be a sufferer from that great drawback of scientific and professional persons–lack of practicability. He appears to have had all his abilities absorbed by ethnological research, and to have none left for the everyday affairs of life which require policy and executive capacity. Consequently he has got into snarls and imbroglios and has been buffeted about by more worldly and self-assertive chiefs of departments, who got things done while Mr. Putnam had to wait." "Prof. Putnam's

Hard Luck: His Difficulties with the Anthropological Exhibit," *New York Times*, 22 May 1893, 9.

Putnam also had to contend with mountains of paperwork. Every employee he hired, for example, had to be confirmed by the fair's Council of Administration; every resignation had to be reported to the same body. Records of these are in the CAM, WCE records CHMRC. In October 1893 when the weather cooled, he wanted to use ten stoves to heat the rooms of the 100,000-square-foot Anthropology Building. They had been used the previous winter, but he had to write to the director general, who took his request to the Administrative Council, which denied it, with the misunderstanding that the stoves would need to be purchased. The process had to go back down the chain of command and back up again for clarification. Minutes of 3 October 1893 and 10 October 1893, in CAM vol. 50, WCE records CHMRC. Putnam, of course, was not the only administrator to be challenged by red tape. Bertha (Mrs. Potter) Palmer, president of the Board of Lady Managers, reported to her organization that she had no direct funds from the U.S. Treasury, despite Congress's support of the Woman's Building. "We have, therefore, to depend absolutely upon the Directory for the supply of the simplest, most necessary, and constant wants, and the complication of authority and administration of the Exposition has been a source of infinite annoyance and trouble to us." "Report to the Board of Lady Managers. Fifth Session, Woman's Building," 7 July 1893, *Addresses and Reports of Mrs. Potter Palmer*, 144–45. This was a typical experience for seemingly simple requests that occurred before, during, and after the run of the fair. Especially in the fair's early months, attendance was low, and much of the grounds remained unfinished. Johnson, ed., *A History of the World's Columbian Exposition*, 1:389.

64. Dreiser, *The Titan*, 327.

3. Native People Collecting for the Fair

1. From biographical sketch in Maj. W. H. Powell, "Records of Living Officers of the U.S. Army," 162, folder C, box 31, HUG 1717.2.12, FWP Papers HUA.
2. Hauptman, *Seven Generations*, 106–7.
3. C. C. Cusick visiting card, folder 1891–1900 C, box 9, HUG 1717.2.1, FWP Papers HUA.
4. Cusick correspondence in folder C, box 31, HUG 1717.2.12, FWP Papers HUA.
5. Cusick to Adjutant General, U.S. Army, 2 March 1891; Cusick to Director General and Manager, World's Fair, 11 May 1891; Cusick to Putnam, 29 May 1891, folder C, box 31, HUG 1717.2.12, FWP Papers HUA.

6. George Brown Goode, 26 May 1891; Goode to Cusick, telegram, n.d. both in folder 2 Outgoing Correspondence of George Brown Goode from Washington, 3 April 1891–26 March 1892, box 37; Horace A. Taylor to Goode, 23 May 1891, folder T, 1891–1893, box 36; Cusick, Fort Assinaboine MT, to Goode, telegram, 1 June 1891, folder C, 1891–1894, box 33, all in SIA RU000070, SIA.

7. Putnam to Secretary of War, 13 June 1891, folder 2, 4653 ACP 1888 (Cornelius C. Cusick), entry 297, Letters Received by the Appointments, Commissions and Personal Branch Document File, Records of the Adjutant General's Office (hereafter 4653 ACP 1888), RG 94, NARA-DC.

8. Putnam to Cusick, 29 July 1891, folder C, box 31, HUG 1717.2.12, FWP Papers HUA.

9. Putnam to Cusick, 13 June 1891; Putnam to Cusick, 20 July 1891; Putnam to Cusick, 29 July 1891; Cusick to Geo. R. Davis, 23 August 1891; Cusick to Putnam, 27 September 1891, all in folder C, box 31; Davis to Putnam, 23 July 1891 and 4 August 1891; Putnam to Davis, 26 June 1891, all in folder D(3), box 32, HUG 1717.2.12, FWP Papers HUA; Davis to Harrison, 9 July 1891; Adjutant General J. C. Kelton to Secretary of War, 21 July 1891, both in folder 2, 4653 ACP 1888, RG 94, NARA-DC.

10. Secretary of the Interior John W. Noble to Secretary of War, 1 July 1891; L. A. Grant, Acting Secretary of War, to Davis, 24 July 1891, both in folder 2, 4653 ACP 1888, RG 94, NARA-DC.

11. Chauncey McKeever, Assistant Adjutant General by command of Major General Miles, Headquarters Division of the Missouri, Special Orders, no. 50, 6 July 1891, Chicago; Kelton, Headquarters of the Army, Special Orders, no. 221, 23 September 1891; Cusick to Assistant Adjutant General, 30 June 1891; Cusick to Adjutant General's Office, 21 September 1891, all in folder 2, 4653 ACP 1888, RG 94, NARA-DC; Cusick to Putnam, 27 September 1891; folder C, box 31, HUG 1717.2.12, FWP Papers HUA.

12. Kelton, Headquarters of the Army, 15 January 1892, folder 1, 4653 ACP 1888, RG 94, NARA-DC.

13. Grant to Davis, 29 August 1891; Davis to Grant, 25 August 1891; G. Norman Lieber, Acting Judge Advocate General, respectfully returned to the Secretary of War, 18 September 1891; Grant to Davis, 25 September 1891; "Details from the Army in connection with the World's Columbian Exposition," sent to Adjutant General's Office, 28 August 1891; Cusick to Adjutant General, 19 February 1892, all in folder 1, 4653 ACP 1888, RG 94, NARA-DC.

14. Putnam to Director General, 10 June 1891, May monthly report, folder World's Columbian Exposition, Monthly Reports to Director General 1891, box 35, HUG 1717.2.13, FWP Papers HUA.

15. Putnam to Cusick, 29 July 1891; Cusick to Putnam, 27 September 1891, folder C, box 31, HUG 1717.2.12, FWP Papers HUA.

16. Cusick to Putnam, 27 September 1891, folder C, box 31, HUG 1717.2.12, FWP Papers HUA.

17. Cusick to Putnam, 7 November 1891, and 15 July 1892, folder C, box 31, HUG 1717.2.12, FWP Papers HUA.

18. Cusick to Putnam, 27 September 1891, and 7 November 1891, folder C, box 31, HUG 1717.2.12, FWP Papers HUA. The 7 November letter indicates from which individuals Cusick made the purchases.

19. Itemized Account of Expenses, 1 July 1892, lists $42.30 for Cusick, and Itemized Account of Expenses, 31 July 1892, lists $65.26. Folder World's Columbian Exposition–Misc. Papers–Administrative and Financial Records, box 37, HUG 1717.2.14, FWP Papers HUA.

20. Cusick to Putnam, 15 July 1892, folder C, box 31, HUG 1717.2.12, FWP Papers HUA.

21. Cusick to Adjutant General, 19 February 1892, folder 1, 4653 ACP 1888, RG 94, NARA-DC.

22. Cusick to Putnam, 15 July 1892; Morgan to U.S. Indian Agents, 27 April 1892, folder C, box 31, HUG 1717.2.12, FWP Papers HUA.

23. Reverend John W. Sanborn, "Report on the New York Indian Exhibit," in *Documents of the Senate of the State of New York*, 499–501. See appendix, "American Indians and Other Indigenous People Affiliated with the United States at the Fair" for a list of names of Iroquois attendees.

24. White, *The Ethnography and Ethnology of Franz Boas*, 31–32.

25. Rohner, *The Ethnography of Franz Boas*, xxiii, 91; Jacknis, "George Hunt," 181.

26. Jacknis, "George Hunt," 177.

27. Jacknis, "Northwest Coast Indian Culture," 111.

28. Johnson, *A History of the World's Columbian Exposition*, 2:344.

29. Putnam to Vowell, 24 September 1892, reel C-10152; Vowell to [S. J. Larke], 18 October 1893, reel C-10153, both in file 85,529, RG 10, Division of Indian Affairs (DIA), LAC.

30. Putnam Report to Director General, October 1891, folder World's Columbian Exposition, Monthly Reports to Director General 1891, box 35, HUG 1717.2.13, FWP Papers HUA; 28 March 1893, CAM vol. 47, WCE records, CHMRC.

31. Summary of Expenses of Department M, n.d., folder World's Columbian Exposition–Misc. Papers–Reports (5), box 36, HUG 1717.2.14, FWP Papers HUA.

32. Putnam report to Director General, October 1891, folder World's Columbian Exposition Monthly Reports to Director General 1891, box 35, HUG 1717.2.13, FWP Papers HUA.

33. Putnam report to Director General, February 1892, folder World's Columbian Exposition Monthly Reports to Director General January–June 1892, box 35, HUG 1717.2.13, FWP Papers HUA.

34. Putnam reports to Director General, May 1892 and June 1892, both in folder World's Columbian Exposition Monthly Reports to Director General January–June 1892; Putnam report to Director General, August 1892; Putnam report to Director General, September 1892, both in folder World's Columbian Exposition Monthly Reports to Director General July–December 1892; all in box 35, HUG 1717.2.13, FWP Papers HUA.

35. Jacknis, "George Hunt," 181–83.

36. Jacknis, "Northwest Coast Indian Culture," 94; list of collections sent to the Field Museum, folder World's Columbian Exposition–Misc. Papers–Lists of Specimens, Etc., box 37, HUG 1717.2.14, FWP Papers, HUA.

37. Atkinson, "One-Sided Conversations," 12. Morison's surname before marriage was Quintal.

38. Atkinson, "The 'Accomplished' Odille Morison," 140, 145, 147–49.

39. Boas diary entry, 21 June 1888, in Rohner, *The Ethnography of Franz Boas*, 93.

40. Morison to Boas, 9 December 1888 and 22 April 1889, both in Franz Boas Papers, APS; Morison, "Tsimshian Proverbs."

41. Atkinson, "The 'Accomplished' Odille Morison," 153.

42. Atkinson, "The 'Accomplished' Odille Morison," 154.

43. Putnam reports to Director General, March 1892 and April 1892, both in folder World's Columbian Exposition, Monthly Reports to Director General January–June 1892; Putnam reports to Director General, July 1892, September 1892, November 1892, and December 1892; Putnam Six Months' Report, October 1892, all in folder World's Columbian Exposition, Monthly Reports to Director General July–December 1892, all in box 35, HUG 1717.2.13, FWP Papers HUA.

44. Cole, *Captured Heritage*, 61, 124.

45. Atkinson, "The 'Accomplished' Odille Morison," 156.

46. Draft of Putnam, "Inception and Organization of the Department," folder World's Columbian Exposition–Misc. Papers–Reports (5), box 36, HUG 1717.2.14, FWP Papers HUA.

47. "Antonio Apache Says He's No Negro," *New York Times*, 4 July 1907, 14. Descriptions of the time and even modern scholarly works have accepted Antonio as an Apache. See Rinehart, "To Hell with the Wigs!" 403; Rydell, *All the World's a Fair*, 63. Browman and Williams, *Anthropology at Harvard*, 252–53, provide evidence of Antonio's fraud and deception. Hinsley and Wilcox, *Coming of Age in Chicago*, suggest that his ethnic heritage "is still unknown," 203n37.

48. Note from Putnam, 29 April 1893, folder A, box 31, HUG 1717.2.12, FWP Papers HUA.

49. Photo caption, Antonio Apache photo, *Oriental and occidental northern and southern portrait types.*

50. "Putnam's Apache Aid, the Ethnological Chief Has a Unique and Valuable Asset," *Chicago Journal,* 14 April 1893; "Antonio, the Apache, Development from a Blanket Indian into a Scientist," *Chicago Inter Ocean,* 16 April 1893, both in box 1, vol. 2, HUG 1717.15, FWP Papers HUA; *Report of the Superintendent of Indian Schools, 1893,* 38.

51. Antonia [*sic*] to Commissioner of Indian Affairs, 21 October 1891, LR 1891:38076, RG 75, NARA-DC.

52. Putnam to Commissioner of Indian Affairs Browning, 16 May 1893, LR 1893:18337, RG 75, NARA-DC.

53. Summary of Expenses of Department M, n.d, folder World's Columbian Exposition–Misc. Papers–Reports (5), box 36, HUG 1717.2.14, FWP Papers HUA. Putnam explained in a letter to Commissioner Morgan, "My agreement with Antonio is simply that I pay his expenses." 2 August 1892, LR 1892:28158, RG 75, NARA-DC.

54. Morgan to U.S. Indian Agents, 22 April 1892, vol. 7, 1:377, CMD-LS; copy in LR 1894:8799, both in RG 75, NARA-DC.

55. Putnam's March 1892 monthly report, 5 April 1892, folder World's Columbian Exposition, Monthly Reports to Director General January–June 1892, box 35, HUG 1717.2.13, FWP Papers HUA.

56. Antonio to Putnam, n.d., in response to 15 June 1892 letter; Antonio an Apache to Putnam, Fort Wingate NM, 17 June 1892, both in folder A, box 31, HUG 1717.2.12, FWP Papers HUA.

57. Antonio an Apache to Putnam, Fort Apache, Arizona, 25 July 1892, Antonio to Putnam, n.d., in response to 15 June letter, both in folder A, box 31, HUG 1717.2.12, FWP Papers HUA.

58. Antonio to Putnam, n.d., in response to 15 June letter; Putnam to Antonio, 4 August 1892, both in folder A, box 31, HUG 1717.2.12, FWP Papers HUA.

59. Putnam to Commissioner of Indian Affairs Browning, 16 May 1893, LR 1893:18337, RG 75, NARA-DC; Antonio to Putnam, n.d., in response to 15 June 1892 letter; [Putnam] to Dr. J. Walter Fewkes, 3 April 1893, both in folder A, box 31, HUG 1717.2.12, FWP Papers HUA.

60. Putnam to Morgan, 2 August 1892, LR 1892:28158, RG 75, NARA-DC.

61. Itemized Account of Expenses, 31 May 1892, folder World's Columbian Exposition–Misc. Papers–Administrative and Financial Records (4), box 37, HUG 1717.2.14; Putnam to Antonio, 4 August 1892, folder A, box 31, HUG 1717.2.12, both in FWP Papers HUA

62. Miller, *Claiming Tribal Identity*, writes about the ways that the modern Oklahoma Cherokee and others have dealt with individuals claiming tribal identities that are not recognized by tribes themselves, 289–93.

63. Minutes, 25 March 1891, folder 2, Executive Committee, January 7, 1891–July 29, 1891, box 7, WCE records, 1893; minutes, 10 November 1892, CAM, vol. 45, WCE records, both in CHMRC; "Division of Anthropology, 1890–1905," folder Administrative, Financial, Etc.–Peabody Museum Harvard Univ., box 22 Administrative, Financial, Etc., HUG 1717.2.2, FWP Papers HUA.

64. Folder 8.13 Dorsey, George A., "South American Archaeology and Ethnology," 378–400 of typed manuscript, box 8 (of 9) Office of Director (FW Putnam), series VII, Records of World's Columbian Exposition Records, 1890–95, Frederic Ward Putnam Peabody Museum Director Records, PMA.

65. Putnam May 1892 report, 1 June 1892, folder World's Columbian Exposition, Monthly Reports to Director General January–June 1892, box 35, HUG 1717.2.13, FWP Papers HUA.

66. Putnam January 1892 report, 8 February 1892, folder World's Columbian Exposition, Monthly Reports to Director General January–June 1892, box 35, HUG 1717.2.13, FWP Papers HUA.

67. Summary voucher with accompanying letter, 2 December 1893, folder World's Columbian Exposition–Misc. Papers–Administrative and Financial Records (3), box 37, HUG 1717.2.14, FWP Papers HUA.

68. Summary voucher with accompanying letter, 2 December 1893, folder World's Columbian Exposition–Misc. Papers–Administrative and Financial Records (3), box 37, HUG 1717.2.14, FWP Papers HUA.

69. For example, John Poli was hired at that rate in March 1893. Minutes, 15 March 1893, CAM, vol. 46, WCE records CHMRC.

4. Department of Ethnology Collecting

1. The Smithsonian and Canadian collecting expeditions are discussed in chapter 5.

2. See, for example, correspondence between Putnam and T. L. Bolton, and Maxwell Riddle to Putnam, 28 June 1891, folder World's Columbian Exposition 1891–93 Ethnological Assets Indexed, box 34, HUG 1717.2.13, FWP Papers HUA.

3. Six Months' Report, October 1892, folder World's Columbian Exposition, Monthly Reports to Director General July–December 1892, box 35, HUG 1717.2.13, FWP Papers HUA.

4. Putnam to Riddle, 24 July 1891, folder World's Columbian Exposition 1891–93 Ethnological Assets Indexed, box 34, HUG 1717.2.13, FWP Papers HUA.

5. Cole, *Captured Heritage*, 1–4, 132.

6. "Report by Boas on North Pacific Coast Exhibit of Indians at World's Columbian Exposition Chicago, 1892–1893," folder World's Columbian Exposition–Misc. Papers–Reports (1), box 36, HUG 1717.2.14, FWP Papers HUA.

7. "Quackuhls Are Here, Arrival of the Vancouver Natives with James Deans," *Chicago Tribune*, 12 April 1893, 1.

8. Deans to Department of Ethnology, 17 May 1892, folder World's Columbian Exposition Moncrieff et al., box 35, HUG 1717.2.13, FWP Papers HUA.

9. Putnam to Mr. Conn, 18 July 1892, folder C, box 31, HUG 1717.2.12; Putnam July 1892 monthly report, 9 August 1892; Putnam monthly report, November 1892, 8 December 1892, both in folder World's Columbian, HUG 1717.2.13; James Dean packing list, 6 June 1892, Memorandum Book, HUG 1717.12, all in FWP Papers HUA.

10. Charles Morison to Boas, 24 March 1893, folder 9.2 Unnumbered case lists, box 38–22 unaccess'd, Frederic Ward Putnam Peabody Museum Director Records, PMA.

11. Northwest Coast tribes were not the only ones controlling shipping costs. Richmond Clow discusses Spotted Tail's role in negotiating freighting costs for the Sicangu Lakota in a forthcoming book, tentatively titled *Spotted Tail*, chap. 12. Rand also discusses the freighting business, observing that Kiowa freighters earned $14,278 in 1880 alone, in *Kiowa Humanity*, 131.

12. Bolton to Putnam, 18 July 1891, folder World's Columbian Exposition 1891–1893 Ethnological Assets Indexed, box 34, HUG 1717.2.13, FWP Papers HUA.

13. Bolton to Putnam, 18 July 1891; Putnam to Bolton, 23 July 1891, both in folder World's Columbian Exposition 1891–1893 Ethnological Assets Indexed, box 34, HUG 1717.2.13, FWP Papers HUA.

14. Bolton to Putnam, 17 August 1891; Putnam to Bolton, 3 September 1891, both in folder World's Columbian Exposition 1891–1893 Ethnological Assets Indexed, box 34, HUG 1717.2.13, FWP Papers HUA.

15. Riddle to Putnam, 9 July 1891; Putnam to Riddle, 24 July 1891, both in folder World's Columbian Exposition 1891–1893 Ethnological Assets Indexed, box 34, HUG 1717.2.13, FWP Papers HUA.

16. For discussion of the introduction of the Dream Dance to the Menominee, see Beck, *The Struggle for Self-Determination*, 36–37.

17. Riddle to Putnam, 31 July 1891, folder World's Columbian Exposition 1891–1893 Ethnological Assets Indexed, box 34, HUG 1717.2.13, FWP Papers HUA; list of material collected by Riddle from Menominee, folder 9.1 Numbered Lists 1891–93, box 38-22, Frederic Ward Putnam Peabody Museum Director Records, PMA.

18. For discussion of the forest economy, see Hosmer, *American Indians in the Marketplace*, and Beck, *The Struggle for Self-Determination*.

19. Ulrich, *The Age of Homespun*, 32.

20. Tisdale to Putnam, 31 October 1893; Tisdale to Putnam, 14 November 1894; Tisdale to Miss Mead, 10 July 1895, all in folder 1, file 94-38, Accession Records, PMA.

21. Tisdale to Putnam, 5 August 1892, folder T, box 33, HUG 1717.2.12, FWP Papers HUA. The travel was described in chapter 2.

22. Tisdale to Putnam, 9 July 1892, folder T, box 33, HUG 1717.2.12, FWP Papers HUA.

23. Phillips, *Trading Identities*, 24.

24. Tisdale to Putnam, 5 August 1892, folder T, box 33, HUG 1717.2.12, FWP Papers HUA.

25. Tisdale to Putnam, 12 August 1892, folder T, box 33, HUG 1717.2.12, FWP Papers HUA.

26. Secretary, Department of Ethnology, to Tisdale, 13 March 1893, folder T, box 33, HUG 1717.2.12, FWP Papers HUA.

27. For correspondence and newspaper clippings regarding the controversial role Sickels played, see folder s (2) E. Sickels, box 33, HUG 1717.2.12, FWP Papers HUA.

28. Sickels to Putnam, 19 October 1891, folder s(2) E. Sickels, box 33, HUG 1717.2.12, FWP Papers HUA.

29. Sickels's vouchers for November and December 1891, folder s(2) E. Sickels, box 33, HUG 1717.2.12, FWP Papers HUA. According to Leroy T. Smith, "The coney hat was a low-priced and staple article" in the hatting business in the nineteenth century. "It was quite an article for barter." Lange, "Then and Now," 50.

30. There was some confusion regarding the role of Henry Mato Najin (Standing Bear) from Rosebud. Standing Bear to T. J. Morgan, 15 January 1891; Frances Mead to Sickels, 19 January 1892; Mead to Standing Bear, 19 January 1892; Sickels to Mead, 22 January 1892, all in folder s(2) E. Sickels, box 33, HUG 1717.2.12, FWP Papers HUA.

31. Sickels to Putnam, 13 December 1891, folder s(2) E. Sickels, box 33, HUG 1717.2.12, FWP Papers HUA.

32. Sickels to Putnam, 17 December 1891, folder s(2) E. Sickels, box 33, HUG 1717.2.12, FWP Papers HUA.

33. "Population, Civilization, Religious, Vital, and Criminal Statistics," ARCIA, 1893, 704–5.

34. Report of Agent Geo. Wright, Rosebud Agency, ARCIA, 1893, 293, 295.

35. Moncrieff list of expenses for Klamath work, submitted from Vladivostok, 13 June 1893, folder World's Columbian Exposition Moncrieff et al., box 35, HUG 1717.2.13, FWP Papers HUA.

36. Stern, *The Klamath Tribe*, 61–64.

37. Employés of Indian Service, Klamath Agency, Oregon, ARCIA 1893, 550.

38. This is based on the national average in the United States in 1893. Table "Amount of Various Articles of Food . . . Which Could Have Been Bought for One Dollar in Each Year from 1890 to 1903," *Eighteenth Annual Report of the Commissioner of Labor, 1903*, 659.

39. Report of Geo. Dorsey, "Explorations in South America," 1893, folder World's Columbian Exposition–Misc. Papers–Reports (1), box 36, HUG 1717.2.14, FWP Papers HUA.

40. Voucher summary, with letter accompanying dated 2 December 1893, folder World's Columbian Exposition–Misc. Papers–Administrative and Financial Records (3), box 37, HUG 1717.2.14, FWP Papers HUA.

41. "Died before Columbus, and Yet They Will Attend the World's Fair," *Globe*, 1 April 1893, box 1, HUG 1717.15, FWP Papers HUA.

42. "Explorations in Honduras," fund-raising pamphlet October 1891, signed by Charles P. Bowditch and Francis C. Lowell, folder 1-1 Correspondence 1891–92, box 1 CAE Records Unaccessioned, PMA.

43. Price to Putnam, 5 December 1891, folder 1-1 Correspondence 1891–92; Price to Putnam, 1 January 1892, folder 1-2 Correspondence 1891–92, both in box 1 CAE Records Unaccessioned, PMA.

44. Bowditch to Putnam, 6 November 1891, folder 1-2 Correspondence 1891–92, box 1 CAE Records Unaccessioned, PMA.

45. List of number of workers from various villages, 1 February 1892, folder 1-2 Correspondence 1891–92, box 1 CAE Records Unaccessioned, PMA.

46. Price to Putnam, 15 December 1891, folder 1-1 Correspondence 1891–92; Price to Putnam, 1 January 1892, Marshall Saville to Putnam, 25 January 1892, folder 1-2 Correspondence 1891–92, both in box 1 CAE Records Unaccessioned, PMA.

47. Marshall Saville to Putnam, 25 January 1892, folder 1-2 Correspondence 1891–92, box 1 CAE Records Unaccessioned, PMA.

48. John G. Owens to T. J. Potts, 2 February 1892, folder 1-3 Correspondence 1891–92, box 1 CAE Records Unaccessioned, PMA.

49. James J. Peterson, U.S. Consul, Tegucigalpa, to Price, 10 February 1892, folder 129 C.A. Exp./Correspondence 1892, Charles Pickering Bowditch Papers, PMA. The expedition leaders also regularly paid out 25 cents for charity—almost the same amount they had initially paid their laborers for a full day's work. Account book 93-27-20/74959.1.10, box 3 CAE Records 93-27, PMA.

50. Owens to Putnam, 19 January 1892, folder 1-2 Correspondence 1891–92, box 1 CAE Records Unaccessioned, PMA. There are two letters under this date, and both are referred to here.

51. Account book 93-27-20/74959.1.18, box 3 CAE Records 93-27, PMA.

52. T. J. Potts to Owens, 28 January 1893, folder Correspondence/ General October 1892–August 1895, box 2 CAE Records 93-27-20, PMA.

53. Putnam to Saville, Owens, Price, and Dodge, 5 November 1892, folder 5-3 PM Correspondence 1891–92, box 5 CAE Records 92-49, PMA.

54. Putnam to Saville, Owens, Price, and Dodge, 5 November 1892, folder 5-3 PM Correspondence 1891–92, box 5 CAE Records 92-49, PMA.

55. Price to Putnam, 1 January 1892; Putnam to Saville, Owens, and Price, 10 February 1892, both in folder 1-2 Correspondence 1891–92, box 1 CAE Records Unaccessioned, PMA.

56. Price to Putnam, 1 January 1892, folder 1-2 Correspondence 1891–92, box 1 CAE Records Unaccessioned, PMA.

57. Saville to Putnam, 29 March 1892, folder 1-2, box 1 CAE Records Unaccessioned; folder 5-6 Expedition Report Saville 1891–92, folder 5-7 Field Notes on the Excavation of Tombs–Owens 1891–92, folder 5-8 Field Notes on the Excavation of Mound 36–Owens 1891–92, box 5 CAE Records 92-49, all in PMA.

58. "List of Articles Procured from the Indian Tribes of the Orinoco River and Its Tributaries, in Venezuela, S.A., by Lieut. Roger Welles Jr., USN 1892," folder 9.1 Numbered Lists, 1891–93, n.d., box 38-22, Frederic Ward Putnam Peabody Museum Director Records, PMA.

59. Safford's inventories are in folder 9.1 Numbered Lists, 1891–93, n.d., box 38-22, Frederic Ward Putnam Peabody Museum Director Records, PMA.

60. Safford to William E. Curtis, 22 June 1891, folder 1 Latin American exhibit September 1890–July 1891, box 40, series 10, SIA RU000070, SIA.

61. Accession 32, Lieutenant George P. Scriver, Accession Records, Anthropology Department, FMNH.

62. 15 March 1893 minutes, Council of Administration Minutes, vol. 46, WCE records CHMRC.

5. Government Agencies Collecting

1. On the scramble, see Cole, *Captured Heritage*, and Beck, "'Collecting among the Menomini.'"

2. Parezo, "The Formation of Ethnographic Collections," 8–14.

3. Parezo, "The Formation of Ethnographic Collections," 8–12.

4. R. Edward Earle to H. W. Henshaw, 1 February 1892, folder Henshaw: Letters Recd by, 1892, in Connection with LCOX Purchases/Not Arranged, box 103, BAE LR 1888–1906, NAA-SI.

5. Otis T. Mason, "Report on the Department of Ethnology in the U.S. National Museum, 1892," folder Dept. of Ethnology Annual Report

1891–92, box 3, Department of Ethnology Annual Reports 1881 to 1894–1895, SIA RU00158, SIA.

6. Goode to Mooney, 2 May 1891; handwritten draft of letter of instruction to Mooney with notes, probably for letter dated 20 December 1892, not signed, both in folder 10 Mooney, James, 1891–1893, box 35; Goode to Dr. W. J. Hoffman, 15 July 1891, folder 13: H, 1891–1894, box 34; Edwin Willits to Mooney, 28 April 1891; Earll to Cox, n.d.; Goode to Mooney, 10 June 1891; Willits to Hoffman, 15 July 1891; Goode to Mooney, 16 May 1892; Earll to Hoffman, 21 May 1892, the latter six in folder 2 Outgoing Correspondence of George Brown Goode from Washington, 3 April 1891–26 March 1892, box 37; Goode to Mooney, 20 December 1892, folder 3 Outgoing Correspondence of George Brown Goode from Washington, 3 November 1, 1892–March 10, 1893, box 37, all in SIA RU000070, SIA; Hoffman to Henshaw, July 3, 1891, box 103, BAE LR 1888–1906, NAA-SI.

7. Moses, *The Indian Man*, 73–74.

8. Goode to Mooney, 16 May 1892, folder 2 Outgoing Correspondence of George Brown Goode from Washington, 3 April 1891–26 March 1892, box 37, SIA RU000070, SIA.

9. Earll to Henshaw, 12 June 1891, describes the vouchers. Folder 2 Outgoing Correspondence of George Brown Goode from Washington, 3 April 1891–26 March 1892, box 37, SIA RU000070, SIA.

10. "Employés of the Indian Service," ARCIA, 1892, 824–25.

11. Report of Agent George G. Day, ARCIA, 1892, 385–87.

12. Report of Agent Charles F. Ashley, ARCIA, 1892, 377.

13. Kickingbird and Ducheneaux, *One Hundred Million Acres*.

14. Mooney to Henshaw, 7 June 1891, folder Henshaw: Letters Recd by, 1892, in Connection with LCOX Purchases/Not Arranged, box 103. He promised to fix the vouchers later. Mooney to Henshaw, 8 June 1891, folder Mooney, James 1891, Mooney, box 109, both in BAE LR 1888–1906, NAA-SI.

15. F. Webb Hodge to Mooney, 27 June 1891, folder Henshaw Copies of Letters Sent re: WCX 1892, box 103, BAE LR 1888–1906, NAA-SI.

16. Mooney to Mr. Gatschet, 14 July 1891, folder Mooney, James 1891, Mooney box 109, BAE LR 1888–1906, NAA-SI.

17. Earll to William V. Cox, 21 January 1893, Voth 288, folder 3, Outgoing Correspondence of George Brown Goode from Washington, 1 November 1892–10 March 1893, box 37, SIA RU000070, SIA; Mooney to Henshaw, 19 May 1891, folder Mooney, James 1891, box Mooney 109, BAE LR 1888–1906, SI-NAA.

18. Goode to Dr. W. J. Hoffman, 15 July 1891, folder 13: H, 1891–1894, box 34, SIA RU000070, SIA.

19. Hoffman, *The Menomini Indians.*

20. Beck, "'Collecting among the Menomini,'" 159.

21. Hoffman to Henshaw, 3 July 1891, folder Hersey-Hough, box 103, BAE LR 1888–1906, BAE, NAA-SI. He had been "authorized to employ interpreters and such other assistance as may be necessary in collecting and transporting the specimens." Earll to Hoffman, 21 May 1892, folder 2 Outgoing Correspondence of George Brown Goode from Washington, 3 April 1891–26 March 1892, box 37, SIA RU000070, SIA.

22. Earll to Hoffman, 21 May 1892, folder 2 Outgoing Correspondence of George Brown Goode from Washington, 3 April 1891–26 March 1892, box 37, SIA RU000070, SIA.

23. Inventory and Memorandum to Registrar, 7 July 1892, both in Accession 25905, microfilm reel 165, SIA RU000305, SIA.

24. "Report of Crow Agency," 22 August 1892, and "Employés of Indian Service," both in *ARCIA* 1892, 284–88, 821.

25. Swan to Goode, 16 July 1891, folder S, 1891–1893, box 36, SIA RU000070, SIA.

26. Mariano Martin, Ascencio Aguilar, Jesus Boson, Juan Galbon, and Jose Anvones Golban, Zia Pueblo, to Matilda Stevenson, 18 December 1891; Stevenson to Henshaw, 6 February 1892, both in folder Henshaw Letters Recd by, 1891, in Connection with WCX Purchases, Not Arranged, box 103, BAE LR 1888–1906, NAA-SI.

27. Henshaw to H[odge], 10 November 1892, folder Henshaw N.D.; 1889–1893; 1905, box 103, BAE LR 1888–1906, NAA-SI.

28. Henshaw, Fruitvale CA, to R. Edward Earll, 15 November 1892, folder 3 Ethnology, box 39, Correspondence and Records Related to Smithsonian Institution Exhibits and Accessions, 1890–1894, SIA RU000070, SIA.

29. Accession 56525, folder 4 Foreign and Domestic Accessions, 1890–1894 Accessions for the World's Columbian Exposition, box 40, SIA RU000070, SIA; Daniel to My dear Prof., 1892, Accession 26525, microfilm reel 169, SIA RU000305, SIA; letter from Daniel, 5 October 1892; Mason to Hodge, 4 November 1892, both in folder Henshaw: Letters Recd by, 1892, in Connection with LCOX Purchases/Not Arranged, box 103, BAE LR 1888–1906, NAA-SI.

30. Report of the Blackfeet Agency, agent George Steell, 15 August 1893, *ARCIA* 1893, 172.

31. A. F. Spiegelberg to Henshaw, 21 September 1892, folder Henshaw: Letters Recd by, 1892, in Connection with LCOX Purchases/Not Arranged, box 103, BAE LR 1888–1906, NAA-SI.

32. Henshaw to Hodge, 3 January 1893, folder Henshaw: Letters Recd by, 1892, in Connection with LCOX Purchases/Not Arranged, box 103, BAE LR 1888–1906, NAA-SI.

33. For a Blackfeet example, see LaPier, *Invisible Reality*, 70.
34. Inventory and Sickels to Mason, 11 July 1892, both in Accession 26105, reel 166, SIA RU000305, SIA; Sickels's inventory with note from Mason, folder Henshaw N.D.; 1889–1893; 1905, box 103, BAE LR 1888–1906, NAA-SI.
35. "Pamunkey Indians and the World's Fair," letter to editor from Terrill Bradley, 3 August [1893], newspaper not identified, box 2, HUG 1717.15, FWP Papers HUA; folder 5 R. Edward Earll allotment account [book], 1893, box 42, series 10, "World's Columbian Exposition (Chicago, 1893), 1886, 1890–1895," SIA RU000070, SIA.
36. Goode to Safford, 5 June 1891, folder 2 Outgoing Correspondence of George Brown Goode from Washington, 3 April 1891–26 March 1892, box 37, series 10, SIA RU000070, SIA.
37. "List of Articles Purchased by F. E. Sawyer," folder 2, box 40, series 10, SIA RU000070, SIA.
38. Report of A. Cameron, P.P., agent, District no. 13, Christmas Island, Cape Breton, Nova Scotia, 20 October 1893, *Annual Report of the Department of Indian Affairs, for the Year Ended 31st December, 1893*, 42.
39. Saunders to Hayter Reed, 12 September 1892, Department of Agriculture Letterbooks, vol. 107, World's Columbian Exposition 1892–1894, Canadian Government Expositions; "Accounts to be accounted for by the Department of Indian Affairs," attached to "Re disposal of the Canadian Pavilion," Department of Agriculture Letterbooks, vol. 76, World's Columbian Exposition 1892–1894, Canadian Government Expositions, both in RG 72; Memo, F. C. Chistrick, 11 January 1894, vol. 746, Agriculture Department Correspondence, RG 17; Circular, R. Sinclair, Acting Deputy Superintendent-General of Indian Affairs, ca. 20 September 1892, reel C-10152; and "World's Columbian Exposition: Amounts to Be Accounted for by the Department of Indian Affairs," reel C-10153, both in file 85,529, RG 10, all in LAC. Sarah Carter argues that despite bureaucratic beliefs that Canadian Indians were either inimical to or culturally unprepared for successful farming, "that along with environmental setbacks, Indian farmers were subject to regulations that denied them the technological and financial opportunities for a strong agricultural base." Carter, *Lost Harvests*, 12.
40. A. Cameron, Indian agent, Christmas Island, Cape Breton to L. Vankoughnet, Deputy Superintendent-General of Indian Affairs, 28 December 1892, reel C-10152, file 85,529, RG 10, LAC.
41. "Wor[l]d's Columbian Exposition: Amounts to Be Accounted for by the Department of Indian Affairs," reel C-10153, file 85,529, RG 10, LAC. Copy also attached to "Re disposal of the Canadian Pavilion,"

9 October 1893, vol. 76, folder 1, Department of Agriculture Letterbooks, 1892–1894, World's Columbian Exposition, Canadian Government Expositions, RG 72, LAC. See also Heald, *A History of the New
Hampshire Abenaki*, 41.

42. Vowell to Deputy Superintendent of Indian Affairs, Ottawa, 19 October 1892; Indian Office to Vowell, 7 November 1892, both in reel
C-10152, file 85,529, RG 10, LAC.

43. "Wor[l]d's Columbian Exposition File."

44. Wm. Laing Meason, Indian agent, Williams Lake Agency, Lesser Dog
Creek, to Vowell, 23 September 1892, reel C-10152, file 85,529, RG 10, LAC.

45. R. E. Loring, Indian agent, Babine Agency to Vowell, 3 October 1892,
reel C-10152, file 85,529, RG 10, LAC.

46. W. H. Lomas, Indian agent, Cowichan Agency to Vowell, 16 September
1892, reel C-10152, file 85,529, RG 10, LAC.

47. Harry Guillod to Vowell, 19 September 1892; J. W. Mackay, Kamloops-
Okanagan Indian Agency, to Vowell, 2 September 1892, both in reel
C-10152, file 85,529, RG 10, LAC.

48. "Wor[l]d's Columbian Exposition." Copy also attached to "Re disposal
of the Canadian Pavilion," 9 October 1893, vol. 76, folder 1, Department of Agriculture Letterbooks, 1892–1894, World's Columbian
Exposition, Canadian Government Expositions, RG 72, LAC.

49. Magnus Begg to Reed, 30 November 1892, Blackfoot Agency Let-
terbook, 1892, vol. 1670, microfilm C-14883, RG 10; Begg to Reed, 19
October 1892, folder Blackfoot Crossing, Gleichen, 1890–1893, vol. 16,
Hayter Reed Fonds, both in LAC.

50. Report of the Blackfeet Agency, Agent George Steell, 15 August 1893,
ARCIA 1893, 172.

51. Report of Farmer of North Blackfoot Reserve, 30 September 1892; Report
of Farmer of South Blackfoot Reserve, 30 September 1892, microfilm
C-14883, vol. 1670, Blackfoot Agency Letterbook, 1892, RG 10, LAC.

52. He made the purchase through the Hudson's Bay Company. A. McDonald, Indian Agent, Crooked Lake Agency, Assiniboia, to Indian Commissioner, Regina, 22 March 1894, reel C-10153, file 85,529, RG 10, LAC.

53. E. D[ewdney] to Saunders, 16 September 1892, reel C-10152, file
85,529, RG 10, LAC.

54. Butler, in *Annual Report of the Department of Indian Affairs, 1891*, 40.

55. Folder September 8, 1891, LR, RG 48, NARA-CPM.

56. Parezo and Fowler, *Anthropology Goes to the Fair*, 274–76; Bokovoy, *The
San Diego World's Fairs*, 115–16, 137.

57. Belt to R. P. Collins, Supt. Indian School, Keam's Canon, 25 March 1893,
144; Belt to Collins, 28 March 1893, 170; Browning to H. A. Taylor, 3 May
1893, P. 329, all in vol. 8, part 2, CMD-LS 1870–1908, RG 75, NARA-DC.

6. Working the Education Displays

1. They did so for both economic and logistical reasons. James Mooney reportedly told Emma Sickels that the Smithsonian was not interested in "an animate exhibit, because although it would be most interesting—an exceedingly important obstacle was in the difficulty of obtaining a competent man, who had the confidence of the Indians, who would attend to the detail of their coming and going and their good care while at the Fair." Sickels to Putnam, 1 January 1892, folder World's Columbian Exposition, Indians etc., box 34, HUG 1717.2.13, FWP Papers HUA. Although the Smithsonian's collection was not so well organized as those by Putnam for the ethnology department, it was intended to show artisan and craft work, technology, games, and ceremony, as well as clothing and "physical characters." Acting on behalf of the Bureau of Ethnology, Frank Cushing organized "a group of the three leading priestly characters" of the Zuni, who put on a "dramatic recital of the epic ritual of creation" for the summer Congress. But otherwise, the Smithsonian exhibit in the government building consisted of seventy plaster life-sized figures of people, primarily Indians from the United States, dressed in clothing and posed with objects of material culture that had been collected for the museum. The museum already owned some of these collections, while others were collected specifically for the fair. Holmes, "The World's Fair Congress," 432–33; C. Bergmann, "List of Figures and Costumes for Exhibition at World's Columbian Exposition in Chicago 189" [sic], MS 7217, NAA-SI. Cushing himself apparently sat as the model for the Sioux warrior on horseback, of which a stereoscope (3-D) photograph was made. Photo lot 2000–14, NAA-SI.

2. "Report by Boas on North Pacific Coast Exhibit of Indians at World's Columbian Exposition Chicago, 1892–1893," folder World's Columbian Exposition–Misc. Papers–Reports (1), box 36, HUG 1717.2.14, FWP Papers HUA.

3. "Notes from the World's Columbian Exposition 1893," Scientific American 59, no. 8 (19 August 1893): 115.

4. Raibmon, Authentic Indians, 51–53.

5. See 14 April 1893, CAM vol. 47, WCE records, CHMRC; Jacknis, "Northwest Coast Indian Culture," 103.

6. Putnam to Davis, 7 April 1893, folder d (2), box 31, HUG 1717.2.12, FWP Papers HUA.

7. "Agreement between F. W. Putnam, Chief, Department of Ethnology World's Columbian Exposition and George Hunt of Beaver Harbor, British Columbia, for the purpose of bringing a certain number of Indians from the vicinity of Beaver Harbor, British Columbia, to the

Ethnographical Exhibition at the World's Columbian Exposition,"
signed by Putnam, 29 September 1892, and by Hunt, 19 January 1893,
folder World's Columbian Exposition–Misc. Papers–Contracts, box
36, HUG 1717.2.14, FWP Papers HUA. Copy in folder World's Columbian
Exposition Moncrieff et al., box 35, HUG 1717.2.13, FWP Papers HUA.

8. Raibmon, *Authentic Indians*, 27.

9. "Quackuhls Are Here, Arrival of the Vancouver Natives with James
Deans," *Chicago Tribune*, 12 April 1893, 1.

10. Putnam to Davis, 6 April 1893; Putnam to Davis, 29 April 1893;
Putnam to Davis, 16 May 1893, all in folder D(2), box 31, HUG
1717.2.12, FWP Papers HUA; Boas to Eltern, 8 May 1893, folder Boas–
Corresp.–1893, April–July, box 6 Boas–Correspondence, November
1887–93, Franz Boas Professional Papers, American Philosophical
Society (FBPP-APS). Translation from German by author.

11. Putnam to Davis, 6 April 1893; Davis to Putnam, 12 April 1893, both in
folder D(2), box 31, HUG 1717.2.12, FWP Papers HUA.

12. "Indians Missed a Meal, Steward Bowen of the Administrative Restaurant Feeding Them Too Well," *Chicago Record*, 14 April 1893, box 1,
HUG 1717.15, FWP Papers HUA.

13. Raibmon, *Authentic Indians*, 55.

14. April 1893 Report, folder World's Columbian Exposition, Monthly
Reports to Director General January–May 1893, box 35, FWP Papers,
HUA; "Quackuhls to Occupy Their Home, Weird and Interesting Cer-
emonies Make Up the Program," *Chicago Tribune*, 6 May 1893, 2.

15. Putnam to Commissioner of Indian Affairs, 29 September 1893, LR
1893:33333, , RG 75, NARA-DC. Copy in folder s(2) E. Sickels, box 33,
HUG 1717.2.12, FWP Papers HUA.

16. These performances are described and analyzed in some detail in
Raibmon, *Authentic Indians*, 55–62.

17. Raibmon, *Authentic Indians*, 59.

18. Raibmon, *Authentic Indians*, 60–62.

19. S. J. Larke to Reverend Albert J. Hall, n.d., reel C-10153, file 85,529,
RG 10, DIA, LAC.

20. Vowell to Larke, 18 October 1893, Microfilm C-10153, file 85,529, RG
10, DIA, LAC. Vowell's letter is almost word for word the response he
got from Agent R. H. Pidcock when he wrote him seeking an explanation of what had occurred at the dance. Pidcock to Vowell, 18
October 1893, reel C-14876, vol. 1648, Kwawkewlth Agency, Alert Bay,
Letterbook 1891–1899, RG 10, DIA, LAC.

21. Putnam to Commissioner of Indian Affairs, 29 September 1893, LR
1893:33333, RG 75, NARA-DC. Copy in folder s(2) E. Sickels, box 33,
HUG 1717.2.12, FWP Papers HUA.

22. Raibmon, *Authentic Indians*, 51–73.

23. The World's Congress Auxiliary of the World's Columbian Exposition of 1893, Programme of the International Congress of Anthropology, folder World's Columbian Exposition, Monthly Reports to Director General June–September 1893, box 35, HUG 1717.2.13, FWP Papers HUA. See also Holmes, "The World's Fair Congress," 429.

24. Jacknis, "Northwest Coast Indian Culture," 111.

25. Raibmon, *Authentic Indians*, 66; Jacknis, "Northwest Coast Indian Culture," 111.

26. "Penobscot Indians on the Ground," *Chicago Record*, 4 May 1893, box 1, HUG 1717.15, FWP Papers HUA; "Local Matters," *Bangor Daily Whig & Courier*, 29 April 1893. The Indian agent George Hunt is no relation to the George Hunt from British Columbia.

27. Putnam's April 1893 report, folder World's Columbian Exposition, Monthly Reports to Director General January–May 1893, box 35, HUG 1717.2.13, FWP Papers HUA.

28. *The Dream City*; Johnson, ed., *A History of the World's Columbian Exposition*, 1:480.

29. "Ere Colon Came, Primitive Life among the North American Indians," *Chicago Inter Ocean*, 9 July 1893.

30. *Columbian Exposition Album*.

31. "Columbian Museum Fund," *Daily Inter Ocean*, 10 November 1893. The Field Museum was briefly called the Columbian Museum at its inception, but is referred to as the Field here to avoid confusion.

32. Zerbe, *Pins from the Plaisance*, 57–58.

33. Folder 10 Notebook, World's Fair, series IV, box 29, Frederick Starr Papers, University of Chicago Library Special Collections Research Center (UCLSCRC).

34. From list in folder World's Columbian Exposition–Misc. Papers–Reports (5), box 36, HUG 1717.2.14, FWP Papers HUA.

35. Report Submitted 20 September 1893 by Daniel Dorchester, *Report of the Superintendent of Indian Schools, 1893*, 37.

36. "The Maharajah of Kapurthala at the Fair," *Chicago Daily Tribune*, 16 August 1893, 1.

37. "In Odd Corners," *Jackson Sentinel* (Maquoketa IA), 17 August 1893.

38. Putnam's June 1893 report, folder World's Columbian Exposition, Monthly Reports to Director General June–September 1893, box 35, HUG 1717.2.13; "Savage Life Illustrated, Five Navajo Indians in Camp at Jackson Park," *Chicago Inter Ocean*, 27 June 1893; "Iroquois Are Coming," *Chicago Daily News*, 21 June 1893; "Six Nations Today, Iroquois Indians Come from New York to the Fair," newspaper not known, July 1893; "Famous Indians Arrive," *Chicago Inter Ocean*, 29

June 1893; "Indians of New York, Famous Six Nations of Iroquois," *Chicago Herald*, 17 July 1893; all in box 1, HUG 1717.15, all in FWP Papers HUA. "Report on the New York Indian Exhibit," by Reverend John W. Sanborn, Director, *Documents of the Senate of the State of New York*, 499.

39. "Ere Colon Came, Primitive Life among the North American Indians," *Chicago Inter Ocean*, 9 July 1893.

40. "Report on the New York Indian Exhibit," by Reverend John W. Sanborn, director, *Documents of the Senate of the State of New York*, 499–500.

41. Bancroft, *The Book of the Fair*, 3:663.

42. Putnam's July and November 1892 reports, both in folder World's Columbian Exposition, Monthly Reports to Director General July–December 1892, box 35, HUG 1717.2.13; "The Indian Exhibit, a Feature to Be Furnished by New-York for the Big Fair," *Buffalo Express*, 8 September 1892, box 1, HUG 1717.15, all in FWP Papers HUA.

43. Putnam to Sanborn, 4 December 1893, folder World's Columbian Exposition, Indians, etc., box 34, HUG 1717.2.13, FWP Papers HUA.

44. "Report on the New York Indian Exhibit," by Reverend John W. Sanborn, director, *Documents of the Senate of the State of New York*, 500.

45. Sanborn to Putnam, 8 August 1893, folder World's Columbian Exposition Moncrieff et al., box 35, HUG 1717.2.13, FWP Papers HUA.

46. Draft of Putnam, "Inception and Organization of the Department," folder World's Columbian Exposition–Misc. Papers–Reports (5), box 36 HUG 1717.2.14, FWP Papers HUA.

47. "In Odd Corners," *Jackson Sentinel* (Maquoketa IA), 17 August 1893.

48. Report Submitted 20 September 1893 by Daniel Dorchester, *Report of the Superintendent of Indian Schools, 1893*, 37; "Report on the New York Indian Exhibit," 500.

49. "In Odd Corners," *Jackson Sentinel* (Maquoketa IA), 17 August 1893.

50. From Gay Leon Dybwad's private collection in NM entry, Dybwad and Bliss, *Annotated Bibliography*.

51. Schrader, *The Indian Arts and Crafts Board*.

52. "Caravels in Port," *Daily Inter Ocean*, 8 July 1893, 3.

53. Johnson, *A History of the World's Columbian Exposition*, 480.

54. "Report on the New York Indian Exhibit," 501; Pratt, *Battlefield and Classroom*, 302.

55. Putnam to Antonio an Apache, 13 May 1892; Antonio an Apache to Putnam, 31 May 1892, both in folder A, box 31, HUG 1717.2.12, FWP Papers HUA.

56. Putnam to Thomas Morgan, 10 March 1892, LR 1892:9248, RG 75, NARA-DC; Morgan to Mrs. Patrick, 1 March 1892, vol. 7, p. 1:118, CMD-LS, RG 75, NARA-DC.

57. Putnam to O. C. French, 6 March 1893; Putnam to D. M. Browning, 16 May 1893; Frank C. Armstrong to Putnam, 23 May 1893; A. F. Willmarth, 27 May 1893; Antonio Apache statement, 17 June 1893; all in folder World's Columbian Exposition, Indians etc., box 34, HUG 1717.2.13, FWP Papers HUA; Putnam to Browning, 16 May 1893, also in LR 1893:18337, RG 75, NARA-DC.

58. McNitt, *The Indian Traders*, 288–89; "Employés of Indian Service," *ARCIA*, 1893, 551. His name is recorded here as Peshli-ki.

59. Report of Navajo Agency, E. H. Plummer, First Lieutenant Tenth Infantry, Acting Agent, 22 August 1893, *ARCIA*, 1893, 110.

60. "Population, Civilization, Religious, Vital, and Criminal Statistics," Navajo Agency, *ARCIA*, 1893, 694–95.

61. Putnam to Browning, 16 May 1893, LR 1893:18337, RG 75, NARA-DC.

62. Plummer to Commissioner of Indian Affairs, 17 June 1893, LR 1893:22869, RG 75, NARA-DC; Antonio Apache statement, 17 June 1893, folder World's Columbian Exposition, Indians etc., box 34, HUG 1717.2.13, FWP Papers HUA.

63. Plummer to Commissioner of Indian Affairs, 17 June 1893, LR 1893:22869, RG 75, NARA-DC.

64. Putnam to Commissioner of Indian Affairs, 25 August 1893, LR 1893:32370, RG 75, NARA-DC; copy in folder World's Columbian Exposition, Indians etc., box 34, HUG 1717.2.13, FWP Papers HUA.

65. "World's Fair Gossip," *Rocky Mountain News*, 10 July 1893, 7.

66. Grocery receipts to Antonio Apache from W. B. Harvey, 18 September 1893, folder World's Columbian Exposition, Indians etc., box 34, HUG 1717.2.13, FWP Papers HUA.

67. Plummer to Herbert Welsh, 19 September 1893, reel 10, *Indian Rights Association Papers* (*IRA Papers*); "Three Navahoe Indians Arrive," *Chicago Tribune*, 29 June 1893, box 1, HUG 1717.15.

68. Antonio to Putnam, n.d., folder A, box 31, HUG 1717.2.12, both in FWP Papers HUA.

69. Letter from Plummer, 27 July 1893, LR 1893:27868 (description available, letter missing from file); Plummer to Commissioner of Indian Affairs, 4 August 1893, LR 1893:29738; Putnam to Commissioner of Indian Affairs, 25 August 1893, LR 1893:32370, all in RG 75, NARA-DC; copy of 25 August 1893 letter also in folder World's Columbian Exposition, Indians etc., box 34, HUG 1717.2.13, FWP Papers HUA.

70. Plummer to Putnam, 26 September 1893, folder World's Columbian Exposition, Indians etc., box 34, HUG 1717.2.13, FWP Papers HUA.

71. C. A. Diehl to Plummer, 31 July 1893, LR 1893:29738, RG 75, NARA-DC.

72. Plummer to Welsh, 22 May 1893; Plummer to Welsh, 16 June 1893; Acting Commissioner of Indian Affairs Frank. C. Armstrong to Welsh,

16 June 1893; Acting Secretary of the Interior to Welsh, 17 June 1893; Armstrong to Secretary of the Interior, 16 June 1893; Plummer to Welsh, 22 June 1893; Fund-raising letter on Indian Rights Association letterhead, 26 June 1893; Plummer to Welsh, 7 September 1893; Plummer to Welsh, 19 September 1893; 26 September 1893 news release, IRA stationery; Plummer to Welsh, 6 September 1893; telegram Plummer to Secretary of Indian Rights Association, 12 October 1893; telegram Plummer to Welsh, 15 October 1893; Commissioner of Indian Affairs D. M. Browning to Welsh, 16 October 1893; telegram Plummer to Welsh, 16 October 1893; Plummer to Welsh, 26 October 1893 (report on trip), all in reel 10; Welsh to Hoke Smith, Secretary of the Interior, 29 May 1893, 765–66; Welsh to Plummer, 29 May 1893, 767–68; Welsh to Executive Committee, Indian Rights Association, 6 June 1893, 788; Welsh to Acting Secretary, Department of the Interior, 14 June 1893, 821; Welsh to Charles C. Painter, 17 June 1893, 828; Welsh to F. Hazen Cope, 29 June 1893, 879; Matthew Sniffen to Plummer, 22 July 1893, 937; all in vol. 9 Letterpress; Welsh to Plummer, 25 September 1893, 21, vol. 10 Letterpress, all in reel 72, all in IRA *Papers*; Welsh to Frank C. Armstrong, Acting Commissioner, 17 June 1893, LR 1893:21957; Plummer to Commissioner of Indian Affairs, 28 July 1893, LR 1893:28727; telegram Welsh, Philip C. Garrett and Gen. O. O. Howard, to Browning, 12 October 1893, LR 1893:38216, all in RG 75, NARA-DC; Browning to Plummer, 30 September 1893, vol 144, nos. 287–288, 25 September 1893 to 31 October 1893, Correspondence Accounts Division, 131, Letters Sent, 1870–1908, RG 75, NARA-DC.

73. Putnam to Colonel O. F. French, State Board of Colorado, 10 March 1893, folder World's Columbian Exposition, Indians, etc., box 34, HUG 1717.2.13, FWP Papers HUA.

74. Putnam to Commissioner of Indian Affairs, 25 August 1893, folder World's Columbian Exposition, Indians, etc., box 34, HUG 1717.2.13, FWP Papers HUA.

75. Willmarth to Antonio Apache, 11 September 1893, folder World's Columbian Exposition, Indians etc., box 34, HUG 1717.2.13, FWP Papers HUA.

76. Putnam to Plummer, 24 August 1893, folder World's Columbian Exposition, Indians etc., box 34, HUG 1717.2.13, FWP Papers HUA.

77. [Putnam] to Plummer, 1 December 1893, folder P, box 33, HUG 1717.2.12, FWP Papers HUA.

78. Plummer to Putnam, 18 December 1893, folder P, box 33, HUG 1717.2.12, FWP Papers HUA.

79. Plummer to Commissioner of Indian Affairs, 26 February 1894, LR 1894:8799, RG 75, NARA-DC.

80. Plummer to Commissioner of Indian Affairs, 26 February 1894, LR 1894:8799, RG 75, NARA-DC.

81. Putnam to Commissioner of Indian Affairs, 9 March 1894, LR 1894:9961, RG 75, NARA-DC. Copy in folder I, box 32, HUG 1717.2.12, FWP Papers HUA.

82. Plummer to Commissioner of Indian Affairs, 15 May 1894, LR 1894:19527, RG 75, NARA-DC.

83. Putnam to Frederick J. V. Skiff, 27 May 1894, folder World's Columbian Exposition, Indians etc., box 34, HUG 1717.2.13, FWP Papers HUA.

84. Putnam to Commissioner of Indian Affairs, 28 May 1894, LR 1894:20605, RG 75, NARA-DC.

85. The fair was originally underwritten by the sale of stock worth $5 million. Johnson, *A History of the World's Columbian Exposition*, 9.

86. "A Land in Miniature: British Guiana's Exhibits at the World's Fair," *New Bethlehem Vindicator*, 11 August 1893, 2.

87. Putnam to Davis, 15 February 1893, folder D(2), box 31, HUG 1717.2.12, FWP Papers HUA.

88. See lists in archaeological reports, in folder World's Columbian Exposition–Misc. Papers–Reports (5), box 36, HUG 1717.2.14, FWP Papers HUA.

89. "Exhibit from British Guiana," *World's Columbian Exposition Illustrated* 3, no. 1 (March 1893): 301.

90. Daniel to Putnam, 22 July 1893, folder D(3), box 31, HUG 1717.2.12, FWP Papers HUA.

91. Daniel to Putnam, 22 July 1893.

92. "Sports in the Lagoon, Guiana Wins the Swimming Race," *Chicago Herald*, 12 August 1892; "Plans for the Swimming Race," *Chicago Tribune*, 11 August 1893, both in Scrapbook, Chicago World's Fair, 1891–1893, vol. 2, 3, HUG 1717.15, FWP Papers HUA.

93. Acting Commissioner R. [V.] Belt to John M. Ewing, 25 March 1893, 142–43; Belt to William B. Creager, 3 April 1893, 196–97; Belt to Creager, telegram, 14 April 1893, 250; Daniel Browning to Samuel Whittington, 4 May 1893, 333–34; Browning to Creager, 4 May 1893, 2:335; all in vol. 8, pt. 2, CMD-LS 1870–1908, RG 75, NARA-DC.

94. "Making Good Indians, Educating Savages at the Government's Expense: The Haskell Institute, Story of the Nation's Great Beneficence–An Indian Artist and His Vivid Pictures," *Chicago Inter Ocean*, 30 August 1893, box 2, HUG 1717.15, FWP Papers HUA; *Indian Helper* 8, no. 47 (11 August 1893): 2.

95. S. B. Whittington to Commissioner of Indian Affairs, 1 July 1893, LR 1893:23939, RG 75, NARA-DC.

96. Whittington to Commissioner of Indian Affairs, n.d., stamped rec'd 3 July 1893, LR 1893:23940, RG 75, NARA-DC.

97. Pratt, *Battlefield and Classroom*, 303, 305.

98. Pratt, *Battlefield and Classroom*, 307.

99. M. B. [Burgess], "Miss Burgess' Trip to and First Impressions of the Big Fair," *Indian Helper* 8, no. 46 (4 August 1893): 4.

100. *Indian Helper* 8, no. 30 (2 May 1893): 3.

101. "Catch Notes at the World's Fair Exhibit," *Indian Helper* 8, no. 47 (11 August 1893): 1.

102. *Indian Helper* 8, no. 51 (8 September 1893): 2.

103. *Indian Helper* 8, no. 52 (15 September 1893): 2.

104. "Catch Notes at the World's Fair Exhibit," 4.

105. *Indian Helper* 8, no. 52 (15 September 1893): 2.

106. Hertzberg, *The Search for an American Indian Identity*, 188; Superintendent, Pierre SD to Yellow Robe, 15 February 1922; Yellow Robe to C. J. Crandall, 20 February 1922; Yellow Robe to C. J. Crandall, 28 February 1922, all in box 20, 1211 Chauncey Yellow Robe, 1921–22, Series: Superintendent's Correspondence, 1917–26 [6007331], Pierre Indian School Collection, RG 75, NARA Central Plains. On Yellow Robe and other boarding school graduates as coaches, see Wade Davies's forthcoming book, tentatively titled *The Rise of Indian Basketball*.

107. Pratt, *Battlefield and Classroom*, 294–307; 12 September 1893, CAM vol. 50, WCE Records, CHMRC.

108. Pratt, *Battlefield and Classroom*, 303; box 1, Boys 1890–1896, Ledgers for Student Savings Accounts, 1890–1918, Records of the Carlisle Indian Industrial School, entry 1336, RG 75, NARA-DC. Records show sixty-six boys withdrawing funds for an entry titled "Chicago" on that date. There is no book available for girls' accounts. For a partial list of Carlisle boys who attended the fair, see "American Indians and Other Indigenous People Affiliated with the United States at the Fair" in appendix.

109. "Indian Girls Received," *Daily Inter Ocean*, 6 October 1893, 7.

110. "Many Attractions This Week," *Daily Inter Ocean*, 2 October 1893, 7.

111. Pratt, *Battlefield and Classroom*, 302.

112. Pratt, *Battlefield and Classroom*, 294–303. One of the number [pseudonym for the author of], "The Carlisle Indian Boys in the Chicago Parade," *Indian Helper* 8, no. 7 (28 October 1892).

113. William Saunders, "Report on the Progress of the Work of the Canadian Section of the World's Columbian Exposition," John Lowe Papers, Department of Agriculture, subject files, vol. 9, E8, MG 29, LAC.

114. News clipping from *Toronto Empire*, 7 October 1893, in Indian Affairs, Black Series files, reel C-10153, file 85,529, RG 10, LAC.

115. William Saunders, "Report on the Progress of the Work of the Canadian Section of the World's Columbian Exposition," 17 December 1892, folder (5) Exhibitions 1876–1893, vol. 9, John Lowe Papers; News clipping from *Toronto Empire*, 7 October 1893, reel C-10153, file 85,529, RG 10, both in LAC.

116. Hayter Reed Memorandum, 6 February 1893, vol. 46, RG 17; Mayne R. Daly to A. R. Angers, Minister of Agriculture, 20 April 1893, folder 2, vol. 76, RG 72, both in LAC.

117. News clipping from *Toronto Empire*, 7 October 1893, reel C-10153, file 85,529, RG 10, LAC; Report of Wilson Morton, Superintendent Liberal Arts, in "Report of the Executive Commissioner for Canada to the World's Columbian Exposition, Chicago, 1893," no. 8g, in *Sessional Papers of the Parliament of Canada*, 41, 44.

118. Folder 10 Notebook, World's Fair, series IV, box 29, Frederick Starr Papers, UCLSCRC.

119. Number 8g, "Report of the Executive Commissioner for Canada to the World's Columbian Exposition, Chicago, 1893," *Sessional Papers of the Parliament of Canada*.

120. Putnam to R. A. Waller, 19 October 1891, folder World's Columbian Exposition 1891–1892, box 34, HUG 1717.2.13; "List of FWP's Assistants Dept M," handwritten, n.d., folder World's Columbian Exposition–Misc. Papers–Administrative and Financial Records (1), box 36, HUG 1717.2.14, both in FWP Papers HUA.

121. Putnam to Davis, 22 November 1893, folder D(1), box 31, HUG 1717.2.12, FWP Papers HUA.

7. Working the Commercial Displays

1. The elevated railroad was also popular, with earnings second only to Cairo Streets. All of these listed earned more than $100,000. "Monthly Report," TNL.

2. Contracts are in *Concession Agreements*, CHMRC.

3. Henry Rightor, "The Esquimau Village," *New Orleans Democrat Times*, 14 July 1893, box 1, HUG 1717.15, FWP Papers HUA.

4. Teresa Dean, "It's Awfully Swell," *Daily Inter Ocean*, 24 April 1893, 2.

5. "The Esquimaux Arrive," *Hamilton [OH] Daily Republican*, 19 October 1892, 1; "News from the Field," *Richmond [IN] Enterprise*, 28 October 1892, 8.

6. "West and South," *Ackley [IA] Enterprise*, November 11, 1892, 2; "Good for the North Pole," *Daily Charlotte Observer*, 2 November 1892, 1. This story was printed in numerous other newspapers as well. Zwick, *Inuit Entertainers*, 16–17.

7. News item, *Springfield Republican*, 6 November 1892, 7; Zwick, *Inuit Entertainers*, 17.

8. *Evelena* passenger list, ancestry.com, accessed 8 June 2016; Zwick, *Inuit Entertainers*, 28.

9. "Notices," *Springfield Republican*, 17 November 1892, 4, is just one example.

10. "World's Fair Gossip: The Esquimaux Basking in the Eager and Nipping Air," *Iola [ks] Register*, 10 February 1893, 7.

11. "Harsh," *Patriot* (Harrisburg PA), 24 April 1893, 7.

12. "Courts of Record," *Daily Inter Ocean*, 4 April 1893, 11.

13. "U.S. Inflation Rate, 1893–2017," http://www.in2013dollars.com/1893 -dollars-in-2017, accessed 25 March 2018.

14. "Are against Furs in Hot Weather," *Chicago Daily Tribune*, 1 April 1893, 1.

15. "Too Warm to Wear Sealskin Coats," *Xenia Daily Gazette and Torchlight*, 1 April 1893.

16. "Esquimaux as Contract Laborers," *World*, 26 April 1893, 4.

17. Agreement with Carpenters and Builders Council, minutes of 3 April 1893, CAM vol. 47, and Minutes of 5 July 1893, CAM vol. 48, both in WCE records CHMRC.

18. "He Says They Are Compelled to Stay," *Chicago Daily Tribune*, 31 March 1893, 1.

19. "An Eskimaux Revolt," *Daily Inter Ocean*, 31 March 1893, 7.

20. "Esquimaux as Contract Laborers," *World*, 26 April 1893, 4.

21. "Courts of Record," *Daily Inter Ocean*, 4 April 1893, 11.

22. "Official Weather Forecast," *Chicago Daily Tribune*, 3 April 1893, 6; "Official Weather Forecast," *Chicago Daily Tribune*, 25 March 1893, 3.

23. Starr, "Anthropology at the World's Fair."

24. "Exodus of Eskimos," *Daily Inter Ocean*, 21 April 1893, 1.

25. "Chicago as a Summer Resort," *Wheeling Daily Intelligencer*, 5 April 1893, 4; untitled opinion, *Knoxville Journal*, 18 April 1893, 4; "Eskimos Break Away," *Weekly Register* (Point Pleasant wv), 25 April 1893, 2.

26. "Are against Furs in Hot Weather," *Chicago Daily Tribune*, 1 April 1893, 1.

27. "Esquimaux Win Habeas Corpus Cases," *Chicago Daily Tribune*, 4 April 1893, 9.

28. "Exodus of Eskimos," *Daily Inter Ocean*, 21 April 1893, 1.

29. Daniel to Putnam, 28 April 1893, folder d(3), box 32, HUG 1717.2.12, FWP Papers HUA.

30. "Exodus of Eskimos," *Daily Inter Ocean*, 21 April 1893, 1; "Eskimos Break Away," *Weekly Register* [Point Pleasant wv], 25 April 1893, 2.

31. "New Incorporations," *Chicago Daily Tribune*, 26 April 1893, 13.

32. "Two Eskimo Villages," *Daily Inter Ocean*, 23 April 1893.

33. "Two Eskimo Villages"; "Esquimaux Win Habeas Corpus Cases."

34. "Indignant Eskimos, at Chicago over the Ill-Bred Actions of Visitors," *Fort Worth Gazette*, 5 June 1893, 7.

35. "Important Decision," *Fort Wayne Sentinel*, 4 May 1893, 1.

36. "Courts of Record," *Daily Inter Ocean*, 23 June 1893, 11; "Courts of Record," *Daily Inter Ocean*, 29 August 1893, 8. Declaration, filed 22 June 1893, Dahms and Langworthy attorneys; Plea, filed 3 July 1893, Prussing and McCulloch attorneys for defendants; Stipulation to dismiss, filed 28 August 1893; all in Peter Pallacier vs. Arctic World's Exposition and P. M. Daniel, United States Circuit Court, Northern District of Illinois, Case file 22885; similar documents in Thomas Pallacier vs. Arctic World's Exposition and P. M. Daniel, United States Circuit Court, Northern District of Illinois, Case file 22884; all in Civil Case files, RG 21, NARA-Great Lakes Branch.

37. "Weird Funeral Rite," *Daily Inter Ocean*, 22 August 1893, 7.

38. Forbush, *Pomiuk*, 57, 125–26; F. N. Graves, "Things at the Fair," *Worcester [MA] Daily Spy*, 7 June 1893, 7; Catherine Cole, "Catherine Cole's Columbian Correspondence," *Daily Picayune*, 15 June 1893, 3. Another children's book was written more than a hundred years after Forbush. It romanticizes the story and, though based on some facts, is fiction. Walsh, *Pomiuk*.

39. Bates, "The Children of the Plaisance."

40. Stephens, "Eskimo Joe and His Foxskin."

41. Zwick, *Inuit Entertainers*, 6–7, 31–68.

42. Cole, "Catherine Cole's Columbian Correspondence."

43. "Bad Day for Fakirs," *Daily Inter Ocean*, 24 July 1893, 1.

44. "Return as Freaks" and "World's Columbian Exposition News," both in *Chicago Tribune*, 1 July 1893, 1.

45. "Red Men Get a Raise," *New Ulm Review*, 9 August 1893, 8.

46. Zerbe, *Pins from the Plaisance*, 53–54.

47. Zerbe, *Pins from the Plaisance*, 49–50, 54–55; "Curly and Rain-in-the-Face to Receive," *Chicago Tribune*, 8 June 1893, 9.

48. *The Dream City*; "Monthly Report and Statement of Collections," TNL.

49. John Lunneen Notebooks, CHMRC.

50. W. O. Smith, Secretary Planters' Labor and Supply Co. to Samuel Parker, Hawaiian Minister of Foreign Affairs, 9 November 1891, folder 1891 Chicago World's Fair, box FO&EX-37, Foreign Office and Executive Chronological Files, 1850–1900, Hawaii State Archives (HSA).

51. Tranquada and King, *The 'Ukulele*, 55–56; Farrell, ed., *Writings of Lorrin A. Thurston*, 83.

52. Thurston, "On Behalf of the Hawaiian Government and the Hawaiian Exhibit" to fair organizers, Chicago, 1 September 1891, folder 1891 Chicago World's Fair, box FO&EX-37, Foreign Office and Executive Chronological files, 1850–1900, HSA; Farrell, ed., *Writings of Lorrin A. Thurston*, 82; Tranquada and King, *The 'Ukulele*, 202n3;

"Thurston's Cyclorama: Description of the Show and the Statue of Pele," *Daily Bulletin* (Honolulu), 13 February 1893, 2.

53. Tranquada and King, *The 'Ukulele*, 56.

54. Advertisement, *Chicago Tribune*, 7 August 1893, 3. Same advertisement 4 August 1893, 6; and 3 August 1893, 6.

55. "Singers for Chicago," *Pacific Commercial Advertiser*, 20 July 1893, 3.

56. "Local and General News," *Daily Bulletin* (Honolulu), 6 September 1893, 3.

57. Workbook 3, John H. Wilson Research Notes, Bob Krauss Workbooks, HSA.

58. Imada, *Aloha America*, 59.

59. Krauss, *Johnny Wilson*, 41–42; notes from Wilson interviews, Workbook 3, John H. Wilson Research Notes, Bob Krauss Workbooks, HSA; local news in Honolulu *Daily Bulletin*, 24 May 1893, 3; Imada, *Aloha America*, 60. The *Hawaiian Gazette*, 15 August 1893, 9, reported that a hula troupe would leave for the fair in late August by the same ship they were reported to have departed on in May. *Pacific Commercial Advertiser*, 14 August 1893, 3, made the same report. *Hawaiian Star*, 14 August 1893, 5, reported that "more hula girls" were heading to Chicago. Perhaps this was another troupe.

60. "Last Living Court Dancer," *Honolulu Star-Bulletin*, 29 May 1960.

61. Interview with Jennie Wilson and Joann Keali'inohomoku, 1 January 1962, HAW 59.3.1, Bishop Museum Archives (BMA).

62. Betty Patterson, "Aunt Jennie at 90 Recalls Her Teens," *Honolulu Sunday Star-Bulletin*, 4 March 1962, Women's Section, 2.

63. Krauss, *Johnny Wilson*, 41–42.

64. From interview by Bob Holman in *Language Matters with Bob Holman*.

65. Patterson, "Aunt Jennie at 90."

66. Interview with Wilson and Keali'inohomoku, 1 January 1962.

67. Honolulu *Daily Bulletin*, 17 August 1893, 3.

68. Imada, "Transnational *Hula*," 165–66.

69. Imada, *Aloha America*, 75, 80; Krauss, *Johnny Wilson*, 42; "That Hula Troupe," *Daily Bulletin*, 23 May 1893, 3.

70. *Hawaiian Star*, 25 November 1893, 5.

71. Interviews with Jennie Wilson and Joann Keali'inohomoku, July 1962, HAW 59.14.1; and 1 January 1962, HAW 59.3.1, both in BMA. Not all of the peoples on the Midway had friendly relations. On 15 April the *Rock Island Daily Argus* reported on a brawl between Arabs and Inuits on Fifty-Fifth Street, 4.

72. Scidmore, "Tea, Coffee, and Cocoa at the Fair."

73. *The Economizer How and Where*, 57.

74. "World's Fair Music," *Chicago Tribune*, 22 August 1893, 4; "Second International Concert," *Daily Inter Ocean*, 22 August 1893, 7.

75. Minutes of 15 September 1893, CAM vol. 50, WCE records CHMRC.

76. "Central America Day at the Fair," *Chicago Tribune*, 3 July 1893, box 1, HUG 1717.15, FWP Papers HUA.

77. *Photographs of the World's Fair*, 309.

78. Caption for "Interior View of the Lapland Village," *The Dream City*.

79. "Caravels in Port," *Daily Inter Ocean*, 8 July 1893, 3.

80. Caption for photo of Columbian Guards, *The Dream City*.

81. Minutes of 5 July 1893, CAM vol. 48, WCE records CHMRC. Cayou reported his employment history in Student Records, Records of the Carlisle Indian Industrial School, RG 75, NARA-DC.

82. See notes on approval of purchase of 500 beds, 1,000 blankets, and 1,000 mattresses for the Guard, minutes of 15 March 1893, CAM vol. 46, WCE records CHMRC.

83. Emily E. Peake entry, Records of the Carlisle Indian Industrial School Data Concerning Former Students ca. 1898, entry 1333, RG 75, NARA-DC. Emily later married attorney Ernest Robitaille (Wyandotte) and they lived in Tulsa. Ernest Robitaille in Student Records of the Carlisle Indian Industrial School RG 75, NARA-DC.

84. Yost, *Buffalo Bill*, 123–27.

85. LaPier and Beck, *City Indian*, chap. 2; Moses, *The Indian Man*, says he leased fifty acres, 79.

86. Maddra, "American Indians in Buffalo Bill's Wild West," 134.

87. Deloria, "The Indians," 52.

88. Yost, *Buffalo Bill*, 236–37.

89. Note, *Chicago Dispatch*, citing *Sioux City Journal*, 9 June 1893, Buffalo Bill Scrapbook, William F. Cody Collection MS 006, MRL-BBCW.

90. Maddra, "American Indians in Buffalo Bill's Wild West," 136.

91. Maddra, "American Indians in Buffalo Bill's Wild West," 136.

92. Warren, *Buffalo Bill's America*, 365.

93. Maddra, "American Indians in Buffalo Bill's Wild West," 138, 140–41.

94. Warren, *Buffalo Bill's America*, 366.

95. Sell and Weybright, *Buffalo Bill*, 147. Deloria says the amount was $50 per month but cites Sell and Weybright.

96. Deloria, "The Indians," 51–53.

97. Warren, *Buffalo Bill's America*, 399.

98. Contracts dated 26 July 1893 are in LR 1893:28007, RG 75, NARA-DC.

99. Zerbe, *Pins from the Plaisance*, 45.

100. "Noble Red Men in Want," *Chicago Record*, 14 June 1893, Buffalo Bill Scrapbook, William F. Cody Collection MS 006, MRL-BBCW.

101. Welsh to R. V. Belt, 8 April 1891, LR 1891:12967, RG 75, NARA-DC.

102. Conversations with Rich Clow and JoAllyn Archambault, Spring 2015.

103. "Wild West and Congress of Rough Riders of the World Programme," Buffalo Bill Scrapbook, William F. Cody Collection MS 006, MRL-BBCW.

104. Warren, *Buffalo Bill's America*, 363–64.
105. "World's Fair Letter," *Herald and Tribune* (Jonesborough TN), 19 July 1893, 1.
106. Note, in *Chicago Globe*, 14 May 1893, Buffalo Bill Scrapbook, William F. Cody Collection MS 006, MRL-BBCW.
107. "Indians See the Show," newspaper not identified, ca. 2 May 1893; "Col. Cody's Indians at the Fair," *Chicago Times*, 2 May 1893; "Indians Greet the Great White Chief," *Chicago Herald*, 2 May 1893; all in Buffalo Bill Scrapbook, William F. Cody Collection MS 006, MRL-BBCW.
108. "Leslie at the Fair," *Chicago Daily News*, 5 May 1893, Buffalo Bill Scrapbook, William F. Cody Collection MS 006, MRL-BBCW.
109. Box 8, folder 10: "The Chicago World's Fair," series 3: Writings, Sub-Series 1: Alexander Proctor, Autobiographical Early Draft, Alexander Phimister Proctor Collection MS 242, MRL-BBCW.
110. Ebner, ed., *Sculptor in Buckskin*, 112.
111. See Beck, "The Myth of the Vanishing Race."
112. Rosaldo, "Imperialist Nostalgia."

8. Those Left Out

1. Blanchard, "Entertainment," 11.
2. "Ready for Crowd," *Chicago Daily Tribune*, 8 October 1893, 1; "Will Be a Great Day," *Inter Ocean*, 9 October 1893, 1; "Red Men Play a Game of Lacrosse," *Chicago Daily Tribune*, 10 October 1893, 9.
3. Copy of document by F. H. Mead, Secretary, 10 February 1892, folder World's Columbian Exposition–Misc. Papers–Administrative and Financial Records (1), box 36, HUG 1717.2.14, FWP Papers HUA.
4. "Wonders of the World's Fair, Great Show of the Native Races," *Springfield Daily Republican*, 20 August 1892. Also reported in "As Seen by Columbus, Native Americans at the Fair, Ethnological Exhibit Will Include Settlements of All the Aboriginal Tribes, Each Living under Conditions Observed at Home," *Chicago Herald*, 18 July 1892. box 1, HUG 1717.15, FWP Papers HUA.
5. Instructions for Collectors of Ethnological Materials, signed by Putnam, n.d., folder Misc. Papers–Administrative and Financial Records (5), box 36, HUG 1717.2.14, FWP Papers HUA.
6. September 1892 F. W. Putnam Report to the Director General, folder World's Columbian Exposition Monthly Reports to Director General July–December 1892, box 35, HUG 1717.2.13, FWP Papers HUA.
7. Memorandum Book, Columbian Exposition, 1892, HUG 1717.12, FWP Papers, HUA.
8. Putnam to Emma Sickels, 3 August 1892, folder World's Columbian Exposition–Correspondence S (2) Sickels, box 33, HUG 1717.2.12, FWP Papers HUA.

9. Tonkovich, *The Allotment Plot.*

10. Fletcher to Putnam, 30 November 1892, folder 1891–1900 F, box 9 1891–1900 C-F, HUG 1717.2.1, FWP Papers HUA.

11. Fletcher to Putnam, 22 May 1891; Fletcher to Putnam, 13 July 1891; Fletcher to Putnam, 30 November 1892, all in folder 1891–1900 F, box 9 1891–1900 C-F, HUG 1717.2.1, FWP Papers HUA.

12. Putnam to Mr. C. Mc C. Reeve, Secretary, [Minnesota] Board of World's Fair Managers, 6 March 1893, folder Ethnology + Archaeology–F. W. Putnam; George R. Davis to Reeve, 4 March 1893; Davis to State Commissioners of Minnesota, 11 March 1893, both in folder Director-General George R. Davis; D. A. Monfort to Reeve, 25 March 1893, folder D. A. Monfort, President, January 1893–April 1893, all in box 1, Correspondence 1891–1894, Board of World's Fair Managers (BWFM) Records, Minnesota Historical Society Library (MHSL).

13. Monfort to Reeve, 17 March 1893; Monfort to Reeve, 23 March 1893, both in folder D. A. Monfort, President, January 1893–April 1893, box 1, Correspondence 1891–1894, BWFM Records, MHSL.

14. Monfort to Reeve, 25 March 1893, folder D. A. Monfort, President, January 1893–April 1893, box 1, Correspondence 1891–1894, BWFM Records, MHSL.

15. Beaulieu to Reeve, 30 March 1893, folder B Miscellaneous 1891–1894, box 2, Miscellaneous Correspondence, BWRM Records, MHSL.

16. Lamphere to Monfort, 29 March 1893, folder George N. Lamphere, 1891–1894, box 1, Correspondence 1891–1894, BWFM Records, MHSL.

17. L. P. Hunt to Reeve, 29 April 1893, folder L. P. Hunt Mn State Superintendent 1891–1893 May, box 1, Correspondence 1891–1894, BWFM Records, MHSL.

18. Putnam to Director General, July 1892, folder World's Columbian Exposition Monthly Reports to Director General July–December 1892, box 35, HUG 1717.2.13, FWP Papers HUA.

19. "Special Exhibit by the Dept. of Indian Affairs," William Saunders, in "Report on the Progress of the Work of the Canadian Section of the World's Columbian Exposition," 17 December 1892, folder (5) Exhibitions 1876–1893, vol. 9, John Lowe Papers, LAC.

20. Magnus Begg to Hayter Reed, 14 April 1893, Blackfoot Agency Letterbook, 1893–1896, vol. 1671, Microfilm C-14883, RG 10, LAC.

21. Putnam to William Curtis, 10 February 1893, folder World's Columbian Exposition, Indians, etc., box 34, HUG 1717.2.13, FWP Papers HUA.

22. Putnam to the Director General, September 1892, folder World's Columbian Exposition Monthly Reports to Director General July–December 1892, box 35, HUG 1717.2.13, FWP Papers HUA.

23. See copious correspondence, primarily to Putnam, in boxes 31–33, HUG 1717.2.12; and boxes 34–35, HUG 1717.2.13, FWP Papers HUA.

24. Petition to President and Cabinet of the United States of America, and Petition to the Commissioners, the Columbian Exposition, 29 June 1891. One witnessed by J. F. Sisson where x marks were made; some were signed. Medicine Bull (Chief), Iron Nation (Chief), Big Mane (Judge), Alex Recountre, Moses Brazean, Standing Cloud, Charley Ellis (Farmer), John Deecks (Police), Frank Liar (Police), Louis Desoitt [?] (Interpreter), Philip Councillor [?], Buck Antelope, Robert Shield (Police), S. Spotted Horse (Police), Battiste C. Bear Bird, Bull Head, Boy Elk, William L. Smith, One to Play With (Chief), Driving Hawk (Chief), Pretty Voice, Thomas Lodge, James Little, Poor Clown, Sam'l M. Bull, Elk Whistle, John, High Elk, Joseph Eagle Star, David Zephier [?] (Herder). The other witnessed by R. J. Dixon and W. R. Buckholder. Signed by [Dixon:] Mark Wells, White Ghost, Wizi, Bull Ghost, Dog Back, Stattering [*sic*] Bear, Fat, His Battle, Surrounded, With Tail, Crow Man, Drifting Goose, Weasel Woman, Little Dog, Frank Black, Blanket, [Buckholder]: Chickpa, Half Day, Hears the Wind, Rain in the Face, Arrow, Smoke Maker, Bad Moccasin, Chas. Parkhurst, Antoine Rondell, Red Water [Dixon], Shoots Enemy, Plays with Iron, Lefthand Bull, Runs all Over, Seeing Elk, Highwalker. Albert C. Hopkins, who had addresses in Milwaukee and Chicago, apparently organized the petition effort. He said that he did not attempt to get "a great number of signatures, but, rather, the endorsening [*sic*] of all the leading and representative Indians, and it will be found that this has been done." Hopkins to Columbian Commissioner, 27 June 1891. The stamped envelope he included with the petitions, with his request to send a set to the president and cabinet, is in the file, unused. See also Hopkins to Director General, 6 May 1891, folder World's Columbian Exposition, Indians etc., box 34, HUG 1717.2.13, FWP Papers HUA.
25. "Miss Sickels Is Answered," *New York Mail and Express,* 31 May 1893. Copy in folder s(2) E. Sickels, box 33, HUG 1717.2.12, FWP Papers HUA.
26. "Indians at the Fair," *Inter Ocean,* 18 August 1892, 5.
27. "World's Fair Notes," clipping, newspaper not identified, n.d., folder s(2), box 33 P-Z, HUG 1717.2.12, FWP Papers HUA; J. H. Clendenning letter, 2 May 1892 (letter missing from file), LR 1892:17570, RG 75, NARA-DC.
28. Morgan to Davis, 6 June 1892, vol. 7, 2:73, CMD-LS, RG 75, NARA-DC.
29. Davis to Morgan, 11 June 1892, LR 1892:21403, RG 75, NARA-DC.
30. John W. Foster to Secretary of the Interior, 23 August 1892, folder August 23, 1892, LR, RG 48, NARA-CPM.
31. Attorney General H. H. Miller to Secretary of State, 25 August 1892, folder August 25, 1892, LR, RG 48, NARA-CPM.

32. "Indians to Make an Exhibit," *Chicago Tribune*, 8 February 1893, 8.

33. Kuehn to William E. Curtis, 22 May 1892; Kuehn to Director General Davis, 15 June 1892, both in folder World's Columbian Exposition, Indians etc., box 34, HUG 1717.2.13, FWP Papers HUA.

34. Putnam to Curtis, 11 June 1892, folder World's Columbian Exposition, Indians etc., box 34, HUG 1717.2.13, FWP Papers HUA.

35. Putnam to Curtis, 10 February 1893, folder World's Columbian Exposition, Indians etc., box 34, HUG 1717.2.13, FWP Papers HUA.

36. Weare to Putnam, 23 June 1891; Putnam to Weare, 29 June 1891, both in folder World's Columbian Exposition, Indians etc., box 34, HUG 1717.2.13, FWP Papers, HUA; Weare to Morgan, 30 July 1891, LR 1891:27942, RG 75, NARA-DC.

37. For a biography of Jaxon, see Smith, *Honoré Jaxon*.

38. Jaxon, Mato Nazin Cinca (Henry Standing Bear), and Molano to Putnam, 15 February 1892, folder J, box 32, HUG 1717.2.12, FWP Papers, HUA.

39. Jaxon to Davis, 24 December 1891; Putnam to Jaxon, 18 January 1892, both in folder J, box 32, HUG 1717.2.12, FWP Papers HUA.

40. Standing Bear to Morgan, 15 January 1891, folder S(2), box 33, HUG 1717.2.12, FWP Papers, HUA.

41. Sickels to Putnam, 17 November 1892, folder S (2), box 33, HUG 1717.2.12, FWP Papers, HUA; Smith, *Honoré Jaxon*, 49–64. The conflict between Sickels and Putnam is well documented in correspondence in folder S (2).

42. Memorandum [by Putnam] in response to Sickels's letter of 17 November 1892, n.d.; Putnam to Davis, 24 November 1892, both in folder S(2), box 33, HUG 1717.2.12, FWP Papers HUA.

43. Daniel Dorchester, Superintendent of Indian Schools, Redfield SD, to Commissioner of Indian Affairs, 6 July 1891, enclosing petition from Santee Sioux Indians. LR 1891:24311, RG 75, NARA-DC.

44. S. Draper, Attorney, to Senator Charles Manderson, 22 February 1892, LR 1892:12255, RG 75, NARA-DC.

45. Newspaper article, "The Santee Indian Band: A Musician's Estimate of the Only Pure American Banh [*sic*] in the World." n.d. (ca. 1888?), reporting on a letter to the Lancaster PA *New Era*; "The Santee Band," *Sioux City Journal*, 6 October 1888. Both in LR 1892:12255, RG 75, NARA-DC. The "Santee Indian Band" article identified the band members as Mr. V. P. Mitchell (E♭ cornet and leader), Mr. Oliver La Croix, Mr. Daniel Graham (Reservation Government Police,) Mr. Charles Frazier, Mr. John Jones, Mr. Joseph Redwing, Mr. Frank Jones, Mr. Stephen B. Smith, Mr. George Redowl, Mr. Eli Abraham, Mr. James W. Garvie, Mr. John Green, Mr. Joseph Kitto, Mr. Job Goodteacher, and Master Charley Graham, side drummer.

46. Morgan to James E. Helms, 30 March 1892, vol. 7, 1:267–68, CMD-LS, RG 75, NARA-DC.

47. Troutman, *Indian Blues*, 111.

48. C. C. Lay inquiry, 4 February 1892, LR 1892:4957, RG 75, NARA-DC; Morgan to Lay, 18 February 1892, vol. 7, 1:61, CMD-LS, RG 75, NARA-DC.

49. Cusick to Putnam, 27 September 1891, folder C, box 31 A-D, HUG 1717.2.12, FWP Papers HUA.

50. Fenollosa to Putnam, 7 September 1892, folder World's Columbian Exposition 1891–93, box 35, HUG 1717.2.13, FWP Papers HUA.

51. Johansen, *Forgotten Founders*; Grinde and Johansen, *Exemplar of Liberty*; Beck, "From Colonization to Self-Determination," 14.

52. Fenollosa to Putnam, 7 September 1892.

53. Holgate to Putnam, 27 July 1891, folder World's Columbian Exposition 1891–93 Ethnological Assets Indexed, box 34, HUG 1717.2.13, FWP Papers HUA.

54. For descriptions of the establishment of this bison herd, see Whealdon, *I Will Be Meat for My Salish*.

55. Miles to Allard, 2 February 1892, LR 1892:11802, RG 75, NARA-DC.

56. Miles to Morgan, 5 February 1892, LR 1892:3317, RG 75, NARA-DC; copy in folder World's Columbian Exposition, Indians etc., box 34, HUG 1717.2.13, FWP Papers HUA.

57. Morgan to Miles, 20 February 1892, vol. 7, 1:86–87, CMD-LS, RG 75, NARA-DC; copy in folder World's Columbian Exposition, Indians etc., box 34, HUG 1717.2.13, FWP Papers HUA.

58. Miles to Putnam, 19 March 1892, folder World's Columbian Exposition, Indians etc., box 34, HUG 1717.2.13, FWP Papers HUA.

59. Hill, *Webs of Kinship*.

60. Ronan to Morgan, 25 March, 1892, LR 1892:11802, RG 75, NARA-DC.

61. Morgan to Ronan, 6 April 1892, vol. 7, 1:302, CMD-LS, RG 75, NARA-DC; copy in folder World's Columbian Exposition, Indians etc., box 34, HUG 1717.2.13, FWP Papers HUA.

62. April 1892 report, folder World's Columbian Exposition, Monthly Reports to Director General January–June 1892, box 35, HUG 1717.2.13, FWP Papers, HUA.

63. Morgan to Ronan, 23 April 1892, vol. 7, 1:379, CMD-LS, RG 75, NARA-DC.

64. Putnam to Morgan, 27 May 1892; Putnam to Miles, 27 May 1892, both in LR 1892:19946, RG 75, NARA-DC.

65. Miles to Putnam, 13 May 1892, LR 1892:19946, RG 75, NARA-DC.

66. "Big Ad for Montana," *Interlake*, 13 May 1892, 1.

67. Putnam to Miles, 27 May 1892, LR 1892:19946, RG 75, NARA-DC.

68. Acting Commissioner Robert V. Belt to Miles, 10 October 1892, vol. 8, 1:18–19, CMD-LS, RG 75, NARA-DC.

69. April 1893 Report; Extra Report, 17 April 1893, both in folder World's Columbian Exposition, Monthly Reports to Director General January–May 1893, box 35, HUG 1717.2.13, FWP Papers, HUA.

70. "Personal and General Notes," *Daily Picayune*, 10 May 1893, 4.

71. "Prof. Putnam's Hard Luck: His Difficulties with the Anthropological Exhibit," *New York Times*, 22 May 1893, 9.

72. "Sioux Indians Coming, Fifteen Will Join Putnam's Anthropological Exhibit," *Chicago Times*, 28 July 1893, box 1, HUG 1717.15, FWP Papers HUA.

73. Evidence of this is scattered throughout the CAM, WCE records CHMRC, for example.

74. Lieutenant Harlon to Mr. Gray, n.d., folder World's Columbian Exposition, Indians etc., box 34, HUG 1717.2.13, FWP Papers HUA.

75. [Frederic] A. Ober notes, n.d.; R. M. Bartleman to Curtis, 18 August 1891; Curtis to Walker Fearn, 15 April 1892; Curtis to Putnam, 25 July 1892; Gustav[o] Aguila Sr., Director Gnal de la Exposicion Universal de Chicago, to Curtis, 1 November 1892; Fernando Gaitan to Curtis, n.d.; Putnam to Curtis, 27 July 1892, all in folder World's Columbian Exposition, Indians etc., box 34, HUG 1717.2.13, FWP Papers HUA.

76. Meeting minutes, "Indian Office Exhibit at the World's Columbian Exposition," 1 February 1892, T. J. Morgan, Frederic Putnam, H. A. Taylor, John M. Ewing, and A. C. Fletcher, folder World's Columbian Exposition, Indians, etc., box 34, HUG 1717.2.13, FWP Papers HUA.

77. Memorandum by Lieut. Safford, n.d., folder World's Columbian Exposition, Indians etc., box 34, HUG 1717.2.13, FWP Papers HUA.

78. Egan, "Exhibiting Indigenous Peoples," 8.

79. Stumpf to Curtis, 3 April 1892, folder World's Columbian Exposition, Indians etc., box 34, HUG 1717.2.13, FWP Papers HUA. Stumpf also warned Curtis of another group's efforts to bring a "musical band of Indians" and indicated his disapproval.

80. E.D. York to Putnam, 30 September 1892, folder World's Columbian Exposition, Indians etc., box 34, HUG 1717.2.13, FWP Papers HUA.

81. Egan, "Exhibiting Indigenous Peoples," 8.

82. Egan, "Exhibiting Indigenous Peoples," 9.

83. Personal communication with Robert Smale, 13 March 2014 and 11 February 2015.

84. Egan, "Exhibiting Indigenous Peoples," 11–12.

85. Egan, "Exhibiting Indigenous Peoples," 6.

86. "Indians and the World's Fair," *New York Mail and Express*, 22 May 1893; "Miss Sickels Is Answered," *New York Mail and Express*, 31 May 1893, both in folder s(2) E. Sickels, box 33, HUG 1717.2.12, FWP Papers, HUA.

87. "Captain Henri Berger Brought from Europe Makes King's Band," *Advertiser*, 15 January 1928. In box 1, notebook 3, September 1891–June 1893, John H. Wilson Research Notes, Bob Krauss Workbooks, HSA.

88. "About the Band," *Pacific Commercial Advertiser*, 4 February 1893, 3.

89. See 1890 census notes from Blount Report, 73–74, in box 1, notebook 3, September 1891–June 1893, John H. Wilson Research Notes, Bob Krauss Workbooks, HSA.

90. Hawaii Nei letter to editor, *Daily Bulletin*, 8 September 1893, 1.

91. "The Hawaiian National Band Want Sufficient Inducement," *Daily Advertiser*, 7 September 1893, 3; "Frisco Gossip," *Pacific Commercial Advertiser*, 7 September 1893, 4; "The Band Will Not Leave," *Daily Bulletin*, 11 September 1893, 2; "The Band Won't Go," *Pacific Commercial Advertiser*, 11 September 1893, 4.

Afterword/Afterward

1. Gilbert, *Whose Fair?* 184.

2. On age-old bison economies, see Brink, *Imagining Head-Smashed-In*.

3. See Indian agent reports in *Annual Report of the Department of Indian Affairs, for the Year ended 31st December, 1893*, in *Sessional Papers of the Parliament of Canada*, 7th Parliament, 4th sess., 1894, vol. 27, no. 10, and correspondence from agents in Agency Records, LAC.

4. Standing Bear to D. M. Browning, 30 April 1893, LR 1893:17350, RG 75, NARA-DC.

5. Clark, *Lone Wolf v. Hitchcock*.

6. Baker, *Anthropology and the Racial Politics of Culture*, 115.

7. Perdue, *Race and the Atlanta Cotton States Exposition*, 53.

8. Denson, *Monuments to Absence*, 8.

9. Perdue, *Race and the Atlanta Cotton States Exposition*, 76–88.

10. Parezo and Fowler, *Anthropology Goes to the Fair*, 100–134. For extensive lists of American Indian participants, broken down by tribal group, with schoolchildren listed separately, see Tables 2.1 and 2.4 through 2.7, 405–8, 410–14.

11. Parezo and Fowler, *Anthropology Goes to the Fair*, 100.

12. Parezo and Fowler, *Anthropology Goes to the Fair*, 194–233; Table 1.1 and Table 1.2, 403–4.

13. Parezo and Fowler, *Anthropology Goes to the Fair*, 104–10, 113, 121–22, 224–25, 242–43.

14. Bokovoy, *San Diego World's Fairs*, 128–37.

Bibliography

Manuscripts and Archives

American Philosophical Society, Philadelphia
  Franz Boas Papers, 1862–1942, MSS B.B61
  Franz Boas Professional Papers, 1860–1942, MSS B.B61p
  Robert Bell Papers, 1874–1908, MSS B.B421
Bishop Museum Archives, Honolulu
  Interviews with Jennie Wilson and Joann Keali'inohomoku
    1 January 1962, HAW 59.3.1
    July 1962, HAW 59.14.1
Buffalo Bill Center of the West, McCracken Research Center, Cody WY
  Alexander Phimister Proctor Collection, MS 242
  James Wojtowicz Collections, 1880–1929, MS 327
  Vincent Mercaldo Collection, 1850–1945, MS 071
  William F. Cody Collection, MS 006
Chicago History Museum Research Center
  Concession Agreements, 1893 World's Columbian Exposition. Printed by
    the Chicago Legal News Co. 7 vols.
  John Lunneen Notebooks
  World's Columbian Exposition Records, 1890–1904
Chicago Public Library, Harold Washington Library Center Special
  Collections
  World's Columbian Exposition Ephemera Collection
Field Museum of Natural History, Chicago
  Anthropology Department
    Accession Records
  Archives
    Cash Book, 1893–95
    George Dorsey Ancon Peru 1893 papers

Payroll Ledgers for F.C.M. 1894

Time Book, 1894–95 (Building Personnel)

World's Columbian Exposition Financial Ledger

Harvard University Archives

Papers of Frederic Ward Putnam

HUG 1717.2.1 General Correspondence 1851–1947

HUG 1717.2.2 Administrative, Financial, Etc.

HUG 1717.2.6 Publications

HUG 1717.2.12 World's Columbian Exposition Correspondence A-Z

HUG 1717.2.13 World's Columbian Exposition Correspondence A-T

HUG 1717.2.14 World's Columbian Exposition Miscellaneous Papers

HUG 1717.12 Memorandum Book, Columbian Exposition, 1892

HUG 1717.15 Scrapbook, Chicago World's Fair, 1891–93

Hawaii State Archives

Foreign Office and Executive Chronological Files, 1850–1900

John H. Wilson Research Notes, Bob Krauss Workbooks

Library and Archives Canada, Ottawa

Hayter Reed Fonds, MG 29, E 106

John Lowe Papers, Department of Agriculture, Subject Files, MG 29, E 18

RG 10. Department of Indian Affairs Records

RG 17. Agriculture Department Correspondence Records

RG 72. Canadian Government Expositions, World's Columbian Exposition, Department of Agriculture Letterbooks, 1892–1894

Minnesota Historical Society Library

Board of World's Fair Managers Records

Correspondence 1891–94

Miscellaneous Correspondence

National Anthropological Archives, Smithsonian Institution

Bureau of American Ethnology, Letters Received 1888–1906

C. Bergmann, "List of Figures and Costumes for Exhibition at World's Columbian Exposition in Chicago 189[3]," NAA MS 7217

Photo Lot 2000–14

National Archives and Records Administration, Central Plains, Kansas City MO

RG 75. Records of the Bureau of Indian Affairs

Pierre Indian School Collection

National Archives and Records Administration, College Park

RG 48. Records of the Department of the Interior

Letters Received and Other Records, 1891–94. Entry 386.

National Archives and Records Administration, Great Lakes Branch

RG 21. Records of District Courts of the United States

Civil Case Files. U.S. Circuit Court for the Northern District of
Illinois, Eastern Division (Chicago)
National Archives and Records Administration, Washington DC
RG 75. Records of the Bureau of Indian Affairs
Letters Received, 1881–1907. Entry 91.
Letters Sent, 1870–1908. Entry 96.
Correspondence Accounts Division
Correspondence Miscellaneous Division
Records of the Carlisle Indian Industrial School
Data Concerning Former Students ca. 1898. Entry 1333
Student Information Cards, 1879–1918. Entry 1329
Student Records, 1879–1918. Entry 1327
RG 94. War Department Records
Records of the Adjutant General's Office
Letters Received by the Appointments, Commissions, and Personal Branch Document File. Entry 297.
4653 ACP 1888 (Cornelius C. Cusick)
Newberry Library, Chicago
Mary E. Chase Diary
"Monthly Report and Statement of Collections, etc. of the W.C.E.
1893." R 1832.0057
Papers of Carlos Montezuma
Peabody Museum of Archaeology and Ethnology Archives, Harvard
University
Accession Records
Central American Expedition Records, 1891–1900
Charles Pickering Bowditch (1842–1921) Papers 1869–1918. Accession 41-7
Frederic Ward Putnam Papers, 1855–1935
Frederic Ward Putnam Peabody Museum Director Records
Smithsonian Institution Archives
SIA RU000070, Smithsonian Institution, Exposition Records of the
Smithsonian Institution and the United States National Museum,
1867–1940
Series 10, World's Columbian Exposition (Chicago, 1893), 1886,
1890–1895
SIA RU000158, United States National Museum, Curators' Annual
Reports, 1881–1964
SIA RU000305, United States National Museum Office of the Registrar
Accession Records, 1834–1958. Microfilm
University of Chicago Library Special Collections Research Center
Frederick Starr Papers, 1868–1935

Published Works

Addresses and Reports of Mrs. Potter Palmer, President of the Board of Lady Managers, World's Columbian Commission. Chicago: Rand, McNally, 1894.

Algren, Nelson. *Chicago: City on the Make.* Garden City NY: Doubleday, 1951.

Annual Report of the Commissioner of Indian Affairs to the Secretary of the Interior, 1892. Washington: Government Printing Office, 1892.

Annual Report of the Commissioner of Indian Affairs to the Secretary of the Interior, 1893. Washington: Government Printing Office, 1893.

Annual Report of the Department of Indian Affairs, 1891 (#14). In *Sessional Papers, Volume 10, Second Session of the Seventh Parliament of the Dominion of Canada*, 1892, vol. 25 A. 1892, pt. 1.

Annual Report of the Department of Indian Affairs, for the Year Ended 31st December, 1893. In *Sessional Papers of the Parliament of Canada Fourth Session, Seventh Parliament*, 1894, vol. 27, no. 10.

Atkinson, Maureen L. "The 'Accomplished' Odille Morison: Tsimshian Cultural Intermediary of Metlakatla, British Columbia." In *Recollecting: Lives of Aboriginal Women of the Canadian Northwest and Borderlands*, ed. Sarah Carter and Patricia McCormack, 135–56. Edmonton: Athabasca University Press, 2011.

——. "One-Sided Conversations: Chapters in the Life of Odille Morison." Master's Integrated Studies Project, Athabasca University, 2008.

Baker, Lee D. *Anthropology and the Racial Politics of Culture.* Durham NC: Duke University Press, 2010.

Baker, Lori E. "Mitochondrial DNA Haplotype and Sequence Analysis of Historic Choctaw and Menominee Hairshaft Samples." PhD diss., University of Tennessee, Knoxville, 2001.

Bancroft, Hubert Howe. *The Book of the Fair: An Historical and Descriptive Presentation of the World's Science, Art, and Industry, as Viewed through the Columbian Exposition in Chicago.* 2 vols. Chicago: Bancroft, 1893.

——. *The Book of the Fair, an Historical and Descriptive Presentation of the World's Science, Art, and Industry as Viewed through the Columbian Exposition at Chicago in 1893.* 5 vols. Chicago: Bancroft, 1893.

Bates, Clara Doty. "The Children of the Plaisance." *St. Nicholas: An Illustrated Magazine for Young Folks* 32, no. 1 (November 1893): 55.

Bauer, William J. Jr. *We Were All Like Migrant Workers Here: Work, Community, and Memory on California's Round Valley Reservation, 1850–1941.* Chapel Hill: University of North Carolina Press, 2009.

Beck, David R. M. "'Collecting among the Menomini': Cultural Assault in Twentieth-Century Wisconsin." *American Indian Quarterly* 34, no. 2 (Spring 2010): 157–93.

——. "From Colonization to Self-Determination: American Indian Higher Education before 1974." *Australian Journal of Indigenous Education* 27, no. 2 (1999): 12–23. Orig. in *Critical Issues in Indian Higher*

Education, ed. Joanna Brown, 16–24. Chicago: American Indian Press, 1995. ERIC number ED 388 478.

———. "The Myth of the Vanishing Race." *Edward S. Curtis's The North American Indian* website. Northwestern University Library and Library of Congress: mounted 2001–2017. Currently located at https://davidrmbeck .files.wordpress.com/2017/09/myth-of-the-vanishing-race-web-grab.pdf.

———. *The Struggle for Self-Determination: History of the Menominee Indians since 1854*. Lincoln: University of Nebraska Press, 2005.

Blanchard, David. "Entertainment, Dance, and Northern Mohawk Showmanship." *American Indian Quarterly* 7, no. 1 (1983): 2–26.

Boas, Franz. "The Anthropology of the North American Indian." In *Memoirs of the International Congress of Anthropology*, ed. C. Staniland Wake, 37–49. Chicago: Schulte, 1894.

Bokovoy, Matthew F. *The San Diego World's Fairs and Southwestern Memory, 1880–1940*. Albuquerque: University of New Mexico Press, 2005.

Bowden, Mark. *Pitt Rivers: The Life and Archaeological Work of Lieutenant General Augustus Pitt Rivers, DCL, FRS, FSA*. Melbourne Australia: Cambridge University Press, 1991.

Brink, Jack. *Imagining Head-Smashed-In: Aboriginal Buffalo Hunting on the Northern Plains*. Edmonton: AU Press, 2008.

Browman, David L., and Stephen Williams. *Anthropology at Harvard: A Biographical History, 1790–1940*. Cambridge MA: Peabody Museum Press/Harvard University Press, 2013.

Burton, Jeffrey. *Indian Territory and the United States, 1866–1906: Courts, Government, and the Movement for Oklahoma Statehood*. Norman: University of Oklahoma Press, 1995.

Cameron, William E., ed. *History of the World's Columbian Exposition*. Chicago: Columbian History, 1893.

———. *The World's Fair, Being a Pictorial History of the Columbian Exposition*. Philadelphia: Home Library, 1893.

Campbell, J. B., ed. *Campbell's Illustrated History of the World's Columbian Exposition in Two Volumes*. Chicago: J. B. Campbell, 1894.

Carter, Robert A. *Buffalo Bill Cody: The Man behind the Legend*. New York: John Wiley, 2000.

Carter, Sarah. *Lost Harvests: Prairie Indian Reserve Farmers and Government Policy*. Montreal: McGill-Queen's University, 1990.

Clark, Blue. *Lone Wolf v. Hitchcock: Treaty Rights and Indian Law at the End of the Nineteenth Century*. Lincoln: University of Nebraska Press, 1994.

Cole, Douglas. *Captured Heritage: The Scramble for Northwest Coast Artifacts*. Seattle: University of Washington Press, 1985.

The Columbian Exposition Album Containing Views of the Grounds. Chicago: Rand, McNally, 1893.

Dedicatory and Opening Ceremonies of the World's Columbian Exposition. Authorized by the Board of Control. Chicago: Stone, Kastler & Painter, 1893.

Deloria, Vine, Jr. "The Indians." In Brooklyn Museum of Art, *Buffalo Bill and the Wild West*, 45–56. Philadelphia: Brooklyn Museum (distributed by University of Pittsburgh Press), 1981.

Denson, Andrew. *Monuments to Absence: Cherokee Removal and the Contest over Southern Memory.* Chapel Hill: University of North Carolina Press, 2017.

Derks, Scott. *The Value of a Dollar: Prices and Incomes in the United States: 1860–2009.* 4th ed. Amenia NY: Grey House, 2009.

Dexter, Ralph W. "Putnam's Problems Popularizing Anthropology." *American Scientist* 54, no. 3 (1966): 315–32.

Documents of the Senate of the State of New York, One Hundred and Seventeenth Session, 1894. Vol. 10, no. 86. "Report of the Board of General Managers of the Exhibit of the State of New York at the World's Columbian Exposition." Transmitted to the Legislature April 18, 1894. Albany: James B. Lyon, State Printer, 1894.

Dorsey, George A. "Man and His Works." *Youth's Companion World's Fair Number*, 1893, 27.

The Dream City: A Portfolio of Photographic Views of the World's Columbian Exposition. St. Louis: N. D. Thompson, 1893.

Dreiser, Theodore. *The Titan.* New York: John Lane, 1914.

Dybwad, G. L., and Joy V. Bliss. *Annotated Bibliography: World's Columbian Exposition, Chicago 1893 Supplement.* Albuquerque: The Book Stops Here, 1999.

Ebner, Katharine C., ed. *Sculptor in Buckskin: The Autobiography of Alexander Phimister Proctor.* 2d ed. Norman: University of Oklahoma Press, 2009.

The Economizer: How and Where to Find the Gems of the Fair. Chicago: Rand, McNally, 1893.

Egan, Nancy. "Exhibiting Indigenous Peoples: Bolivians and the Chicago Fair of 1893." *Studies in Latin American Popular Culture* 28 (2010): 6–24.

Eighteenth Annual Report of the Commissioner of Labor, 1903: Cost of Living and Retail Prices of Food. Washington: Government Printing Office, 1903. Serial Set CIS no. 4739.

Ewers, John C. "A Century and a Half of Blackfeet Picture Writing." *American Indian Art Magazine* 8, no. 3 (Summer 1983): 52–61.

Farrell, Andrew, ed. *Writings of Lorrin A. Thurston.* Honolulu: Advertiser, 1936.

Fogelson, Raymond D. "The Red Man in the White City." In *Columbian Consequences: The Spanish Borderlands in Pan-American Perspective*, ed. David Hurst Thomas, 3:73–90. Washington DC: Smithsonian Institution Press, 1991.

Forbush, William Byron. *Pomiuk, a Waif of Labrador: A Brave Boy's Book for Brave Boys.* Boston: Pilgrim Press, 1903.

Freed, Stanley A. *Anthropology Unmasked: Museums, Science, and Politics in New York City.* Wilmington OH: Orange Frazer Press, 2012.

Gerlach, Dominic B. "St. Joseph's Indian Normal School, 1888–1986." *Indiana Magazine of History* 69, no. 1 (March 1973): 1–42.

Gilbert, James. *Perfect Cities: Chicago's Utopias of 1893.* Chicago: University of Chicago Press, 1993.

———. *Whose Fair? Experience, Memory, and the History of the Great St. Louis Exposition.* Chicago: University of Chicago Press, 2009.

Grinde, Donald A., Jr., and Bruce E. Johansen. *Exemplar of Liberty: Native America and the Evolution of Democracy.* Los Angeles: American Indian Studies Center, UCLA, 1991.

Gruber, Jacob W. "Ethnographic Salvage and the Shaping of Anthropology." *American Anthropologist* 72 (1970): 1289–99.

Harmon, Alexandra. *Rich Indians: Native People and the Problem of Wealth in American History.* Chapel Hill: University of North Carolina Press, 2010.

Hauptman, Laurence M. *Between Two Fires: American Indians in the Civil War.* New York: Free Press Paperbacks, 1995.

———. *Seven Generations of Iroquois Leadership: The Six Nations since 1800.* Syracuse: Syracuse University Press, 2008.

Hawthorne, Julian. *Humors of the Fair.* Chicago: E. A. Weeks, 1893.

Heald, Bruce D. *A History of the New Hampshire Abenaki.* Charleston SC: History Press, 2014.

Hertzberg, Hazel W. *The Search for an American Indian Identity: Modern Pan-Indian Movements.* Syracuse: Syracuse University Press, 1971.

Hill, Christina Gish. *Webs of Kinship: Family in Northern Cheyenne Nationhood.* Norman: University of Oklahoma Press, 2017.

Hinsley, Curtis M. "Anthropology as Education and Entertainment: Frederic Ward Putnam at the World's Fair." In *Coming of Age in Chicago: The 1893 World's Fair and the Coalescence of American Anthropology.*, ed. Curtis M. Hinsley and David R. Wilcox, 1–77. Lincoln: University of Nebraska Press, 2016.

———. "Frederic Ward Putnam, 1839–1915." In *Encyclopedia of Archaeology: The Great Archaeologists*, ed. Tim Murray, 1:141–54. Santa Barbara: ABC-Clio, 1999.

———. "The Museum Origins of Harvard Anthropology, 1866–1915." In *Science at Harvard University: Historical Perspective*, ed. Clark A. Elliot and Margaret W. Rossiter, 121–45. Bethlehem PA: Lehigh University Press, 1992.

Hinsley, Curtis M., and David R. Wilcox, eds. *Coming of Age in Chicago: The 1893 World's Fair and the Coalescence of American Anthropology.* Lincoln: University of Nebraska Press, 2016.

Hoffenberg, Peter H. *An Empire on Display: English, Indian, and Australian Exhibitions from the Crystal Palace to the Great War.* Berkeley: University of California Press, 2001.

Hoffman, Walter James. *The Menomini Indians.* New York: Johnson Reprint Organization, 1970. Originally published as one of several reports attached to the *14th Annual Report of the U.S. Bureau of Ethnology, 1892–93.* Washington: Government Printing Office, 1896.

Holmes, W. H. "The World's Fair Congress of Anthropology." *American Anthropologist* 6, no. 4 (October 1893): 423–34.

Hosmer, Brian C. *American Indians in the Marketplace: Persistence and Innovations among the Menominees and Metlakatlans, 1870–1920.* Lawrence: University Press of Kansas, 1999.

Hosmer, Brian C. and Colleen O'Neill, eds. *Native Pathways: American Indian Culture and Economic Development in the Twentieth Century.* Boulder: University Press of Colorado, 2004.

Hulst, Cornelia Steketee. *Indian Sketches: Pere Marquette and the Last of the Pottawatomie Chiefs.* New York: Longmans, Green, 1918.

Hunt, Lynn. *Writing History in the Global Era.* New York: W. W. Norton, 2014.

Imada, Adria L. *Aloha America: Hula Circuits through the U.S. Empire.* Durham: Duke University Press, 2012.

———. "Transnational *Hula* as Colonial Culture." *Journal of Pacific History* 46, no. 2 (2011): 149–76.

Indian Rights Association Papers, 1868–1968. Glen Rock NJ: Microfilming Corporation of America, 1974.

Jacknis, Ira. "George Hunt, Collector of Indian Specimens." In *Chiefly Feasts: The Enduring Kwakiutl Potlatch.* , ed. Aldona Jonaitis, 177–225. Seattle: University of Washington Press, 1991.

———. "Northwest Coast Indian Culture and the World's Columbian Exposition." In *Columbian Consequences: The Spanish Borderlands in Pan-American Perspective,* ed. David Hurst Thomas, 3:91–118. Washington DC: Smithsonian Institution Press, 1991.

Johansen, Bruce E. *Forgotten Founders: How the American Indian Shaped Democracy.* Boston: Harvard Common Press, 1982.

Johnson, Carolyn Schiller. "Performing Ethnicity: Performance Events in Chicago, 1893–1996." PhD diss., University of Chicago, 1998.

Johnson, Rossiter, ed. *A History of the World's Columbian Exposition Held in Chicago in 1893.* By Authority of the Board of Directors. 4 vols. New York: D. Appleton, 1897–98.

Kickingbird, Kirke, and Karen Ducheneaux. *One Hundred Million Acres.* New York: Macmillan, 1973.

Krauss, Bob. *Johnny Wilson: First Hawaiian Democrat.* Honolulu: University of Hawaii Press, 1994.

Lange, Gustav, Jr. "Then and Now: A Series of Interviews with Well-Known Men Whose Recollections of Their Early Associations in the Hat Trade Make Interesting Reading in Contrast with Present Methods." *American Hatter* 27, no. 1 (August 1897): 47–50.

Language Matters with Bob Holman. Film. David Grubin Productions and Pacific Islanders in Communications, 2014.

LaPier, Rosalyn R. *Invisible Reality: Storytellers, Storytakers, and the Supernatural World of the Blackfeet.* Lincoln: University of Nebraska Press, 2017.

LaPier, Rosalyn R., and David R. M. Beck. *City Indian: Native American Activism in Chicago, 1893–1934.* Lincoln: University of Nebraska Press, 2015.

Larner, John William, ed. *The Papers of Carlos Montezuma, M.D., including the Papers of Maria Keller Montezuma Moore and the Papers of Joseph W. Latimer.* Wilmington DE: Scholarly Resources, 1984. Microfilm.

Maddra, Sam. "American Indians in Buffalo Bill's Wild West." In *Human Zoos: Science and Spectacle in the Age of Colonial Empires,* ed. Pascal Blanchard, Nicolas Bancel, Gilles Boëtsch, Éric Deroo, Sandrine Lemaire and Charles Forsdick, trans. Teresa Bridgeman. Liverpool: Liverpool University Press, 2008.

Martinez, Matthew J. "Travels and Image Making in the Land of Enchantment." *Mellon Tribal College Research Journal* 1 (2013): 1–27.

Mason, Otis T. "Ethnological Exhibit of the Smithsonian Institution at the World's Columbian Exposition." *International Congress of Anthropology,* 1894, 208–16.

McNenly, Linda Scarangella. *Native Performers in Wild West Shows: From Buffalo Bill to Euro Disney.* Norman: University of Oklahoma Press, 2012.

McNitt, Frank. *The Indian Traders.* Norman: University of Oklahoma Press, 1962.

Meyer, Carter Jones, and Diana Royer, eds. *Selling the Indian: Commercializing and Appropriating American Indian Cultures.* Tucson: University of Arizona Press, 2001.

Midway Types: A Book of Illustrated Lessons about the People of the Midway Plaisance, World's Fair, 1893. Chicago: American Engraving, 1894.

Miller, Mark Edwin. *Claiming Tribal Identity: The Five Tribes and the Politics of Federal Acknowledgment.* Norman: University of Oklahoma Press, 2013.

Morison, Mrs. O. "Tsimshian Proverbs." *Journal of American Folk-Lore* 7 (1889): 285–86.

Moses, L. G. *The Indian Man: A Biography of James Mooney.* Urbana: University of Illinois Press, 1984.

———. "Indians on the Midway: Wild West Shows and the Indian Bureau at World's Fairs, 1893–1904." *South Dakota History* 21, no. 3 (1991): 205–29.

"Notes from the World's Columbian Exposition Chicago 1893." *Scientific American* 49, no. 8 (19 August 1893): 115.

Oriental and occidental northern and southern portrait types of the Midway plaisance; a collection of photographs of individual types of various nations from all parts of the world who represented, in the Department of ethnology, the manners, customs, dress, religions, music and other distinctive traits and peculiarities of their race. St. Louis: N. D. Thompson, 1894.

Parezo, Nancy. "The Formation of Ethnographic Collections: The Smithsonian Institution in the American Southwest." In *Advances in Archaeological Method and Theory*, ed. Michael B. Schiffer, 10:1–49. San Diego: Academic Press, 1987.

Parezo, Nancy J., and Don D. Fowler. *Anthropology Goes to the Fair: The 1904 Louisiana Purchase Exposition.* Lincoln: University of Nebraska Press, 2007.

Perdue, Theda. *Race and the Atlanta Cotton States Exposition of 1895.* Athens: University of Georgia Press, 2010.

Phillips, Ruth B. *Trading Identities: The Souvenir in Native North American Art from the Northeast, 1700–1900.* Seattle: University of Washington Press, 1998.

Photographs of the World's Fair. Chicago: Werner, 1894.

Pokagon, Chief [Simon]. "The Red Man's Greeting." Hartford MI: C. H. Engle, 1893.

Pratt, Richard Henry. *Battlefield and Classroom: Four Decades with the American Indian, 1867–1904.* 1964; rpt. Lincoln: University of Nebraska Press, 1987.

Putnam, Frederic Ward. "A Problem in American Anthropology." *Science* 243 (25 August 1899): 225–36.

Raibmon, Paige. *Authentic Indians: Episodes of Encounter from the Late-Nineteenth-Century Northwest Coast.* Durham: Duke University Press, 2005.

———. "Theatres of Contact: The Kwakwaka'wakw Meet Colonialism in British Columbia and at the Chicago World's Fair." *Canadian Historical Review* 81, no. 2 (June 2000): 157–92.

Rand, Jacki Thompson. *Kiowa Humanity and the Invasion of the State.* Lincoln: University of Nebraska Press, 2008.

Rasenberger, Jim. *High Steel: The Daring Men Who Built the World's Greatest Skyline.* HarperCollins: 2004.

Report of the Superintendent of Indian Schools, 1893. Washington: Government Printing Office, 1893.

Report to the Governor of the Board of General Managers of the New York State Exhibit at the World's Columbian Exposition. 31 December 1892. Albany: James B. Lyon, State Printer, 1893.

Rinehart, Melissa. "To Hell with the Wigs! Native American Representation and Resistance at the World's Columbian Exposition." *American Indian Quarterly* 36, no. 4 (2012): 403–42.

Rohner, Ronald P., ed. *The Ethnography of Franz Boas: Letters and Diaries of Franz Boas Written on the Northwest Coast from 1886 to 1931.* Chicago: University of Chicago Press, 1969.

Rosaldo, Renato. "Imperialist Nostalgia." *Representations* 26 (Spring 1989): 107–22.

Rountree, Helen C. *Pocahontas's People: The Powhatan Indians of Virginia through Four Centuries.* Norman: University of Oklahoma Press, 1990.

Russell, Don. *The Lives and Legends of Buffalo Bill.* Norman: University of Oklahoma Press, 1960.

Rydell, Robert W. *All the World's a Fair: Visions of Empire at American International Expositions, 1876–1916.* Chicago: University of Chicago Press, 1985.

Sandburg, Carl. *Chicago Poems.* New York: Henry Holt, 1916.

Schrader, Robert Fay. *The Indian Arts and Crafts Board: An Aspect of New Deal Indian Policy.* Albuquerque: University of New Mexico Press, 1983.

Scidmore, Eliza Ruhamah. "Tea, Coffee, and Cocoa at the Fair." *Harper's Bazaar,* 30 September 1893, 813–16.

Sell, Henry Blackman, and Victor Weybright. *Buffalo Bill and the Wild West.* Basin WY: Big Horn Books for Buffalo Bill Historical Center, 1979.

Sessional Papers of the Parliament of Canada, 4th sess., 7th Parliament, 1894, vol. 27, no. 7.

Shepp, James W., and Daniel B. Shepp, *Shepp's World's Fair Photographed.* Chicago: Globe Bible, 1893.

Silkenat, David. "Workers in the White City: Working Class Culture at the World's Columbian Exposition of 1893." *Journal of the Illinois State Historical Society* 104, no. 4 (Winter 2011): 266–300.

Smith, Carl. *The Plan of Chicago: Daniel Burnham and the Remaking of the American City.* Chicago: University of Chicago Press, 2006.

Smith, Donald B. *Honoré Jaxon: Prairie Visionary.* Regina Saskatchewan: Coteau Books, 2007.

Starr, Frederick. "Anthropology at the World's Fair." *Popular Science Monthly,* 1 September 1893, 610.

Stephens, C. A. "Eskimo Joe and His Foxskin." *Youth's Companion* 75, no. 14 (4 April 1901): 173.

Stern, Theodore. *The Klamath Tribe: A People and Their Reservation.* In *Monographs of the American Ethnological Society,* vol. 41, ed. June Helm. Seattle: University of Washington Press, 1966.

Thrush, Coll. *Indigenous London: Native Travels at the Heart of Empire.* New Haven: Yale University Press, 2016.

Todd, F. Dundas. *"Snap Shots" or World's Fair from a Camera through Recent Photos.* St. Louis: Woodward and Tiernan, 1893.

Tonkovich, Nicole. *The Allotment Plot: Alice C. Fletcher, E. Jane Gay, and Nez Perce Survivance*. Lincoln: University of Nebraska Press, 2012.

Tozzer, Alfred M. *Biographical Memoir of Frederic Ward Putnam, 1839–1915*. Washington DC: National Academy of Sciences, 1933.

Tranquada, Jim, and John King. *The 'Ukulele: A History*. Honolulu: University of Hawaii Press, 2012.

Troutman, John W. *Indian Blues: American Indians and the Politics of Music, 1879–1934*. Norman: University of Oklahoma Press, 2009.

Trujillo, Dennis P. "The Commodification of Hispano Culture in New Mexico: Tourism, Mary Austin, and the Spanish Colony Arts Society." PhD diss., University of New Mexico, 2003.

Ulrich, Laurel Thatcher. *The Age of Homespun: Objects and Stories in the Creation of an American Myth*. New York: Alfred A. Knopf, 2001.

U.S. Bureau of the Census. *Historical Statistics of the United States: Colonial Times to 1970*. Pt. 1. Washington DC: Government Printing Office, 1975.

Viola, Herman. *Diplomats in Buckskins: A History of Indian Delegations in Washington City*. Washington DC: Smithsonian Institution Press, 1981.

Von Baeyer, Edwinna. "Walking Tall: Mohawk Iron Workers." In *Hidden in Plain Sight: Contributions of Aboriginal Peoples to Canadian Identity and Culture*, ed. Cora Jane Voyageur, David R. Newhouse, and Dan Beavon, 65–82. Toronto: University of Toronto Press, 2011.

Walsh, Alice. *Pomiuk, Prince of the North*. Vancouver BC: Beach Holme, 2004.

Warren, Louis S. *Buffalo Bill's America: William Cody and the Wild West Show*. New York: Alfred A. Knopf, 2005.

———. *God's Red Son: The Ghost Dance Religion and the Making of Modern America*. New York: Basic Books, 2017.

———. "Wage Work in the Sacred Circle: The Ghost Dance as Modern Religion." *Western Historical Quarterly* 46, no. 2 (2015): 141–68.

Whealdon, Bon I. *I Will Be Meat for My Salish: The Federal Writers Project and the Buffalo of the Flathead Indian Reservation*. Helena: Montana Historical Society, 2002.

White, Leslie A. *The Ethnography and Ethnology of Franz Boas*. Bulletin of the Texas Memorial Museum 6. Austin: Texas Memorial Museum, 1963.

White, Richard. *Railroaded: The Transcontinentals and the Making of Modern America*. New York: W. W. Norton, 2011.

Winslow, Charles S., ed. *Indians of the Chicago Region*. Chicago: Soderlund Printing, 1946.

Wolfe, Patrick. "Settler Colonialism and the Elimination of the Native." *Journal of Genocide Research* 8, no. 4 (2006): 387–409.

Wolfe, Patrick. *Settler Colonialism and the Transformation of Anthropology: The Politics and Poetics of an Ethnographic Event*. London: Cassell, 1999.

Yost, Nellie Snyder. *Buffalo Bill: His Family, Friends, Fame, Failures, and Fortunes.* Chicago: Swallow Press, 1979.

Zerbe, Ida. *Pins from the Plaisance.* Cleveland: Borrows Brothers, 1893.

Zwick, Jim. *Inuit Entertainers in the United States: From the Chicago World's Fair through the Birth of Hollywood.* West Conshohocken PA: Infinity, 2006.

Index

Chavez, Pedro (Mayan), 156
Chavez, Samuel (Mayan), 156
Cheeno (Navajo), 117, 120
Cherokee Indians: unable to attend
  fair, 176, 177
Cheyenne and Arapaho Agency: col-
  lecting from, 85–86; conditions
  on, 86
Cheyenne and Arapaho Indians, xxiv
Cheyenne Indians: unable to attend
  fair, 169. *See also* Northern Chey-
  enne Indians
Chicago: as modern city, xix–xxi,
  34–35; as site of fair, xx
Chicago Day, 7, 167
Chicago Jim (Kwakwạka'wakw),
  109, 110
Chickasaw Indian exhibit: at Cotton
  States Exposition, 197
Chilcoton Indians: collecting from, 95
Chilocco Indian Agricultural
  School, 130
Chippewa Indians. *See* Ojibwe Indians
Choctaw Indians: unable to attend
  fair, 172, 176
Christmas Island, Nova Scotia: collecting from, 94
Cleveland, Grover, xx, 128, 164
Clow, Richmond, 243n11
Cody, William "Buffalo Bill," xvii;
  22–24, *23*, 26, 28, 30, 46, 135, 139,
  147, 158–65, 178, 186, 199
collecting: for Canadian government
  exhibit, 83–84, 92–99; for fair, 30,
  39, 44–45, 51–101. *See also* collectors; Smithsonian Institution
collectors: Canadian, 69, 75, 92–99;
  for fair, 32, 36–37, 51–52, 67, 68–69,
  70, 170; for museums, 83; role of,
  37–38, 66. *See also* Apache, Antonio; Bertolette, Daniel; Boas, Franz;
  Bolton, T. L.; Cusick, Cornelius C.

(Tuscarora); Daniel, Z. T.; Emmons,
  George; Hodgkins, C. L.; Hoffman,
  Walter James; Holgate, Thomas;
  Hunt, George (Kwakwạka'wakw);
  Laurent, Joseph (Abenaki); Mon-
  crieff, Scott; Morison, Odille
  (Tsimshian); Owens, John; Riddle,
  Maxwell; Safford, William E.; Sav-
  ille, Marshall; Sawyer, Fran; Sickels,
  Emma; Thompson, Edward; Tis-
  dale, Archibald; Welles, Roger
Colombian Indians: unable to
  attend fair, 187
colonialism, 101, 193–94, 196–97. *See
  also* imperialism
Colorado: sponsoring living exhibit,
  46, 65, 107, 117, 121, 200
Columbian Guard, 141, 142, 158
Comanche Indians: unable to
  attend fair, 169
commercial displays, xxvii, xxviii,
  7, 9–11, 22–25, 30, 32, 135–66. *See
  also* Buffalo Bill's Wild West and
  Congress of Rough Riders of the
  World; T. R. Roddy's American
  Indian village
Copan: collecting from, 77–80, 81;
  exhibit, 17
Cornplanter (Seneca), 114
Costa Rican Indians: unable to
  attend fair, 187
Cotton States Exposition, Atlanta
  1895, 197–98
Cowichan Agency: collecting from,
  95–96
Crazy Horse (Lakota), 56
Cree Indians: collecting from, 99;
  on fairgrounds, 107
Crook, George, 62
Crooked Lake Agency: collecting
  from, 99
Crow Creek Sioux, 175

Crowfoot (Blackfoot), 97
Crow Indians: collecting from, 88–89; unable to attend fair, 178
Crow Reservation: conditions in, 89
Crystal Palace Exhibition, xxi
cultural continuity, xxv, 9, 12, 163, 196
cultural mediators, 61, 69
Cummins, Frederick, 198
curio trade. *See* Indian curio trade
Curtis, William, 177, 187
Cushing, Frank, 112, 251n1
Cusick, Cornelius C. (Tuscarora), 53, 115, 180–81; as collector, 18, 51, 52–58, 63, 66, 67, 94; as ethnologist, 52–55, 58; and U.S. Army, 52–55
Cusick, James, 52
Cusick, Nicholas, 52

Dahomey village exhibit, 27–28, 136
Dakota Indians: on fairground, 46; unable to attend fair, 172
Daniel, Adolphus (Arawak), 46, 107, 123–25, 126, 134
Daniel, P. M., 137, 139, 141–44, 147
Daniel, Z. T.: as collector, 90
Davis, George, 43, 54, 176
Deans, James, 13, 70–71
Deer, Thomas (Inuit), 139, 142, 158; wages of, 125, 139, 199
Degoulick (Inuit), 144
Deloria, Vine, Jr., 159, 161
Denson, Andrew, 197
Department of Ethnology and Archaeology (Department M), 18, 35, 168
Department of Indian Affairs, Canada, 94; display, 93–94
Department of Justice, U.S., 176–77
"Digger" Indians: unable to attend fair, 169
Doctor of Clayoquot (Atlu), 96
Dole, Sanford, 190

Dorsey, George, 21–22, 112; collecting in Peru, 40–41, 66, 76–77, 81
Drabble, John (Kwakwaka'wakw), *109*, 112
Drabble, Mrs. (Kwakwaka'wakw), *109*
Dreiser, Theodore, 47

economic change, xvii, xix, xxiii–xxiv, 81, 106
economic conditions: in Indian country, xv–xvi, xvii, xxiii, xxiv, 68, 69–70, 75–76, 85–86, 89, 90, 92–93, 97–99, 117, 121–22, 163, 193–95, 196. *See also* cash economy
Egan, Nancy, 188–89
Eliot, Charles W., 32
Ellison, E. H., 186–87
Emmons, George, 70
Eneutseak, Esther (Inuit), 138, 144–45; as entrepreneur, 144–46; at Luna Park, 145; and wages working for Barnum and Bailey, 145–46
Eskimo village exhibit, 24–25, 26, 136, 137–47, *138*, *146*; at Cotton States Exposition, 197
Esquimau Bay, 137
Esquimaux Exhibition company, 142
Esquimaux village. *See* Eskimo village exhibit
ethnographers. *See* ethnologists
ethnological exhibit. *See* anthropological exhibits; Putnam, Frederic Ward: and anthropological exhibits
ethnological village, 12–16, 17, 28, 30, *45*, 46, 57, 106–27, 135; early plans for, 37–38, 42–44
ethnologists, 34; at Anthropological Congress, 18; as collectors, 37, 39
Exposition Universelle, Paris 1889, 29

lage, 24, 136, 147; unable to attend
  fair, 172; wages of, 147, 166, 200
Hodgkins, C. L., 38
Hoffenberg, Peter, xxi
Hoffman, Walter James: as collector,
  84–85, 88–90; salary of, 126
"Hoguel-get" Indians: collecting
  from, 95
Holgate, Thomas: as collector, 41, 182
Holmes, William Henry, 85
Honduran government: collecting
  at Copan, 79
Hopi Indians: collecting from, 85
Hopkins, Albert C., 176, 266n24
hula dancers, 151–54, 199
human remains: collected for fair,
  40–41, 42, 66, 76, 235n47
Hunt, David (Kwakwaka'wakw), *109*
Hunt, George (Kwakwaka'wakw),
  59; as collector, 18, 51, 58–61, 66,
  67, 71, 94, *109*; and contract, 107;
  as ethnologist, 18, 58, 112; on fairgrounds, 65, 108, 109–12; organizing Kwakwaka'wakw exhibit, 107;
  wages of, 125, 133, 173, 199–200
Hunt, Lynn, xvii–xviii

identity, xvi
Imada, Adria, 154
images of Indians, xxi–xxiii, 4, *14*,
  178–79, 191, 195. *See also* American
  Indians: representation of by others; American Indians: representation of by selves; caricatures
imperialism, xix, 29; cultural, xvii.
  See also colonialism
impostors, 65. *See also* Apache, Antonio; Indian Arts and Crafts Act
  (1935); Jaxon, Honoré Joseph
Indian Arts and Crafts Act (1935), 116
Indian curio trade, xxii, xxiii, 113–14,
  115–16, 148. *See also* tourist trade

Indian guides, 74
Indian Rights Association, 228n15;
  and Navajos at fair, 119
Indian school exhibit. *See* boarding
  school exhibit, Canadian; boarding school exhibit, U.S.
Indian Territory, 176; legal status of,
  176–77
indigenous people: on display, 29
industrialization, 193. *See also*
  modernization
International Colonial and Export
  Exhibition, Netherlands 1883, 29
interpreters, 75, 85, 88
Inuits: in Chicago before fair, 137–
  39; at Eskimo village display, 24–
  25, 137–47, 191; protesting their
  conditions, 139–44; wages of,
  125, 137, 139, 142, 144, 166, 200;
  and weather, 138–39, 141; working outside fairgrounds, 142,
  158, 197
Iroquois Indians. *See* Haudenosaunee Indians

Jack, Luther (Tuscarora), 114, 115
Jacknis, Ira, 45, 58, 112
Jackson Park, xx–xxi
Jaxon, Honoré Joseph, 178–79, 191, 197
Jibara Indians: unable to attend
  fair, 187
Joe. *See* Nallook (Inuit)
Johnny Jump Up (Yoo-Ka-Lucke), *140*
Johnson, Andrew, 52
Johnson, Carolyn Schiller, xviii
Johnson, Rossiter, xx
Jones, Frank (Santee Sioux),
  267n45
Jones, Henry M. (Santee Sioux), 179
Jones, John (Santee Sioux), 267n45
Jones, Wilson N. (Choctaw), 176
Josefina (Mayan), 79

Orinoco River: collecting at, 80
Osage Agency, 38
Osage Indians, 38
Osage Boarding School, 11, 130
Owens, John: as collector, 79–80

Pablo, Michel (Salish), 183–84
Paiute: economy, xxiv
Pallacier, Peter (Inuit), *143*, 143–44, 147
Pallacier, Thomas (Inuit), 141, 143–44
Palmer, Bertha (Mrs. Potter), 237n63
Palmer, Nancy Helene Columbia
  (Inuit), 138
Pamunkey Indians, 7–8
Panama-California Exposition, San
  Diego 1915, 198–99
Papago Indians: unable to attend
  fair, 169
Parezo, Nancy, 84, 198
Parker, Ely (Seneca), 56, 114
Parker, Quanah (Comanche), 85;
  salary of, 127
Patagonian Indians: unable to
  attend fair, 187
Peabody Museum, Harvard, 32, 35,
  77, 79; collections, 74
Peake, Emily (Ojibwe): as inter-
  preter, 158; salary of, 127, 158
Pend d'Oreilles Indians: unable to
  attend fair, 169, 183–86
Penobscot Indians: described in
  newspapers, 12; on fairgrounds,
  46, 107, 112–14, *113*, 116, 134, 157–
  58, 191, 199
Perdue, Theda, 197
performers. *See under* American
  Indians; Native Hawaiians; Mayan
  Indians
Peru: collecting from, 91–92
Peshlakai (Peshloki), 117, 120
Peshloki (Navajo), 117, 120
Phillips, Ruth B., xxii

Piegan Indians, 90, 97; unable to
  attend fair, 169, 185, 186
Pima Indians: unable to attend
  fair, 169
Pinao, Pauahi (Native Hawaiian),
  152, *155*
Pine Ridge Reservation, 161, 169;
  collecting from, 91; conditions
  on, 162, 194–95
Plenty Horses (Lakota), *15*; contract, *162*
Plummer, E. H., 117–19, 120–21
Poire, Napua Stevens (Native Hawaiian), 152
Pokagon, Leopold (Potawatomi), 7
Pokagon, Simon (Potawatomi), 5–7,
  6, 9, 167, 175; and "Red Man's
  Greeting," 7, 10, 11
Pomiuk (Inuit), 144, *145*; earnings
  of, 125
Potawatomi Indians: and Chicago
  treaty, 7; on fairgrounds, 46, 107;
  playing lacrosse, 167; at Santos's
  funeral, 189; and T. R. Roddy's
  Indian village, 24, 136, 147; wages
  of, 147, 166, 200
potlatch, 110, 112
Powell, Frank, 176
Powell, John Wesley: and linguistic
  classification, 18
Pratt, Richard Henry, xxii, 14, 20–21,
  130, 131–32
Pretty Face (Lakota), 147, 148
Price, Hiram, 77
Prince Pomiuk. *See* Pomiuk (Inuit)
Proctor, Alexander, 165
Putnam, Frederic Ward, xxvii, 7,
  29–48, *33*, 51, 54, 61–62, 66, 68,
  71–72, 83–84, 94–95, 100, 173, 176,
  182; and anthropological exhibits,
  16–18, 54, 105–6; and anthropology, 35; and archaeology, 35;

Putnam, Frederic (*continued*)
collecting human remains, 41;
and control of Indian exhibits,
31, 32, 35, 105, 135, 167–70, 173–
74, 177–78, 180–81, 183–91; and
ethnological village, 20, 28, 42–
44, 106–27, 135; and instructions
to collectors, 37, 40, 41, 44, 45,
63, 70; and Kwakwaka'wakw controversy, 111; and politics, 46–47,
236n63; and portrayal of Indians,
25; salary of, 126

Q!wélelas (Kwakwaka'wakw), *109,
110, 111*
Quaguhl Indians. *See* Kwakwaka'wakw Indians
Queen Charlotte Islands BC, 71, 82
Queen Lili'uokalani (Native Hawaiian), 152, 190; overthrow of, 136,
150, 190
Quelch, J. J., 124

racism, 27–28
Raibmon, Paige, xix, 107, 111, 112
railroads, xxv
Rain-in-the-Face (Lakota), 147–48,
149, 164–65
Rand, Jacki, xvii, xix, xxiii
Randall, Delia (Bannock), 21
Red Bird, 167
Red Cloud, 167
Red Cloud, Jack (Sioux), 165
Red Crow (Blackfoot), 97
Red Jacket (Seneca), 56
Red Owl, George (Santee Sioux),
267n45
Redwing, Joseph (Santee Sioux),
267n45
Reed, Hayter, 97, 174
Reeve, Charles McCormick, 172
Reeves, Emma (Abenaki), 11–12, 115

Reichel, Keali'i (Native Hawaiian),
152–54
religion: suppression of, 111–12
Rensselaer Indian School, 130
representation. *See under* American
Indians
Reuben, James (Nez Perce), 170
Riddle, Maxwell, 70, 73
Riel's Rebellion, 179
Rocky Bear (Lakota), 164
Roddy, Thomas R., 27, 147, 200
Rohl-Smith, Carl, 24
Ronan, Peter, 184
Rosaldo, Renato, 166
Rosebud Reservation: conditions
on, 75–76
Ross, Joshua (Cherokee), 176
Round Valley Indian community,
California, xxiii
Royer, Diana, xvii
Rydell, Robert, xix, xxi

Safford, William E.: as collector, 80,
91–92, 188
Salish Indians, Montana, 183; unable
to attend fair, 169, 183–86
Salsbury, Nate, 158–59, 178
salvage ethnology, 34
Sami village, 136, 156–57, 191; wages
of, 157
Sanborn, John Wentworth, 114, 115
Sandburg, Carl, xx
Santee Sioux brass band, 11, 179–80,
182, 197
Santos (Aymara), 189
Saville, Marshall: as collector, 79–80
Sawyer, Fran: as collector, 92
scholars: in Indian country, 39, 101
schoolchildren, Native: at fair, xxviii,
20, 134, 168. *See also* boarding
school exhibit, Canadian; boarding school exhibit, U.S.

Tozzer, Alfred, 29

trade: in material culture, xviii, 68; pre-Columbian, xviii. *See also* fur trade; Indian curio trade; tourist trade

traders, 86–88. *See also* Keam, Thomas V.; Voth, Henry

transportation, xxv–xxvi; railroads, xxv

treaty: at Chicago, 1833, 7

tribal sovereignty, 177

Troutman, John, 180

T. R. Roddy's American Indian village, 28, 126, 147; popularity of, 27, 136, *157*, and wages, 147, 148, 166, 167

Trujillo, Dennis, xxi

Tsilhqot'in Indians. *See* Chilcoton Indians

Tsimshian Indians: collecting from, 61

Tuktootsina, Christopher Columbus (Inuit), 138

Turner, Frederick Jackson, xv, xxi–xxii

Tuscarora Indians, 51, 56

Two Boots Standing Together (Luther Jack, Tuscarora), 114, 115

U.S. Army: and the fair, 54

U.S. government exhibit: plans for, 99–100

Ute Indians: unable to attend fair, 169

Vancouver Island BC, 60; collecting from, 95–96

vanishing race trope, xxi–xxii

Venezuelan Indians: unable to attend fair, 187

Voth, Henry, 88

Vowell, A. W., 60, 95, 110

wage labor market. *See* cash economy

Walker, Mrs. (Navajo), 117–18, 120

War Department: and the fair, 52–55

Warren, Charles, 152

Warren, Louis, xvii, xix, xxiii–xxiv, 161, 163

Warren, Tyler (Ojibwe), 173

Warren, William (Ojibwe), 173

Washington, George, 52

Weare, P. B., 178

Webster, Thomas (Onondaga), 114

Welles, Roger, 80

West, Gerald, 57

westward expansion, 194

White, Richard, xxv

White Beaver (Frank Powell), 176

The Whole Truth (Nathaniel Kennedy, Seneca), 114

Whonnock, John (Kwakwa̱ka̱'wakw), *109*

Whonnock, Mrs. John (Kwakwa̱ka̱'wakw), *109*

Wichita Indians: unable to attend fair, 169

Wild West shows, xxii, xxvi, 9, 10–11, 37, 135, 198, 228n15. *See also* Buffalo Bill's Wild West and Congress of Rough Riders of the World; Miller Brothers 101 Ranch Wild West Show

Willmarth, A. F., 118–20

Wilson, Jack (Wovoka), xxiv

Wilson, Jennie (Kini Kapahukula-okamāmalu, Native Hawaiian), 152–55, *153*, *155*, 199

Winnebago Indians, 231n53; collecting from, 171. *See also* Ho-Chunk Indians

Wisconsin Dells, 200

work. *See* labor

workers. *See* labor

World's Columbian Exposition: as symbol of modernity, xxi

World's Columbian Exposition Company, 136

world's fairs. *See* Centennial Exposition, Philadelphia 1876; Cotton States Exposition, Atlanta 1895; Exposition Universelle, Paris 1889; International Colonial and Export Exhibition, Netherlands 1883; Panama-California Exposition, San Diego 1915; Tertio-Millennial Exposition, Santa Fe 1883
Wounded Knee massacre, 160–61
Wovoka, xxiv

Yellow Robe, Chauncey (Sioux), 130–31

Yoo-Ka-Lucke (Inuit), *140*
Yost, Nellie, 159
Young Man Afraid (Lakota), 75

Zacharias (Inuit), 142, 146, 147; wages of, 139
Zapotec Indians: at Cotton States Exposition, 197
Zelaya, Jeronimo, 78
Zerbe, Ida, 147–48
Zia Pueblo: collecting from, 89
Zuni Indians: and fair, 251n1
Zwick, Jim, xix

Lightning Source UK Ltd.
Milton Keynes UK
UKHW010843240519
343257UK00007B/303/P